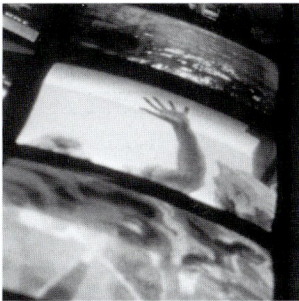

Media Technologies, Markets and Regulation

This publication forms part of an Open University course *Understanding Media* (DA204). The complete list of books for DA204 is as follows:

Understanding Media: Inside Celebrity (editors: Jessica Evans and David Hesmondhalgh)
Media Audiences (editor: Marie Gillespie)
Media Production (editor: David Hesmondhalgh)
Analysing Media Texts (editors: Marie Gillespie and Jason Toynbee)
Media Technologies, Markets and Regulation (editors: Richard Collins and Jessica Evans)

Details of this and other Open University courses can be obtained from the Student Registration and Enquiry Service, The Open University, Milton Keynes, MK7 6YG, United Kingdom: tel. +44 (0)1908 653231, email general-enquiries@open.ac.uk.

Alternatively, you may visit The Open University website at http://www.open.ac.uk where you can learn more about the wide range of courses and packs offered at all levels by The Open University.

To purchase a selection of Open University course materials visit http://www.ouw.co.uk, or contact Open University Worldwide, Michael Young Building, Walton Hall, Milton Keynes MK7 6AA, United Kingdom for a brochure. tel. +44 (0)1908 858785; fax +44 (0)1908 858787; email ouwenq@open.ac.uk

Media Technologies, Markets and Regulation

Edited by Richard Collins and Jessica Evans

The Open University

Edited and designed by The Open University.

Typeset in India by Alden Prepress Services, Chennai.

Printed and bound in Malta by Gutenberg Press.

ISBN 0 7492 6830 1

1.1

Contents

The Open University Course Team

Tony Aldgate, Arts Faculty Advisor
Geoff Austin, Leading Technical Developer
Hedley Bashforth, Associate Lecturer and Study Guide Author
Melanie Bayley, Media Project Manager
Tony Bennett, Chapter Author
Chris Bissell, Chapter Author, Faculty of Technology
Kathleen Calder, Editorial Media Developer
Fiona Carey, Editorial Media Developer
Elizabeth Chaplin, Associate Lecturer and Study Guide Author
James Chapman, Reading Member
Giles Clark, Publishing Advisor
Richard Collins, Chapter Author and Book Editor
Lene Connolly, Print Buying Controller
Shanti Dass, Editorial Media Developer
Alison Edwards, Editorial Media Developer
Jessica Evans, Chapter Author and Book Editor
Tot Foster, Consultant Producer, Sound & Vision
Marie Gillespie, Deputy Course Chair, Chapter Author and Book Editor
Richard Golden, Production and Presentation Administrator
Lisa Hale, Media Assistant, Compositor
Alma Hales, Rights Advisor
R. Harindranath, Critical Reader, 2002–3
Celia Hart, Picture Researcher
David Herbert, Chapter Author & Arts Faculty Advisor
David Hesmondhalgh, Course Chair, Chapter Author and Book Editor
Jonathan Hunt, Publishing Advisor
Denise Janes, Course Secretary, 2002–3
Tim Jordan, Critical Reader, 2002–3
Wendy Lampert, Course Manager
Alex Law, Associate Lecturer and Study Guide Author
Sylvia Lay-Flurrie, Course Secretary
Hugh Mackay, Staff Tutor, Teaching Advisor and Critical Reader
Margaret McManus, Media Assistant, Rights
Katie Meade, Contracts Executive
Diane Mole, Graphics Media Developer
Martin Moloney, Associate Lecturer and Study Guide Author
Dave Morris, Interactive Media Developer
Jason Toynbee, Chapter Author and Book Editor
Howard Twiner, Graphics Media Developer

Consultant Authors

Frances Bonner, University of Queensland
Gill Branston, Cardiff University
Nick Couldry, London School of Economics and Political Science
John Downey, Loughborough University
Jostein Gripsrud, University of Bergen
Sonia Livingstone, London School of Economics and Political Science
Nick Stevenson, University of Nottingham
Gillian Ursell, Trinity and All Saints College, University of Leeds

External Assessors

Ann Gray, University of Lincoln
Peter Golding, Loughborough University

Book preface

Media Technologies, Markets and Regulation is Book 5 of an Open University course, *Understanding Media*. Unlike the other books on the course, it is available only to Open University students. The other four books on the course have been published as a series, also entitled *Understanding Media*. The four books in this series are as follows:

Understanding Media: Inside Celebrity, edited by Jessica Evans and David Hesmondhalgh

Media Audiences, edited by Marie Gillespie

Media Production, edited by David Hesmondhalgh

Analysing Media Texts, edited by Marie Gillespie and Jason Toynbee (with DVD-ROM)

The first book introduces four elements central to any investigation of the media (history, texts, production and audiences) via an analysis of the important media phenomenon of celebrity. The next three books in the series then examine texts, production and audiences in greater detail. This, the fifth and final book on the course, examines the way that societies attempt to organise and control various technological properties of the media, via two contrasting mechanisms: markets and states.

Across these different topics, the course addresses three *themes* in media analysis, which the course team believe are fundamental to any appreciation of the importance and complexity of the media. These are

- power
- change and continuity
- knowledge, values and beliefs

These elements and themes can be traced via the index of each book, but the book introductions and conclusions will also help follow how they are pursued across the series.

Understanding Media covers a great deal of media studies curriculum, but of course it still isn't possible for us to cover everything. Nevertheless we have aimed to cover a wide range of media examples, both historically and geographically, and to introduce a number of differing and often competing approaches.

The chapters are designed to be rigorous but student-friendly, and we have sought to achieve this in a number of ways. We have provided clear outlines of the aims of each chapter at its beginning, and summaries at the end, with careful explanations along the way. Activities are built into the chapters, and are designed to help readers understand and retain the key concepts of the course. Just under half of these activities are based around *readings* – extracts drawn from books, academic articles and the media themselves – which are integral to the discussion contained in the chapter. These readings are indicated by a coloured line next to the margin. Each book is thoroughly indexed, so that key concepts can be tracked across the different books in the series. Further reading is indicated at the end of each chapter. Finally, although each book is self-contained, references to other books in the series are indicated by the use of bold type.

Media studies has taken its place as a familiar academic discipline in schools and universities, embraced in large numbers by students, but crassly dismissed by commentators who in most cases seem never to have read a serious analysis of the media. The need to think carefully about the media's role in modern societies is as great as ever. We hope that you find these books a stimulating introduction to this vitally important area of study.

Open University courses are produced by course teams. These teams include academic authors, from The Open University and from other institutions, experienced tutors, External Assessors, editors, designers, audio and video producers, administrators and secretaries. The Open University academics on the *Understanding Media* course team were based mainly in the Sociology discipline, within the Faculty of Social Sciences, but we also drew upon the expertise of colleagues in the Faculty of Arts, in order to construct a course with interdisciplinary foundations and appeal. While book editors have had primary responsibility for each book, the assignment of editors' names to books cannot adequately convey the collective nature of production at The Open University. The names of the *Understanding Media* course team are listed at the front of this book.

I'd like to thank all my colleagues on the course team for their hard work and good humour, especially Wendy Lampert, who has been a really excellent and efficient Course Manager.

David Hesmondhalgh, Course Chair
On behalf of the *Understanding Media* course team

Technology, media and society

Richard Collins and Jessica Evans

We live in a world pervaded by media and communications — and media and communications shape that world. They are not just widely present; our world is inconceivable without them. You may well have felt the hairs on your neck rise on reading this. How many times have you read something like this before? How can the writers not recognise, you may well be thinking, that this is true only for the north, the 'developed' world, the rich! Do they not know that much of the world is illiterate? That most of the world's population does not have a personal telephone? That those with no access to electricity are excluded from watching television, from access to the internet and, often, from reading books and newspapers outside the hours of daylight? This is true. But, is it not also true that the whole world is now deeply interconnected? Environmental change originating from the developed world's activities has impacts on the whole world. The price of basic commodities throughout the world is influenced by demand in the developed world. Military power is applied by the developed world to the rest of the world and not vice versa. 'First world' tourists are now everywhere (and refugees and asylum seekers from the rest of the world are almost as pervasive). All of these global interconnections are inconceivable and unsustainable without modern media and communications.

In this book we examine three of the key relationships and forces that inform such large-scale impacts of the media:

- technology
- markets
- regulation.

These matters take us to the question which, implicitly or explicitly, haunts media studies: How powerful are media and communications? The question is often posed in terms of the media's influence on audiences: What are the effects of film on children? How far does people's newspaper reading influence their voting behaviour? Is television advertising uniquely powerful? But, in this book, we formulate the question rather differently and ask: What is the large-scale social impact of media and communication?

We consider the impact of technology in making modern media and communications what they are, and the fundamental economic characteristics of media and communications (and show how these are, in important ways, different from the economic characteristics of other goods and services), and we examine the reciprocal shaping of society by the media and media by society, focusing on the key issue of regulation. The reasons for doing this are straightforward and simple, whether we approach the question from a media- or society-centred starting point. Media and communications are important constitutive forces in modern societies (that is, society would be very different without them) and, looking at the question from a media-centred point of view, modern media and communications are shaped by social forces. This is one of the most important reasons why media are different in different societies.

However we pose the question of media power we are led to ask what measures, if any, should we take to mitigate what are seen as undesirable media effects (or reinforce what are seen as positive effects). Such measures are often referred to as regulation of the media. And, although technology changes both the way in which we communicate and the effects of our media and communication systems, so too do we change media and communications, through regulation. In order to accentuate the positive and minimise the negative, children (and sometimes adults) are barred from seeing certain films; democratic societies strive to ensure that there are several sources of political information; television advertising is regulated more stringently than other forms of advertising; and consumers of the mass media – viewers, listeners and readers – are thought to need media education to improve their media literacy and strengthen their defences against the media's baleful influence. Perhaps that is why you are reading this book!

You may have asked yourself, when reading the preceding paragraph: Who is the 'we' here?, for such matters are sometimes strongly contested. The 'we' who change media and communication through regulation may quickly become divided into rival 'them' and 'us' groups. 'They' might advocate stricter control of media content whereas 'we' might think something lighter and more permissive is to be preferred, or vice versa. Regulation, like most important concepts and practices (think of the many meanings that can be attributed to terms such as 'citizenship', 'wealth', 'justice', and so on) can be defined in different ways. But, in its broadest sense, by 'regulation' we mean the actions we collectively take to secure particular outcomes – more of some things and less of others.

However, for our purposes in this book, that is too wide a definition. Media and communication regulation, in the sense that we use it (see in particular Chapter 4) is the combination of actions taken through use of the law, specialist institutions (such as the UK Office of Communications – Ofcom), and public support, which is designed to change the conduct of people and institutions in the media and communication field. And, of course, a system of shared but often contested values lies behind regulators' actions, whether the regulators are formally constituted by

government – such as the UK's Ofcom, the United States' Federal
Communications Commission (FCC) or South Africa's Independent
Communications Authority of South Africa (ICASA) – or by the media
and communications industry as self-regulatory agencies (such as the
UK's Press Complaints Commission or the many film censorship and
classification bodies, for example, Germany's Frei willige selbst Kontrolle
or the British Board of Film Classification). Accordingly, we consider the
contested nature of some of these value systems that underpin regulation –
notably the rival claims of the principles and values of freedom of
expression and a right to privacy.

These kinds of questions, answers and social responses imply that
society is somehow outside media and communications and that the
media is a thing on which society can act. There is a truth to this, but
it is not the whole truth. For, as well as society shaping media and
communications (with different configurations of knowledge, values and
beliefs about the media producing different outcomes – for example,
censorship to check undesirable media behaviour and/or subsidy to
encourage desirable behaviour), media and communications can be seen
as a force shaping society over the long term. Our political and social
institutions, our patterns of intimate behaviour, the very connectedness to
others which defines the boundaries of our social world are all, arguably,
shaped by media and communications. In this book we will consider
some examples of how this large-scale shaping of society by modern
media and communications has taken place, and of how the media have
a constitutive role acting on and transforming social institutions and
practices, as well as exploring the ways in which societies act on and
transform the media. Here is an example (taken from a writer whose
work we consider in Chapter 2) of the kind of proposition about the
constitutive effect of the media with which we are concerned:

> Television removes much of the doubt as to what subjects one's
> children or parents know about. Any topic on any popular situation
> comedy, talk show, news program, or advertisement – be it death,
> homosexuality, abortion, male strippers, sex-change operations,
> political scandals, incest, rape, jock itch or bras that 'lift and separate' –
> can be spoken about the next day in school, over dinner, or on a
> date, not only because everyone knows about such topics, but also
> because everyone knows that everyone knows. [...] The public and
> all-inclusive nature of television has a tendency to collapse formerly
> distinct situations into one. In a society shaped by the segregated
> situations of print, people may secretly discuss taboo topics, but with
> television, the very notion of 'taboo' is lost.
>
> Meyrowitz, 1985, p.92

Meyrowitz is making claims about the large-scale impact of modern media and communications. Television, for him, constitutes society on a new basis. Two sorts of questions obviously arise. Firstly, is what he claims true? What evidence is there to confirm or qualify his claim? And secondly, if he is right, what (if anything) should we as a society do? This book thus focuses on the effect of the media in constituting society; that is, on the large-scale effects of media and communications. No book can do everything and the authors of this one make no claims to have done so (phew, you may say quietly as the hairs on your neck fall back into place). But what have they done exactly? How do we make the arguments in the four chapters which follow?

The first chapter proposes that there is a reciprocal relationship between technology and society. Technology both shapes and is shaped by society. One of the most important instances of this relationship is a tendency towards standardisation in the way we communicate with each other. Consider the persuasive examples of standardisation explored in Chapters 1 and 2, largely drawn from an early communication technology – printing. Printing, the argument which you will find set out fully later contends, led to the adoption of a particular kind of spoken and written English – a standardisation of English. Similar claims are made in respect of later communication technologies such as film, broadcasting and the internet which, perhaps, echo many of the effects of printing.

However, Chapter 1 also argues that although technology exerts considerable power for change, it is often hard to anticipate quite what these changes will be. The ultimate effect of new communications technologies may be very different from those envisaged by their producers. For example, the use of mobile phones for texting: many phone users employ the SMS function, originally built into the network for engineers, to send written messages rather than use the voice capability for which the phone and its network had been primarily designed. Texting means that the mobile phone has become a medium which requires literacy to use it fully. It has lower costs per message than network operators initially envisaged (though texting may well have contributed to a more rapid uptake of mobile telephony than would otherwise have been the case, with consequential improved revenue flows for operators), and has opened the door to a new generation of multimedia mobile communication devices which are a long way from simple instruments for communication by voice over distance.

User demand is thus a very important force that qualifies the power exerted by the factor of technological momentum outlined in Chapter 1. Chapter 1 identifies a shift to the consumer in modern communication technologies; for example, instead of watching a television programme at the time it is transmitted, the video/DVD recorder enables us to watch it at our convenience. And, instead of consuming information provided by a small group of others working for the mass media, we can now communicate our own messages; for example, through internet blogs or podcasting.

In the second chapter, we take up the general theme of the power exerted by technological change and both extend Chapter 1's account of technology's impact on the media and consider the large-scale effects of media and communications technologies on society. We reflect more extensively on the case of printing and argue that the standardising effect of printing produced 'modern English' – what you are now reading. Doubtless a similar argument could be made for other languages. We also consider another comparable case – Joshua Meyrowitz's argument that television has changed several important aspects of contemporary life. For example, he claims that it has redrawn the boundaries between the public and the private, between the worlds of adults and children, and has changed the skills needed by a successful politician.

In Chapter 2 we also take up an issue that runs through all the chapters in this book – media regulation. Chapter 1 proposed that society shapes technology as well as technology shaping society. Regulation is an important instance of this social shaping whereby societies act on shared beliefs and try to secure shared values. Societies, through their media regulators, make rules that influence the shape, size and mode of operation of the media. They exert power to secure ends in keeping with their values and beliefs. Some activities and effects are encouraged while others are countervailed, but there is seldom complete agreement about what should be encouraged and what resisted. Reasonable people can, and do, disagree on what is desirable. Different societies regulate their media and communications systems in different ways, and any particular society may use different regulatory instruments at different times to secure whatever social goals are prioritised.

In this context, we consider two different and influential 'takes' on the impact and effects of media technology and on whether, and how, the media should be regulated. The ideas in question are those of the German philosopher Jürgen Habermas and the American scholar Ithiel de Sola Pool. Broadly, their analyses of the relationship between the modern media of communication and society point towards different regulatory strategies – one towards liberalisation and the other towards control.

In the third chapter we turn to the economics of the media for two reasons. Firstly, understanding the distinctive economics of media and communications helps us understand *why* the media are so pervasive and *why* the issues of power and control associated with them are both inescapable and intractable. And secondly, there has been a profound and pervasive recent shift towards the use of markets, rather than state or government direction, as the principle that is governing modern media and communications. If we understand the economics of the media we will better know how media markets work and do not work. You will learn that media markets have some very distinctive features which make them different from many other markets. If we know the meaning of terms such as scale economies, network externalities, public goods, and so on we will better understand how media power is exercised and why the media may need regulating. We will know where regulation is likely to succeed and where it might fail.

In the fourth and final chapter of this book we focus our attention on the regulatory history of broadcasting and telecommunications in the UK and on how these media have moved between public and private ownership. We also begin a more fine-grained consideration of regulation by identifying different kinds of regulatory institutions and practices (notably law, statutory regulation and self-regulation) and the value conflicts which, almost inevitably, arise when regulation is under consideration. Should, for example, belief in the value of freedom of expression prevail? How far can John Stuart Mill's classic case for freedom of expression provide a valid and viable basis for media policy today? In what circumstances do individuals' entitlements to privacy outweigh others' rights to know? Are the rules different for celebrities than for ordinary people? And, if so, why should there be a difference?

Working through these four connected chapters we hope that you will see, on the one hand, the relationship between technology as a force that shapes both communications and society and, on the other hand, the regulation through which societies often respond to the power exerted by media and communication. This leads us to consider possible alternative institutional arrangements for shaping and regulating both technology and its social consequences. Should markets prevail? And if so, what, if anything, should be done about the distinctive and sometimes unwelcome outcomes that flow from the fundamental economic properties of modern media and communications? If markets are used, do they need regulating? If so, how? Through the general law or through self or statutory regulation? If we do not use markets, what sort of public provision is appropriate? What are the values and beliefs which inform our decisions on such matters? What grounds are there for deciding between rival courses of action? Which of the opposing beliefs and values, such as a right to privacy and a right to freedom of information, should govern our decisions? Read on!

Reference

Meyrowitz, J. (1985) *No Sense of Place: The Impact of Electronic Media on Social Behaviour*, New York, Oxford University Press.

Technology and the media

Chapter 1

Chris Bissell

Contents

1 Introduction: what is technology?

The range of contemporary technological tools for communication and entertainment is staggering – mobile phones, 24-hour news broadcasting, MP3 and DVD players, iPods, the internet and a television channel for every day of the year! How have we reached this technological position? Is it empowering us, and bringing us useful and enjoyable new products and services, or is it a threat to more traditional values? Are we powerless in the face of such rapid technological change, or can we control and regulate such technologies?

This chapter aims to prepare you for a later, more detailed look at issues of technology policy, media markets, and regulation. In particular, I want to encourage you not to take things for granted, but to challenge some of the generally accepted views of technology, particularly in the context of media technologies.

Let us begin with an examination of what, precisely, we mean by 'technology' in the context of the media.

Activity 1.1

Think about the word 'technology'. What does it mean to you? Start by listing a few terms or phrases including the words 'technology' or 'technological'. Look at your list and, after you have completed it, look at my list below. Do the words 'technology' and 'technological' always have the same meaning? ▪ ▪ ▪

When I think of the word 'technology' the terms that occur to me are: 'information technology', 'new technology', 'office technology', 'digital technology', 'communication technology', 'biotechnology', 'nanotechnology', 'science and technology', 'technological revolution'. However, there are many others, so I would expect your list to be quite different. It is clear that a whole range of meanings is implied by these terms. 'Office technology' and perhaps 'new technology' seem to refer primarily to hardware: computers, printers, scanners, fax machines, etc. 'Biotechnology' and 'nanotechnology' seem to refer to specific disciplines, each with their own practices and techniques. 'Digital technology' describes a particular way of implementing a range of functions electronically, so we have digital watches, mobile phones or televisions in contrast to earlier 'analogue' devices. And the phrases 'science and technology' and 'technological revolution' suggest a particular ideological approach or view of the world, and call out for critical analysis.

The word 'technology', then, is problematic. It is particularly so in the English language. Many other European languages distinguish between *technique* and *technologie* (French) or *Technik* and *Technologie*

(German) – although it is also true to say that the distinction has become blurred somewhat in such languages in recent years, perhaps due to the influence of English. Historically, though, *technique/Technik* refers to artefacts and the means of producing them (often better translated into English as 'engineering'), while *technologie* refers more to the body of knowledge relating to such practices. Some writers in English have used the term 'technics' for the *technique/Technik* aspect of technology.

Activity 1.2

Look up a dictionary definition of technology. How do the definitions you find relate to the above? ■ ■ ■

I found the following definition of technology in the *Collins English Dictionary*:

■ the application of practical or mechanical sciences to industry or commerce;

■ the methods, theory and practices governing such application;

■ the total knowledge and skills available to any human society for industry, art, science, etc.

There is not a hard and fast distinction, but the first definition seems to relate more to engineering/'technics', while the third is technology proper. The second definition appears to combine aspects of both.

1.1 Science and technology

'Science and technology' was one of the phrases I picked out in my discussion of Activity 1.1. The fact that the phrase is so often used suggests that the two concepts are closely related or even that there is a single something called 'science and technology'. You will even come across the term 'technoscience'.

We can identify two extreme positions in the 'science and technology' debate. The first claims that science and technology are two distinct activities. Science aims to understand the world and generate theories to explain it. Practical application of scientific knowledge is strictly of secondary importance. Technology, on the other hand, is concerned with exploiting scientific and other knowledge to make things of practical importance; understanding the natural world is not particularly relevant. A result of this distinction is the common view that technology is applied science: science comes up with new descriptions, models or explanations of the world and then these are applied to practical purposes as 'technology'. Much of the current political rhetoric about science and technology is predicated upon this theoretical position, even though it is not often made explicit.

The second extreme position, which owes much to late twentieth-century neo-Marxist analysis, sees science and technology as more or less the same thing – this is the 'technoscience' position. In this view, both science and technology are determined by the institutional arrangements (funding, politics, economics, etc.) of modern capitalist societies. The idea that science strives after truth, generating disinterested knowledge that can then be applied to practical problems, is seen as naïve and even dangerous.

Unsurprisingly, neither of these extreme positions is adequate for explaining the science–technology relationship. But it is useful to bear this general dichotomy in mind when looking at media technologies. Take television, for example. Clearly, television is only possible because of scientific discoveries about electricity, electromagnetic radiation, thermionic valves, semiconductors, and so on. But television as a social phenomenon relies on the large-scale socio-technological systems conditioned by political and commercial interest, regulatory bodies, and the like. By a 'large-scale socio-technological system' in this context I mean things like the electricity generation and supply network, or the complex process of converting raw materials into the various television components, and so on.

1.2 Science, technology and change

When people talk about science and technology, it is usually not long before you hear the word 'change' – the 'rapid pace of technological change', for example, or 'new scientific discoveries that are going to change the world'. One interesting feature about scientific and technological change can be summed up as follows: in general, new science comes from old science; new technology from old technology. Examples can be found from all periods, but let us consider some recent developments in media technologies. Digital broadcasting, DVDs, mobile phones, the internet, computer-generated special effects, etc., have involved very little 'new science'. Rather, they have resulted from the refinement of mid-twentieth-century technology: increasing miniaturisation of electronic devices, improvements in battery technology, applications of nineteenth- and early twentieth-century mathematics, and so on. A phrase that is often used to characterise this phenomenon is 'technological momentum'. Rather than resulting from the application of science, technological developments are driven by the demands of a particular technology and the society in which it operates.

Having said this, however, we need to be careful. Like all generalisations it cannot be pushed too far. For example, quite a lot of recent scientific and mathematical advances have only become possible because of the digital computer: here a new technology has given rise to new science and maths.

So far, what I have said has related to technology in general, so let us now begin to focus on *media* technologies, while continuing to develop a critical approach to the wider technological domain.

2 How society and technology interact

Reading 1.1 Activity

Now read the following extract, 'The technology and the society', from Raymond Williams's book, *Television, Technology and Cultural Form* (1974). When you come to Williams's nine statements about cause and effect, study his precise words very carefully. Some of the statements are very similar, but with crucial differences. Then try to do the following:

■ explain in your own words what Williams means by 'technological determinism';

■ pick out some crucial words in Williams's nine statements, and explain them.

It should help if you bear in mind these tasks as you read, and make a few notes as you go along.

Reading 1.1

Raymond Williams, 'The technology and the society'

It is often said that television has altered our world. In the same way, people often speak of a new world, a new society, a new phase of history, being created – 'brought about' – by this or that new technology: the steam-engine, the automobile, the atomic bomb. Most of us know what is generally implied when such things are said. But this may be the central difficulty: that we have got so used to statements of this general kind, in our most ordinary discussions, that we can fail to realise their specific meanings.

For behind all such statements lie some of the most difficult and most unresolved historical and philosophical questions. Yet the questions are not posed by the statements; indeed they are ordinarily masked by them. Thus we often discuss, with animation, this or that 'effect' of television, or the kinds of social behaviour, the cultural and psychological conditions, which television has 'led to', without feeling ourselves obliged to ask whether it is reasonable to describe any technology as a cause, or, if we think of it as a cause, as what kind of cause, and in what relations with other kinds of causes. The most precise and discriminating local study of 'effects' can remain superficial if we have not looked into the notions of cause and effect, as between a technology and a society, a technology and a culture, a technology and a psychology, which underlie our questions and may often determine our answers.

It can of course be said that these fundamental questions are very much too difficult; and that they are indeed difficult is very soon obvious to anyone who tries to follow them through. We could spend our lives trying to answer them, whereas here and now, in a society in which television is important, there is immediate and practical work to be done: surveys to be made, research undertaken; surveys and research, moreover, which we know how to do. It is an appealing position, and it has the advantage, in our kind of society, that it is understood as practical, so that it can then be supported and funded. By contrast, other kinds of question seem merely theoretical and abstract.

Yet all questions about cause and effect, as between a technology and a society, are intensely practical. Until we have begun to answer them, we really do not know, in any particular case, whether, for example, we are talking about a technology or about the uses of a technology; about necessary institutions or particular and changeable institutions; about a content or about a form. And this is not only a matter of intellectual uncertainty; it is a matter of social practice. If the technology is a cause, we can at best modify or seek to control its effects. Or if the technology, as used, is an effect, to what kinds of cause, and other kinds of action, should we refer and relate our experience of its uses? These are not abstract questions. They form an increasingly important part of our social and cultural arguments, and they are being decided all the time in real practice, by real and effective decisions.

It is with these problems in mind that I want to try to analyse television as a particular cultural technology, and to look at its development, its institutions, its forms and its effects, in this critical dimension. [...]

Versions of cause and effect in technology and society

We can begin by looking again at the general statement that television has altered our world. It is worth setting down some of the different things this kind of statement has been taken to mean. For example:

(i) Television was invented as a result of scientific and technical research. Its power as a medium of news and entertainment was then so great that it altered all preceding media of news and entertainment.

(ii) Television was invented as a result of scientific and technical research. Its power as a medium of social communication was then so great that it altered many of our institutions and forms of social relationships.

(iii) Television was invented as a result of scientific and technical research. Its inherent properties as an electronic medium altered our basic perceptions of reality, and thence our relations with each other and with the world.

(iv) Television was invented as a result of scientific and technical research. As a powerful medium of communication and entertainment it took its place with other factors – such as greatly increased physical mobility, itself the result of other newly invented technologies – in altering the scale and form of our societies.

(v) Television was invented as a result of scientific and technical research, and developed as a medium of entertainment and news. It then had unforeseen consequences, not only on other entertainment and news media, which it reduced in viability and importance, but on some of the central processes of family, cultural and social life.

(vi) Television, discovered as a possibility by scientific and technical research, was selected for investment and development to meet the needs of a new kind of society, especially in the provision of centralised entertainment and in the centralised formation of opinions and styles of behaviour.

(vii) Television, discovered as a possibility by scientific and technical research, was selected for investment and promotion as a new and profitable phase of a domestic consumer economy; it is then one of the characteristic 'machines for the home'.

(viii) Television became available as a result of scientific and technical research, and in its character and uses exploited and emphasised elements of a passivity, a cultural and psychological inadequacy, which had always been latent in people, but which television now organised and came to represent.

(ix) Television became available as a result of scientific and technical research, and in its character and uses both served and exploited the needs of a new kind of large-scale and complex but atomised society.

These are only some of the possible glosses on the ordinary bald statement that television has altered our world. Many people hold mixed versions of what are really alternative opinions, and in some cases there is some inevitable overlapping. But we can distinguish between two broad classes of opinion.

In the first − (i) to (v) − the technology is in effect accidental. Beyond the strictly internal development of the technology there is no reason why any particular invention should have come about. Similarly it then has consequences which are also in the true sense accidental, since they follow directly from the technology itself. If television had not been invented, this argument would run, certain definite social and cultural events would not have occurred.

In the second − (vi) to (ix) − television is again, in effect, a technological accident, but its significance lies in its uses, which are held to be symptomatic of some order of society or some qualities of human nature which are otherwise determined. If television had not been invented, this argument runs, we would still be manipulated or mindlessly entertained, but in some other way and perhaps less powerfully.

For all the variations of local interpretation and emphasis, these two classes of opinion underlie the overwhelming majority of both professional and amateur views of the effects of television. What they have in common is the fundamental form of the statement: 'television has altered our world'.

It is then necessary to make a further theoretical distinction. The first class of opinion, described above, is that usually known, at least to its opponents, as *technological determinism*. It is an immensely powerful and now largely orthodox view of the nature of social change. New technologies are discovered, by an essentially internal process of research and development, which then sets the conditions for social change and progress. Progress, in particular, is the history of these inventions, which 'created the modern world'. The effects of technologies, whether direct or indirect, foreseen or unforeseen, are as it were the rest of history. The steam-engine, the automobile, television, the atomic bomb, have *made* modern man [*sic*] and the modern condition.

The second class of opinion appears less determinist. Television, like any other technology, becomes available as an element or a medium in a process of change that is in any case occurring or about to occur. By contrast with pure technological determinism, this view emphasises other causal factors in social change. It then considers particular technologies, or a complex of technologies, as *symptoms* of change of some other kind. Any particular technology is then as it were a by-product of a social process that is otherwise determined. It only acquires effective status when it is used for purposes which are already contained in this known social process.

The debate between these two general positions occupies the greater part of our thinking about technology and society. It is a real debate, and each side makes important points. But it is in the end sterile, because each position, though in different ways, has abstracted technology from society. In *technological determinism,* research and development have been assumed as self-generating. The new technologies are invented as it were in an independent sphere, and then create new societies or new human conditions. The view of *symptomatic technology,* similarly, assumes that research and development are self-generating, but in a more marginal way. What is discovered in the margin is then taken up and used.

Each view can then be seen to depend on the isolation of technology. It is either a self-acting force which creates new ways of life, or it is a self-acting force which provides materials for new ways of life. These positions are so deeply established, in modern social thought, that it is very difficult to think beyond them. Most histories of technology, like most histories of scientific discovery, are written from their assumptions. An appeal to 'the facts', against this or that interpretation, is made very difficult simply because the histories are usually written, consciously or unconsciously, to illustrate the assumptions. This is either explicit, with the consequential interpretation attached, or more often implicit, in that the history of technology or of scientific development is offered as a history on its own. This can be seen as a device of specialisation or of emphasis, but it then necessarily implies merely internal intentions and criteria.

To change these emphases would require prolonged and co-operative intellectual effort. But in the particular case of television it may be possible to outline a different kind of interpretation, which would allow us to see not only its history but also its uses in a more radical way. Such an interpretation would differ from technological determinism in that it would restore *intention* to the process of research and development. The technology would be seen, that is to say, as being looked for and developed with certain purposes and practices already in mind. At the same time the interpretation would differ from symptomatic technology in that these purposes and practices would be seen as *direct*: as known social needs, purposes and practices to which the technology is not marginal but central.

Reading source

Williams, 1974, pp.9–14 ■ ■ ■

I asked you to do the following:
- Explain what is meant by 'technological determinism';
- Pick out some crucial words in Williams's nine statements, and explain them.

Here are my responses. By 'technological determinism', Williams means that technology determines, to a great extent, the processes of social change. Technology (and science as well) is autonomous and linked to the notion of 'progress'. In this view, technologies such as 'the steam-engine, the automobile, the atomic bomb' and, we can now add, the computer, are what have made modern society.

When I started to pick out key words from Williams's nine statements, I first noted the distinction between 'invented', 'discovered' and 'became available', in the opening sentence of the statements. 'Invented' certainly carries connotations of determinism; 'discovered' much less so; while 'became available' suggests that social as much as technological influences were the determining factor. Then I noted how the term '[technological] power' was downgraded as we went from the 'technological determinism' to the 'symptomatic technology' end of the spectrum. But there are many other key words such as 'society' or 'behaviour' that you might have picked out of Reading 1.1.

Activity 1.3

Now re-read the last two paragraphs of Reading 1.1. What does Williams claim is inadequate about both technological determinism and symptomatic technology? Try to answer this before reading on. ■■■

Williams points to the fact that both the technological determinism approach and the symptomatic technology approach tend to isolate technology from other factors, in particular the way in which social needs or desires can be converted into technological intent. In fact, he calls attention to the general lack of theoretical work on the technology–society relationship at that time (mid-1970s). To a large extent this lack was addressed in the 1980s and 1990s; a particularly useful perspective being the 'social construction of technology (SCOT)' approach developed by Wiebe Bijker, Thomas Hughes and Trevor Pinch, and others (Bijker et al., 1987).

In one of the earliest and now classic SCOT analyses of technological change, Bijker et al. considered the development of the bicycle from the 'penny farthing' into essentially its modern form during the period 1880 to 1900. The story they tell is a far cry from technological determinism. Rather, the various competing designs were championed by very different social groups, who had very different requirements. For example, the 'boy racers' favoured the penny farthing, whose enormous front wheel allowed high speeds to be achieved, albeit at considerable risk. Women and more elderly riders chose smaller-wheeled designs for reasons of modesty or safety. The modern design, claim Bijker et al., was accepted by all only when pneumatic tyres could be shown to allow higher speeds to be achieved with smaller wheels, as well as improved comfort and safety. The modern bicycle, in this view, was *socially* constructed as much as – or even more than – *technologically* constructed.

The SCOT approach, at least in its initial form, concentrated on the social shaping of technology and tended to ignore what is sometimes called 'the reciprocal relationship between artefacts and social groups'. This means, as Williams points out in Reading 1.1, it is a mistake to think of technology and social relations as separate: technology and society are mutually constitutive. Media technologies are a good example. Not only does society influence the technological developments used to produce and distribute media products, but the technologies themselves can favour the emergence of new forms of social relationships.

Box I.I Regulation

Regulation is particularly important for large-scale socio-technological systems. There will be much more about regulation and markets in the following chapters, but it is worth setting the scene straight away, in the context of media regulation.

I mentioned 'regulatory bodies' earlier in the main text – what are they? One answer would be to say that they are bodies like the UK's Office of Communications (Ofcom), Canada's Canadian Radio, Television and Telecommunications Commission (CRTC) or the US's Federal Communications Commission (FCC). But that sort of answer does not tell us what these bodies actually do! Let us turn again to the dictionary. The *Oxford English Dictionary* defines 'regulate' as 'to control, govern or direct, to subject to guidance or restriction, to adapt to circumstances or surroundings'. These definitions give us useful clues – they point to regulation as something societies do to achieve desired ends, as a flexible process that adapts to circumstances but that operates through control and restriction.

Different countries have organised regulation differently. In the UK, there was for a long time a state monopoly in both wired communication (through the Post Office) and broadcasting (through the BBC). In the USA there was a virtually private monopoly (Bell–AT&T) in telephony until the 1980s, while broadcasting was highly commercial and competitive from the early days of the sector. This meant that regulation in the UK was 'internalised' within the organisation (the BBC is a contemporary example of this with its regulator, the BBC Governors, who are part of the organisation). In the USA, on the other hand, regulation was 'externalised' and undertaken by separate bodies – notably the FCC.

Historically, there have been three major aspects to media regulation: technology, content, and ownership. The demands of technology meant that there had to be national and international agreements from the days of telegraphy onwards. Compatible systems for telegraphy and then telephony had to be agreed; and radio and television broadcasting had to be organised so that there was no interference between channels, or between broadcasting and the use of radio by, for example, the emergency services.

The regulation of content is thought to be particularly important for broadcasting because of the universal availability of programmes, and the need to avoid indecency and political bias. In the UK, the BBC was (and at the time of writing, in 2005, still is) expected to regulate itself through its Governors. With the introduction of commercial broadcasting, a separate regulatory body appeared, first known as the Independent Television Authority (ITA). In 2003 in the UK, all the non-BBC communications regulatory bodies were merged into Ofcom, with a wide brief ranging across the telecommunications and electronic media markets. In the USA, the FCC was established in 1934 to cover both broadcasting and wired telecommunications. Its brief includes both technical and content aspects of communications.

The internet is often said to be unregulated. Certainly, there are few controls over content (although some internet service providers offer filtering of content, and there is a wide range of software designed to control access to websites by, for example, children). As far as the technology is concerned, however, there is a great deal of regulation – through bodies such as the Internet Engineering Task Force (http://www.ietf.org/).

Questions of ownership are important because it is considered desirable to avoid concentration of both technological provision (telephony, for example) and content (radio and television) in too few hands. With the breaking up of commercial monopolies (such as that of Bell–AT&T in the USA in the 1980s) and state monopolies (such as many European telephone providers), regulatory bodies play an important role in monitoring and controlling the telecommunications industry. They also often regulate commercial mergers and takeovers of media companies.

Look at the development of SMS (texting) in mobile phones. Originally somewhat of an afterthought in the original mobile phone standard, texting has now become both a major feature of life and an important determinant in the design of mobile phones. (SMS was slower to take off in the USA owing to the later introduction of interoperability between different mobile providers than in the UK.) The rise of texting as a widespread communication medium has meant that mobile phones now come with electronic dictionaries and sophisticated software to predict a word from its first few letters. The social context has certainly shaped the technology as the following passage indicates:

> The first short message was sent in December 1992 from a Personal Computer to a mobile phone on the Vodafone GSM network in the UK. At the time, SMS was never intended for use as a consumer-to-consumer messaging service. Consumers, however, embraced the facility despite its limitations and SMS became an unexpected success that took the mobile industry completely by surprise. Few would have expected how this hard-to-use service would take off.
>
> Several factors combined to make this the messaging medium of choice for the younger generation. First, it is cheaper to send a message by SMS than to phone – the charges that network operators levy on SMS messaging are much lower than those they levy on calls. For cash-strapped younger consumers, low-cost SMS was a strong enough draw for them to overlook the usage-related difficulties and limitations of the medium – factors that acted as significant barriers to adoption for less cost-conscious older mobile phone users. In fact, some argue that it is precisely because of the manual dexterity needed to master the telephone keypad for text entry and the arcane chat-room vocabulary adopted by inveterate SMS users, and the difficulty in mastering these skills, that makes SMS so popular among younger people. While it would be fatuous to claim that older mobile phone owners are less likely to embrace SMS because of an apparent inability to grasp new technology, learn new skills, or that they lack manual dexterity, the overall age profile of a typical SMS user does nevertheless reflect a marked bias towards the younger demographics. There is an opinion that older people have generally been unwilling to use the service because other, simpler, mediums for communication exist, while younger people are such avid users of the medium precisely because it is so difficult to master.
>
> Maximiser, 2004

Activity 1.4

To what extent do you agree that there is such an 'age divide' in the use of texting? ■■■

My personal feeling is that the use of SMS is now far more common among 'older people' than this extract would suggest. As SMS has become easier to use, it has been adopted almost as a 'chat medium' by a wide variety of groups, including the middle-aged. There is evidence that women tend to use it more frequently than men (as with the telephone itself).

The main aim of this section is to emphasise that there is no simple answer to the question about how any technology has 'altered our world'. This remainder of this chapter investigates just a few aspects of this complex issue in the context of the media.

3   Time, space and media technologies

One interesting feature of media technologies (and, indeed, communication technologies in general), is the way in which they are associated with changing social practices in time and space.

Activity 1.5

Read the following quotation, from which I have deleted the reference to a particular media technology. What do you think the author is referring to, and why? ■ ■ ■

> Even while communal solidarity was diminished, vicarious participation in more distant events was also enhanced; and even while localities were loosened, links to larger collective units were being forged. [This technology] encouraged silent adherence to causes whose advocates could not be found in any one parish and who addressed an invisible public from afar. New forms of group loyalty began to compete with an older, more localised nexus of loyalties.
>
> Eisenstein, 1983, pp.95–6

The quotation in Activity 1.5 is from Elizabeth Eisenstein's 1983 book *The Printing Revolution in Early Modern Europe* (Eisenstein, 1983). If you correctly identified the 'media technology' in question as print, what gave it away? My feeling is that the reference to 'parish' implies that it is an old technology, since we would not normally use this word today. But if we changed 'parish' to 'location', it seems to me that much the same could be said about broadcasting, film or even the internet.

Now, you might think that print is very old hat in a twenty-first century course about media. But there are a number of important features that are generally applicable to modern media. For example, one of the revolutionary aspects of print was that it was standardised: everyone had an identical copy, unlike manuscripts. Indeed, it is a great problem for scholars of manuscript literature to reconstruct the original form of a text from the various divergent copies that survive. In contrast, a standard printed text meant that people could engage with the same text at different times and in different places. Networks of scholars, particularly scientists and philosophers from the seventeenth century onwards, were able to correspond about printed texts. Both 'time' and 'space' are *reorganised* through the new medium.

Occasionally, of course, the new print technology also allowed errors to be widely promulgated; the most famous, perhaps, being the so-called 'Wicked Bible', where the critical word 'not' was omitted from the injunction on adultery! (See Figure 1.1.) But the fact that many people were then viewing the identical error also meant it could be more easily identified and corrected – and the printers were fined £300!

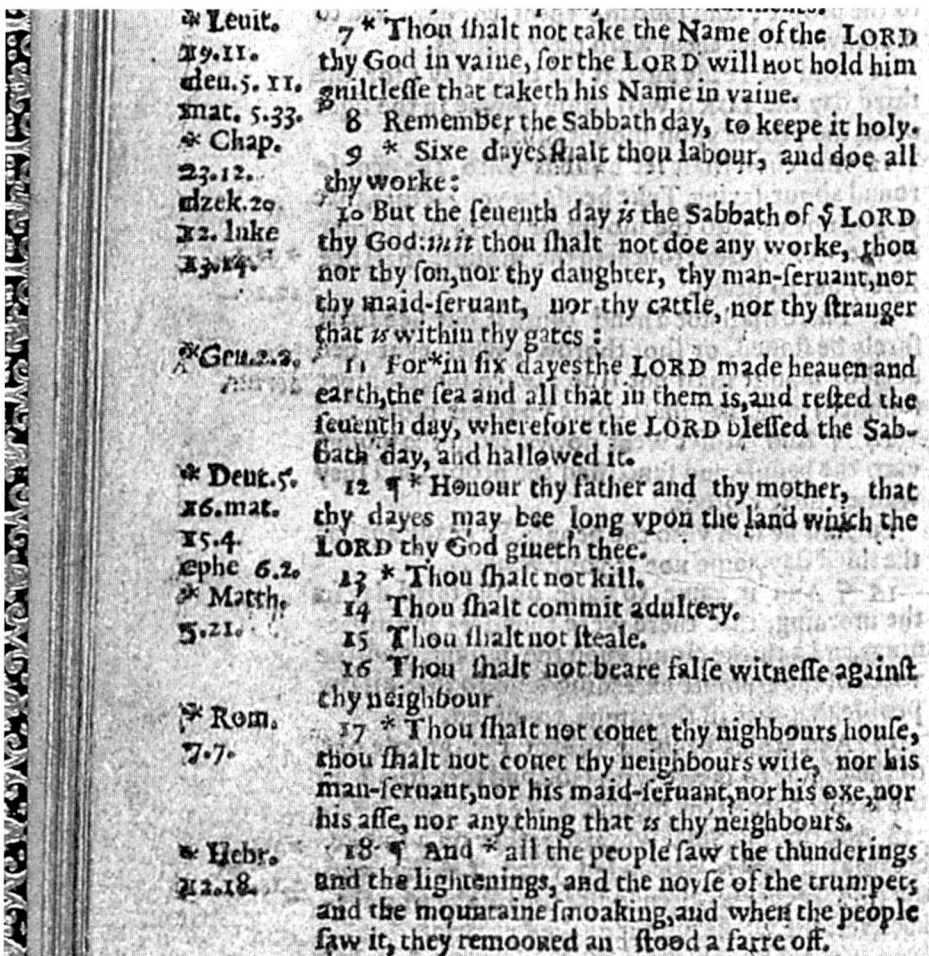

Figure 1.1 *The Wicked Bible (1631). Printing technology reproduced a thousand copies of a version of the Bible in which a printing error stated as one of the Ten Commandments: 'Thou shalt commit adultery'*
Source: The British Library

Activity 1.6

Consider some other media technologies: broadcasting, film, video/DVD, the internet. How do they 'alter time and space' for the user? (Are there constraints on where and when media technologies can be used?) ■ ■ ■

Broadcasting is independent of the location of the recipient (within geographical limits, and providing there is an electricity supply) but restricted in time. You have to tune in at the time a programme is on (unless you have recording facilities). Film is independent of both time and space, since in principle it can be shown anywhere, at any time. But in practice, you have to visit a particular cinema at a certain time. Video/DVD is independent of both time and space to a greater extent, at least within large towns with a good range of video shops or libraries.

The internet is independent of both time and space (providing there is network access). This is one reason why broadcasters are increasingly making programmes and programme archives available via the internet. Electrical and electronic delivery systems are particularly relevant to perceptions of time and space. The communication historian James Carey made the point particularly clearly in his study of the telegraph in *Communication as Culture* (Carey, 1989). Leaving aside earlier semaphore telegraph systems, electrical communication technology decisively separated the message from the messenger: for the first time communication no longer implied transportation.

Rapid and accurate information flow by telegraph over a wide network brought hitherto unimaginable possibilities for the co-ordination and control of industrial society. Carey singles out the change in nineteenth-century commodity markets and the introduction of standard time zones as two major examples. With the introduction of the telegraph and the corresponding flow of information on a national basis, differentials in commodity prices between cities were greatly reduced. Speculation therefore moved from the geographical realm into the temporal realm of what is known as futures trading. Because of the telegraph, everyone was effectively in the same place for the purposes of trade; time was opened up to the forces of commerce. Again because of the telegraph (and the railways), a set of standard time zones could be kept in synchrony with a single clock – despite the protests of those who thought such divorcing of time from the local position of the sun unnatural or even blasphemous. A similar point can be made about media technologies: broadcasting, for example, became enormously influential in structuring daily life around news bulletins, serials, concerts, soap operas, and so on.

Thus far we have emphasised the large-scale effects of media technologies. However, this power is never absolute and is always shaped and modified by social institutions. To use another of Carey's examples, telecommunications may have ironed out geographical differences in markets, but when Boston began to rival the New York Stock Exchange (as a result of the elimination of the information gap between them), telephones were quickly banned from the New York trading floor. New York's resulting 30-second lead in trading information was sufficient to ensure its continuing advantage! A slight enough example, perhaps, but sufficient to make the point that technical systems, and large-scale technical systems in particular, arise as a result of a complex interaction between technology, economics, politics, bureaucracy, and so on. So, the power of the media and the technologies on which it is based is not absolute but relative and *regulated* by social institutions reflecting particular interests.

The mobile phone is, perhaps, the most striking contemporary reorganiser of time and space. The most portable of devices, it is ideal for instant communication anywhere and at any time. Yet it also allows the storage and retrieval of both text and voice messages (and, increasingly, still and moving images) at both a time and place of the user's choosing.

4 Standards, systems and the shift to the consumer

In this section I shall examine three crucial aspects of the relationship between media technologies and social shaping: the importance of standards and the relationship between standards and regulation; the significance of large-scale socio-technical systems; and the recent shift in technological complexity to the consumer side of delivery systems.

4.1 Standards

The importance of standardisation has already been mentioned in the context of a very old media technology, print.

Activity 1.7

Think about other media technologies and the technologies that support them. List some features that have become standardised, and then read on. ■■■

There are plenty of examples of technologies that support media and that have become standardised, for example:

- electricity: standard voltage and mains alternating current frequency; standard battery formats;
- broadcasting: standard systems for radio and television transmission (channel frequencies, technical specifications, etc.);

- recording: standard sizes and electro-mechanical/electronic characteristics of recording and playback systems for vinyl records, audio and video cassettes, and DVDs;
- film: standard size of film and number of frames per second; standard for film soundtrack;
- computers: standard file formats for text, audio and images; standard hardware from different manufacturers.

Standardisation takes place in two major ways. The first is when an official regulatory body draws up rules to be followed by everyone in a particular sector. Standards for electricity supply fall into this category, as do those relating to broadcasting and telephony. Such standards are termed *de jure* standards, since they have a quasi-legal status: unless you conform to the standard you are simply not allowed to participate. Other standards emerge from industry and commerce, when one particular way of doing things becomes so common that it is called a de facto standard. Examples are audio and video cassette, CD, DVD and the PC. Unlike electricity, broadcasting and telephony, there are no formal regulations governing the products (although they may also use *de jure* standards in the way they operate). What has happened in the case of audio and video cassette and the PC is that one manufacturer achieved such a great market share that others began to conform to the particular standard. Or, sometimes, a group of manufacturers and other interested parties get together to agree a standard even before products are manufactured, in which case the standard has a much more *de jure* flavour. This was the case for digital mobile telephony and the DVD.

Standardisation often brings benefits for both producers and consumers of media products. Once a standard has emerged, as long as it is an 'open' standard and not confined to one firm, increased competition between manufacturers and distributors tends to bring prices down. And the existence of a common standard brings about 'interoperability', so that, for example, any CD can be played on any CD player (at least in principle – anti-piracy technologies can restrict this).

Standards issues (particularly de facto standards) are closely linked to issues of copyright and intellectual property. This is not the place to discuss these in detail, but it is interesting to observe the existence of widely differing approaches to proprietary control. One reason for the success of the IBM format PC in the 1980s and 1990s against its major competitor (Apple Macintosh) was the fact that details of the operating system of the former were made freely available to software developers, whereas details of the Macintosh system were kept highly restricted. In the hardware arena, Philips took the approach of licensing its patented audio compact cassette so that other manufacturers could use the same format. This contributed greatly to the audio cassette rapidly becoming a de facto standard. The IBM and Philips standards were open whereas the

Macintosh standard was not. And in the software field, there is currently (2005) an ongoing battle between the 'open source' software movement, which believes in allowing free access to computer code, and many software companies, such as Microsoft, who believe that ownership of software products should be protected.

Activity 1.8

Can you think of examples where the absence of a single common standard causes problems – or has caused problems in the past – for media and communication technologies? (Look back at my discussion of Activity 1.5 at the beginning of Section 3.) Apart from moving to a common standard, what measures do you know of that have been used to overcome such problems? ■ ■ ■

Perhaps the most common everyday example of a situation in which the absence of a standard causes problems for media and communication technologies (although not restricted to media and communication technologies) is the electricity supply. Even within Europe, with its common 220 volts, 50 cycles per second, different mains plugs are used. The USA uses 120 volts, 60 cycles per second. Within Europe, this problem is overcome by special adaptors that allow one style plug to be used to connect to a different style socket. But this is no help for people moving between North America and Europe. One answer, for certain devices, is to build 'dual standard' equipment. For example, electric shaver sockets in the UK often have two outlets, one for the European, one for the US standard.

Moving to media technologies proper, historically, three different colour television standards emerged – NTSC from the USA (also used in Japan), SECAM from France (also used in Russia) and PAL from Germany (also used in the UK and elsewhere). Since television tends to be used in one particular location, this has not been a great problem, but the answer for border areas or for very small portable television receivers has been to produce dual- or multi-standard devices. A similar situation exists for mobile telephony.

An example from film is the way in which early silent movies were hand cranked at various numbers of frames per second (usually between 16 and 18 frames per second). The (motorised) rate of 24 frames per second was standardised in 1927, when sound was introduced. So unless particular measures are taken, projecting early films from before this period on 'modern' equipment gives the characteristic 'speeded up' effect.

So, standards, although they may seem at first sight to be a long way from the cutting edge of science and technology, are vital for both production and consumption. Without widely accepted standards, no one will wish to invest in media production and consumers will not wish to purchase devices such as television sets, CD or DVD players, or computers.

4.2 Large-scale socio-technological systems

The historian of technology Thomas Hughes (1983) developed what he called the 'system builders' approach to shed light on technological development. His work related to the development of the electricity supply network, but is of much wider relevance, particularly to media technologies. He argued that much of the technical change in the early years of the twentieth century was a consequence of the building of the electricity supply network, and that the form that this took was determined as much by decisions of the financiers and entrepreneurs who wanted to control the networks as by technical issues. He coined the term 'reverse salient' to explain one particular feature of technological advance. 'Salient' is a military term used to describe the situation when a small force advances beyond the rest of the front, exposing itself to the enemy. A technological 'reverse salient' is when technological advance in general is held up by a particular problem. In Hughes's analysis, in such a situation huge forces (technological, financial, etc.) are devoted to the particular problem in order to resolve it.

Adopting Hughes's approach we can view some recent developments in digital media technology as an example of the overcoming of a reverse salient. To appreciate this, you need first to understand the basic principle of digital technology, outlined in Box 1.2.

Box 1.2 Numbers for everything

Any media product (text, images, sound) can be represented digitally – that is, by numbers. The numbers are normally transmitted as a binary code. In other words, only two symbols are used. For much of the internet these symbols, transmitted over optical fibres, are a very short flash of laser light, normally represented as the binary symbol 1 or an equivalent period of darkness represented by the symbol 0.

In the case of text, we can use a numerical code for every alphabetic character, number, punctuation mark, etc. Table 1.1 shows part of a standard code used for such purposes, where the codes are given in denary (decimal) form rather than the binary code that would normally be used for data storage or transmission. Originally known as the American Standard Code for Information Interchange (ASCII), it is now more properly termed International Alphabet 5 (IA-5).

Table 1.1 Some ASCII (IA-5) codes

Character	Code	Character	Code	Function	Code
A	65	a	97	back space	8
B	66	b	98	tab	9
C	67	c	99	new line	10
D	68	d	100	carriage return	11
E	69	e	101		
F	70	f	102	space	32
G	71	g	103		
H	72	h	104		
I	73	i	105		
J	74	j	106		
K	75	k	107		
L	76	l	108		
M	77	m	109		
N	78	n	110		
O	79	o	111		
P	80	p	112		
Q	81	q	113		
R	82	r	114		
S	83	s	115		
T	84	t	116		
U	85	u	117		
V	86	v	118		
W	87	w	119		
X	88	x	120		
Y	89	y	121		
Z	90	z	122		

Activity 1.9

Using the coding in Table 1.1, decode the following sequence: 77 69 68 73 65 32 83 84 85 68 73 69 83.

Now suppose the value 32 is added to each of the 13 alphabetic character codes in the sequence listed immediately above (so that the number 77 becomes '109', for example). What do the resulting numbers signify? Go to the end of this chapter to find the answer. ■ ■ ■

The simple example in Box 1.2 and Activity 1.9 is an illustration of how text processing can be carried out using numerical operations: the instruction 'add 32 to every upper-case code' converts the sequence to lower case. Such numerical processing is the key to what we call the 'information revolution': it allows us to code and process text, sound, images, moving pictures. Images can be represented digitally, by using numerical codes for brightness levels and colour, although (unlike text) many millions of codes are needed for a good representation of an image. Sound can be captured digitally by representing the strength of the sound wave at any particular instant by a numerical code.

There are many advantages in using digital representations: for example, the final quality of the product can be much better; and it is possible to use computer technology to process text, images and audio in ways that were just not possible with earlier technologies. But – and here is the 'reverse salient' in Hughes's terminology – until recently there was an enormous problem in exploiting the potential of digital technology for the production and dissemination of media products. Coding such products digitally results in huge amounts of data, which made it impracticable to use digital techniques for terrestrial broadcasting, mobile telephony or video recording. So, during the 1980s and 1990s, enormous efforts were put into developing the new technologies (including a number of remarkably influential standards) needed to overcome this problem. We can view such activities as a very large-scale socio-technological system (or an interconnection of a number of such systems). Important players were:

■ governments and supranational bodies (for example, the European Union in defining the GSM standard for mobile telephony);

■ manufacturers, for the research and development of new electronic hardware;

■ consortia of commercial and industrial bodies, such as the Motion Pictures Expert Group (MPEG), which began by addressing the problem of digital television, but came up with techniques that are now also used in CD-ROMs, mobile phones, the internet, DVDs and mp3 players.

4.3 The shift to the consumer

The third important aspect of media technology is what I call 'the shift to the consumer'. This is both a technological and a social shift and – unsurprisingly – the two are connected.

Early media technologies demanded little on the part of a user's equipment. Print needs nothing (except, perhaps, a pair of spectacles) and even early radio receivers could be easily built at home. As a child in the 1960s I remember building a 'foxhole radio' of the type Second World War soldiers were said to have used (see Figure 1.2). All you need is a pair of headphones, some thin copper wire, a pencil lead, and a razor blade. With such rudimentary technology you can easily still pick up AM radio transmissions. I also remember using a paper cone and a sewing needle to play back 78 rpm records!

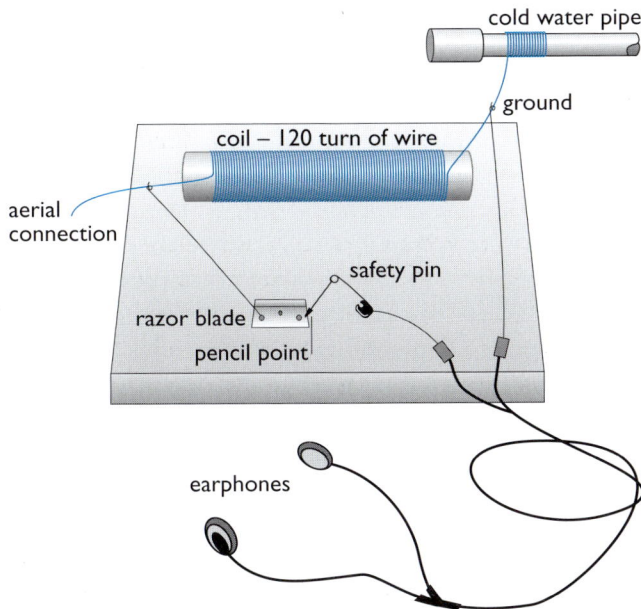

Figure 1.2 *A foxhole radio was the ultimate in keeping technology simple at the user's end. Soldiers could construct a functioning radio using basic parts that were easily available, even during hostilities*

The point is that the technology required by the user was kept simple to keep down costs. All the complicated technology was at the production end – whether in printing, broadcasting or recording. To a large extent, this general maxim remained true until the last couple of decades. Even with the invention of FM broadcasting, magnetic tape recording, television or stereo broadcasting, the receivers/players were comparatively simple: it just was not possible to have highly complicated (and expensive) electronics in mass-produced consumer goods.

All this has changed with digital technology. Digital radio and television receivers, DVD players and even mobile phones now have far more processing power than the early digital computers. Of course, such developments went hand in hand with the development of new production technologies that resulted in a huge reduction in the price of digital components.

It is the availability of sophisticated electronics and digital signal processing at the receiver end as well as at the production end that has allowed the fundamental drawback of digitised media products – the huge amount of data – to be overcome. One major advance has been in so-called 'compression' techniques, which allow the amount of digital data stored or transmitted to be reduced without noticeably reducing the quality. Some of these compression techniques are highly complicated, and this certainly is not the place to discuss them. But the basic point is this: in early AM radio, the radio signal is essentially a radio wave version of the original sound waveform and is very simple to turn back into a soundwave. Early gramophone records simply had the soundwave 'engraved' onto the disc. A needle to pick up the vibrations, and a horn (even a paper cone) to amplify the sound, was all that was required to reproduce a version (admittedly 'low fidelity') of the original. Compare this now with what is involved in digital technology. In digital radio and television broadcasting the original signal is in effect 'chopped up' and distributed simultaneously over thousands of different broadcasting frequencies. It can only be 'put back together' by means of complicated processing at the receiver. The mp3 format for music involves an algorithm that analyses the sound in terms of human perception and suppresses elements that we cannot hear, since there is no need to transmit or record them. In the MPEG standards for digital video the data is compressed by (among other techniques) examining how similar consecutive frames are and, if there has not been much change, transmitting only the differences. GSM (the standard used for most mobile telephones in Europe at the time of writing) digital mobile phones include a process whereby the characteristics of the speaker's voice are analysed and enough information is transmitted for a sufficiently close replica to be synthesised at the other end. What all these techniques have in common is the huge amount of processing required both at the production/transmission end and also – and this is what is so new – at the player/receiver end.

I have stressed the importance of digital technology at the consumer end, but we must not forget the changes on the production side. The same improvements in digital recording and storage technologies mean that films and television programmes can be recorded, stored and manipulated (for editing and special effects) much more easily than with earlier technology. Such digital production systems became available before the associated digital consumer products, since the necessarily high investment in hardware and software was possible from producers, while consumers needed to be able to continue to use their existing equipment. But the advantages of unifying the technologies of production and consumption were also a significant driver in the move to digital media technologies.

Now, this has all been rather technical and, you might think, remote from the study of the media. In a moment we shall look in more detail at the relation between technology, regulation and society in the context of two specific media technologies – video recording and the internet. But before we do this think about the relevance of the material of this chapter for understanding the media and the relationship between media and society.

Activity 1.10

First, think of standardisation. Who does this empower: the manufacturers and producers or the consumer? Then, consider 'large-scale socio-technical systems' and 'systems builders' – what power relationships are involved here? Finally, think about technology and social change. In the light of what you have just read, do you think that technology drives social change? Or does society determine the way technology advances? ■ ■ ■

It seems to me that there are a number of important aspects of technology and the power relationships associated with it. As far as standardisation is concerned, the existence of common standards often results in increased competition, an expansion of the market, a tendency for no single provider to dominate the market and greater consumer choice. However, the opposite can also be the case, particularly when government monopolies are involved – for example, the long domination of the BBC in UK broadcasting, or the Post Office telephone monopoly in the UK until the 1980s (apart from the city of Kingston-upon-Hull and adjacent region, which had its own telephone service). Or take the example of Microsoft. The fact that Microsoft products became a virtual standard for PC software certainly improved such aspects as interoperability, but many observers have criticised both the quality of many of the products and also the dangers of Microsoft's virtual global monopoly. Recently, however, other software providers have exploited the existence of Microsoft 'standards' to produce much cheaper (or sometimes even free) alternatives. The StarOffice suite of software, for example, can read most Microsoft Office files and store files in a compatible format.

The 'systems builders' approach reminds us of the complexity of the power relationships in large-scale socio-technological systems, and also that modern hi-tech systems can often only be created as the result of a high degree of collaboration between interested parties, especially when huge efforts are needed to overcome reverse salients (see Section 4.2). The shift of processing power to the user end, it can be argued, has also shifted a certain amount of power to the consumer. Digital techniques in principle offer a greater choice (although this can be contested, certainly in quality terms) and a degree of interactivity with such formats as DVD or digital television, where the viewer can select different options, or even transmit opinions to the broadcaster.

Turning to the relationship between technology and social change, I think my discussion supports the 'social construction' (SCOT) viewpoint rather than any simple, linear, technologically determined chain of cause and effect along the lines of:

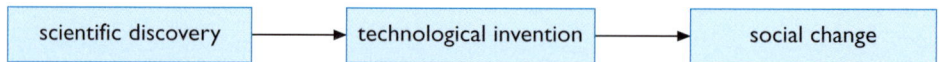

Figure 1.3 *Such a technologically determinist model does not reflect the complexity of the relationship between society and technology*

Certainly new media technologies have been accompanied by social change, but enormous, deliberate, social efforts have also been made to bring about the technology. Digital mobile telephony is an excellent example. The origin was a political imperative on the part of the EU to develop a pan-European digital system to replace the incompatible, analogue systems of the 1980s. Similarly, the pressure to produce a digital system for movies that would eventually lead to the DVD came initially from the motion picture industry.

I do not expect you to have come up with these particular examples, since my commentary has referred to things not discussed specifically in previous sections. But I hope you were able to identify some of the main features of what is a very complex situation, both technologically and socially.

5   Case study 1: video recording

This section and the next are devoted to two case studies that exemplify the points discussed so far. Firstly, video tape recording.

Table 1.2 lists the chronology of some of the major technical developments in video recording on tape and digital disc. (It is not intended to be complete.)

Table 1.2 The development of the video recorder

1956	First video recorder, standing nearly 2 m high, recorded 15 mins on a 20-inch reel of tape, required air conditioning because of heat generated by valves
1957	More 'compact' machine (approx. 1 x 1 x 1.5 m), no air conditioning needed, still used valves
1967	First Japanese transistorised, colour, reel-to-reel video recorder, retail price around £500 (price of a small car)
1974	Philips video cassette recorder with 1 hr play time (£450) on a £20 cassette tape
1978	Large-format laserdisc introduced, but never achieved huge market success
1979	Three-hour cassettes introduced, several competing incompatible standards
1982	VHS standard emerged as winner, three-hour cassettes down to £10
1995	Philips/Sony announced and demonstrated *MMCD* system. Toshiba and Warner announced and demonstrated *SD* system. Agreement reached on a common standard to become known as DVD
1996	First DVD players sold in Japan (November)
1997	DVD Forum established

This is a linear story of technological development of the type often given after the event. But it hides a more complex and much more interesting story.

5.1 The VCR

First, look at the timescale. Brian Winston, in his book *Media, Technology and Society* (1998), studied a wide range of media technologies, and identified a typical lead time of three or four decades for the establishment of a new technology from early prototypes, and a lot longer from the scientific basis of the technology. This was true for the VCR and is useful to bear in mind when reading any claim about 'revolutionary' media technologies. Second, consider one of the key technological developments: the replacement of valves by solid-state (transistorised) electronics. The transistor was invented in 1947, but early products using transistors were not particularly successful or reliable. However, because of its enormous potential to replace the valve in many applications (with the advantages of reduced power consumption and heat generation, for example), huge efforts were devoted over the following decades to improving the technology. Particularly important was the invention of the integrated circuit, in which many transistors and other components were fabricated on a single silicon chip, rather than as individual devices that then had to be interconnected.

But technological improvements were only part of the story.

Reading 1.2 Activity

Read the following two extracts from *Which?* magazine reports. What strikes you about price, reliability, maintenance and expected use, compared with VCR or DVD machines of the early twenty-first century? (In 1977 a young teacher's entry salary was around £3,200, compared with about £19,000 in 2005; and a VCR or DVD in 2005 could be bought for as little as £30.)

Reading 1.2a

Consumers' Association, 'Inside story: video cassette recorders'

A video cassette recorder (VCR) is a machine which enables you to record television programmes and play them back on your television screen [...]

The only video cassette recorder made specifically for home use at the moment is the Philips N1502 (list price £649, though you may find it for £600 or less if you shop around). It's about the size of a 22 in suitcase. [...]

What our members found

The main reasons they gave for buying a VCR was missing programmes by being out or asleep when they were shown, and to resolve programme clashes. Very few regretted buying one; several said they'd be lost without their recorder. They divided about equally as to whether their recorders were reliable or unreliable [...]. Nearly all thought the picture quality acceptable. Main complaints:

- **tapes or tape mechanism faulty**
  Tapes (various brands) got 'churned', 'chewed', 'twisted' or 'stuck', or tapes broke.
- **recording time too short**
  At the moment, the longest running tape plays for only an hour. Members found either that they wanted to record longer programmes than this, or that they had preset their recorders for an hour's programme which had started a few minutes late, and so lost the closing sequences. Philips tell us that they are

introducing a new model this month – N1700 – which will record for a maximum of 2hr 10min, by running the present 1hr cassettes more slowly.

- **tapes expensive**
  The longest-playing cassette costs about £23, though you can find them at around £17 if you shop around (or buy in bulk).

- **video heads expensive**
  Some members were disappointed with how long these lasted (Philips tell us they should last 1,000hr), or thought them expensive to replace (£40 to £60).

Reading source

Consumers' Association, 1977

Reading 1.2b

Consumers' Association, 'The rival systems'

There are four basic *systems* of video recorder – **VCR**, **Beta**, **VHS** and **SVR**.

Some brands of recorder use one system, others another. This is the way these systems have developed:

- **VCR** is the Philips system. The first Philips machine (and the first real domestic video recorder) was the N1500 launched in 1974. The N1501 and N1502 versions followed in late 1975 and 1976 – but, like the N1500, were restricted to one hour of playing time. In late 1977, Philips brought out the N1700 – incompatible with the early N1500 series – giving a longer recording time (this version is sometimes called VCR-LP)

- **Beta** was introduced by the Japanese company of Sony in 1975. The Beta II format (which, again, gave a longer recording time) followed in early 1977

- **VHS** is the other Japanese system. It was developed by JVC, launched in 1976, and became available in the UK with three hours' playing time in 1978

- **SVR** is a development by Grundig of the VCR system. The VCR 4000 was launched in early 1977, giving two hours' playing time. After Philips brought out the N1700, Grundig brought out the SVR 4004 – capable of four hours' playing time.

In the long run, one system may triumph over the others, and become the standard system. But there's no sign of this happening at present.

The four existing systems are **incompatible** – which means that you can't change tapes between *systems*, though you can still do so between brands *using the same system* (except that N1500-series VCR recorders are also incompatible with N1700-series VCR models). Blank SVR tapes can be used on VCR machines – though not *vice versa*. But this is unlikely to matter to most people – members didn't often use their video recorders for playing-back pre-recorded tapes, or tapes made on another machine.

Reading source

Consumers' Association, 1979 ■ ■ ■

From Readings 1.2a and 1.2b it should be apparent that the early machines cost a fortune – nearly 20 per cent of a teacher's salary compared with less than 0.2 per cent of a teacher's salary in 2005! Running costs were also high, with expensive tapes and the need to replace recording heads quite frequently. Most surprising, perhaps, is the view of the Consumers' Association in 1979 that incompatibility between the different systems was unimportant.

In fact, the resolution of the incompatibility problem turned out to be one of the key drivers in the development of the technology. Once the VHS system had won out, there was far more incentive to purchase a machine. Users *did* want to swap tapes. Video shops and libraries could invest with confidence in a stable market. Economies of scale meant that manufacturers could lower prices and different companies competed more vigorously once they all used the same system. Interestingly, the VHS system is often claimed to be inferior in terms of reproduction quality to one of its rivals (Beta), and is presented as a rather ironic success story. But whether or not this is true, it misses the point. The success or otherwise of a media technology depends on price, design, marketing, convenience and many other aspects, as well as supposed 'technological superiority'.

With the success of the VHS format, new forms of cultural practice emerged. It became commonplace for friends to meet to watch a video at home, for example; and the desire of people to keep track of favourite serials or soaps while on holiday encouraged manufacturers to add new features, such as timers that allowed several episodes to be recorded automatically, and 'long play' options that gave extra recording time for such purposes. Machines became available with two tape drives, to enable users to copy tapes. The development of the video recorder is a classic example of the complexities of socio-technical change.

5.2 The DVD

The DVD offers an interesting contrast to the VCR. The idea of a disc, rather like an audio CD but with a vastly increased capacity capable of storing a whole movie, came out of an informal Hollywood committee in 1994. By the following year, two competing systems had been proposed, but unlike the VCR experience the relevant manufacturers agreed on a common standard *before* launching their products. The first discussions were acrimonious, but the two competing designs were brought together as a compromise, in part at least because of actions by the major software and hardware giants, who put pressure on the original companies and joined a consortium to develop a common standard. Although the road to standardisation was not easy and a good deal of bickering and jostling for position took place for many years, the result was a technology that introduced a number of novel coding techniques and gained a market share much more rapidly than was the norm (although it should not be forgotten that DVD technology is firmly based on CD technology and compression standards for digital television, which date from the early 1980s).

The pre-competition standardisation of the video and audio aspects of the DVD was not, however, repeated when it came to recordable and re-writable discs. Here, a number of competing and incompatible formats were developed. (By the time you read this, the problem may have been resolved, but it was certainly a problem in the early days of this technology.)

Like other digital technologies, the key to the DVD is the enormous processing power in the receiver, which cannot only cope with the 'decompression' necessary to recover the original data, but also offers interactivity, multiple sound tracks and many other features.

6 Case study 2: the internet

Table 1.3 gives you the opportunity to stand back from contemporary developments and analyse the long-term characteristics of another media technology, this time the internet. (Again, it makes no attempt to be complete.)

Table 1.3 The development of the internet

1967	Ann Arbor meeting of ARPA (Advanced Research Projects Agency) on computer networking
1969	Networking project at Bolt, Beranek & Newman begins. ARPANET established
1972	Washington Conference on Computer Communication
1973	First international email
1974	Emergence of standard Transmission Control Protocol (TCP)
1975	Creation of mail lists
1979	ARPANET transferred to Defence Communication Agency CompuServe founded
1983	ARPA-INTERNET established, separate from MILNET
1985	US National Science Foundation agrees to build and manage a backbone network linking its five supercomputing sites
1990	Tim Berners-Lee, working at CERN, conceives the http standard (protocol for hypertext) and World-Wide Web
1993	First internet 'browser' program (Mosaic) introduced
1994	Netscape introduced
1995	Microsoft (belatedly) realises the importance of the world wide web and bundles Explorer with Windows

Activity 1.11

What similarities do you notice between Table 1.3 and the earlier discussion of video recording technology? ■ ■ ■

Three things spring to mind when I look at Table 1.3. Firstly, there was again a three-decade interval between the origins of the internet in the 1960s and the widespread adoption of the technology by the public in the mid-1990s. Secondly, standards were again important. Two examples are the TCP and http protocols, but also the falling-in-line of Microsoft at a relatively late stage. The third commonality is the fact that the new technology was used extensively for applications not envisaged at the outset. Email is the classic example of a key driver for the development of computer network technologies that was not a major aim of the early networks. Video libraries and exchange of tapes were similarly an outcome of early video recorders, which had been designed initially with the aim of recording television programmes.

6.1 The social context

Read the following quotation from the sociologist Manuel Castells, on the internet. How does Castells characterise the effects of the internet on modern societies? ■ ■ ■

> The Internet is the fabric of our lives. If information technology is the present-day equivalent of electricity in the industrial era, in our age the Internet could be likened to both the electrical grid and the electric engine because of its ability to distribute the power of information throughout the entire realm of human activity. Furthermore, as new technologies of energy generation and distribution made possible the factory and the large corporation as the organizational foundations of industrial society, the Internet is the technological basis *for* the organizational *form* of the Information Age: the network. [...]
>
> In the last quarter of the twentieth century, three independent processes came together, ushering in a new social structure pre-dominantly based on networks: the needs of the economy for management flexibility and for the globalization of capital, production, and trade; the demands of society in which the values of individual freedom and open communication became paramount; and the extraordinary advances in computing and telecommunications made possible by the micro-electronics revolution. Under these conditions, the Internet, an obscure technology without much application beyond the secluded worlds of computer scientists, hackers, and counter cultural communities, became the lever for the transition to a new form of society – the network society – and with it to a new economy.
>
> Castells, 2001, pp.1–2

Castells likens the transformative powers of the internet to those of the new electrical technologies of an earlier age (which he calls the 'industrial era'). He compares the ways in which electrical technologies made possible new organisational structures of factories and corporations with the ways in which modern information and communication technologies (ICTs) have ushered in a 'network society'.

Reading 1.3 Activity

Now read the following extract from Brian Winston's book, *Media, Technology and Society*, and write a few sentences summarising Winston's arguments, comparing them with those of Castells in the quotation given in Activity 1.12.

Reading 1.3

Brian Winston, 'This grand system'

By July 1995 there were supposedly anything from 6.5 million machines worldwide to 10.3 million in the US alone connected to the net. The popular figure of Internet users of between 35 and 45 million appears to have been obtained by simply multiplying the 6.5 million by seven – perhaps because in the earliest days of the ARPANET, seven users per terminal was a norm. The range of estimates does not inspire confidence and seems, on the face of it, to be absurd. At this time, some net demographers were putting the user figure at about one-tenth of the high estimate, that is some 3 million. This would seem to be far nearer to the mark: in Britain for example, only 20 per cent of 4 million home computers were even claimed as connected in 1996 (while, at the same time, surveys claiming up to six million British users were regularly published without explanation as to how such a figure could be reached).

And who were these users, these 'early adopters'? 'According to the Georgia Institute of Technology, in the most comprehensive survey of Internet users to date (1994), 90% were men, 80% white, 70% North Americans, 50% spent 40 hours or more a week computing and 30% are graduates' (Winston and Walton, 1996, p.79).

From the very beginning it has been clear that the most unambiguously valuable facility provided by the net is e-mail. That would seem to hold for current users as it did for the ARPANET pioneers. There is no more efficient or cheaper way to communicate, especially when time zone differences are so great that no working hours are shared. It is also probably the case that, again as happened with the pioneers, shared professional or, especially, academic concerns can lead to useful multi-person exchanges. However, the radical impact of such a system on the academy, say, will be contained for the foreseeable future by traditional requirements of authorship and publication. Other uses such as the creation of a virtual social community seem to have less, if any, purpose except as a sort of hobby.

There were several other reasons for viewing the reality of the net, as opposed to the inflated rhetoric surrounding it, with a certain cynicism. The more users, the more slowly the system sent. Experience suggested that California needed to be asleep if any chance of reasonable access were to be achieved. [...] The internet represents the final disastrous application of the concept of commoditisation of information in the second half of the twentieth century. By the mid-1990s there was talk of abandoning the whole system in favour of a second Internet which could be kept preserved from the information detritus suffocating the original.

There is also little to support the idea that the net will become a crucial method for selling goods and services. Every system for avoiding shopping from the mail-order catalogue to the cable television shopping channel has never done more than provide, albeit often profitably, niche services. One of the sillier facets of Information Revolution rhetoric is the belief that technology is urgently required to help people avoid going shopping or travelling on business. People like shopping and travelling – just as they like being told, or reading, stories. So we do not need stories to be any more 'interactive' than they have been since the dawn of time; a liking for travel is why business people have avoided the lure of the video-conference phone for nearly two-thirds of the twentieth century; and we so love shopping we have made the shopping mall (as the latest incarnation of the nineteenth century arcade) into our emblematic public space. Why the slow, cluttered and inefficient Internet should be more significant than previous distant buying systems is not clear. It seemed that in the early years the only effective marketers on the vaunted Information Highway were pornographers.

[...]

Beyond the hype, the Internet was just another network. This is to say its social effects could (and would) be as profound as, for example, those of that far more ubiquitous network, the telephone. As profound ... and as unrevolutionary.

Reference

Winston, B. and Walton, P. (1995) 'Review of the News', in Eldridge, J.E.T. (ed.) *Glasgow Media Group Reader Volume 1: News Content, Language and Visuals,* London, Routledge.

Reading source

Winston, 1998, pp.334–6 ■ ■ ■

At first sight Winston takes a very different line from Castells. Winston is dismissive of the notion of an 'information revolution' and critical of the statistics used to support the notion. He points to email as the overwhelmingly important application and is sceptical about the internet becoming a major force in the supply of products and services (including media products).

Castells, although he does not use the term 'revolution' in this quotation, does attribute very strong transformative powers to the internet. By attributing so much power to technology, he tempts us to assume that he is taking a primarily technological determinist approach – and, indeed, Castells has been criticised for this by a number of commentators on his work. It is true that the quotation from Castells has a rather determinist flavour, but elsewhere he is more circumspect, emphasising the fact that society and technology are mutually constitutive:

> The point of departure of [my] analysis is that people, institutions, companies, and society at large, transform technology, any technology, by appropriating it, by modifying it, by experimenting with it. This is the fundamental lesson from the social history of technology, and this is even more so in the case of the Internet, a technology of communication. Conscious communication (human language) is what makes the biological specificity of the human species. Since practice is based on communication, and the Internet transforms the way in which we communicate, our lives are deeply affected by this new communication technology. On the other hand, by doing many things with the Internet, we transform the Internet itself. A new socio-technical pattern emerges from this interaction.
>
> Moreover, the Internet was purposely designed as a technology free communication, for historical and cultural reasons that I will present in this book. It is not the result of this project that we are free at last thanks to the Internet – as I hope I will be able to show: it all depends on context and process. But it follows that the Internet is a particularly malleable technology, susceptible of being deeply modified by its social practice, and leading to a whole range potential social outcomes – to be discovered by experience, not proclaimed beforehand.
>
> Castells, 2001, pp.2–3

Where the two writers do differ is with respect to the degree of change that can be attributed to new media technologies and particularly to the Internet. Winston prefers to emphasise that the social effects of the Internet are just as 'profound' but 'non-revolutionary' as the telephone, while Castells sees something quite new in the global networks. It all depends, I suppose, on how you define 'revolutionary' – enormous social change and shifts in the balance of power were also associated with the telephone, but again, the key term is 'mutually constitutive'.

6.2 An information revolution

Since the words 'revolution' and 'revolutionary' are so often used in the context of the new media technologies, it is instructive to tease out what is meant by these terms.

Firstly, it is worth noting that the word 'revolution' has an interesting history. Its original meaning of a turning, or a periodically repeating cycle, seems to have been applied only comparatively late to political events – and at first, to use Simon Shapin's phrase – in the sense of 'fortune's wheel' (Shapin, 1996, p.3). That is, a political or social revolution (when the word was used at all) was not a radical overturning or reordering of things, but rather a potentially repeating change rather like an economic cycle. The modern meaning of the word as we use it when we speak of an industrial, scientific, political, or – of course – an *information* revolution dates back to the *philosophes* of the French Enlightenment, and may well have been applied to the notion of a revolution in science before being used to describe irreversible political events.

One of the most striking features of the rhetoric about 'the information revolution' is the way in which we are promised a utopia. Information and communication technologies, we are told, promise us virtually unlimited access to information and entertainment; instantaneous communication with anyone in the world; increased leisure and quality of life; and even new, improved forms of society. Such claims have been made about all kinds of technologies: canals, steam engines, electricity, the telegraph, motion pictures ... the list, if not endless, is pretty long!

My point is that there is nothing new about much of the rhetoric surrounding the internet and ICT in general. However, while I am sceptical about extreme claims about an 'information revolution', I think we can pick out some real changes of high significance for media students:

1   The internet, much more than any earlier media technology, is centred around user *demand*. Media products such as newspapers (and their archives), radio programmes (and archives), MP3 music files, etc. are available as and when the user wishes. There are still problems shipping around the huge data files involved, particularly for high-quality video, but there is as yet no slowing down of higher and higher data rates to consumers.

2   Individuals now have much greater opportunities to create and manipulate their own media products – digital photography and video, for example. And the world wide web offers the user-friendly 'home page' as a route to the construction of other home-made media products and also for the maintenance of personal identity or identities. (The plural is particularly noticeable where WWW home page authors offer 'professional' and 'personal' options – sometimes

via different servers.) Indeed, it is now common for 'internet-active' organisations and individuals to offer their URL as an alter ego – from company PR front ends, through commercial business cards, to university academics exchanging details of research areas and publications at conferences. School and university students are invited to produce personal or group web pages as part of assignments – and in contrast to previous exercises in interpersonal and teamworking skills, such efforts are now often visible globally as media products. And not only as a finished product, as Daniel Chandler (1998) has remarked:

> The 'personal home page' is a new genre brought into existence by that branch of the internet which is known as the World-Wide Web. Personal home pages are online multi-media texts which address the question, 'Who Am I?'... In such sites, what are visibly 'under construction' are not only the pages but the authors themselves.
>
> Chandler, 1998

3   The rise of the 'weblog' or 'blog' is another interesting phenomenon which has shifted power to the individual. A weblog might be thought of as a modern version of the centuries-old 'commonplace book' (a notebook in which quotations, poems and other items that strike the author are recorded). A weblog is a sort of online equivalent, but containing hot links to the items that have attracted the author's attention, as well as the author's comments. Like other web pages, and unlike the commonplace book, it is available as a media product to anyone with a connection to the internet. Again, unlike the commonplace book, some weblogs allow others to post material. Weblogs came to wide public attention at the time of the Iraq War of 2003, when a number of Iraqis used personal weblogs to make available detailed and continuously updated information from the heart of the war. Recently we have seen a version of the 'blog' developing in the form of 'podcasting' where consumers can download sound, 'radio', news programmes onto their iPod (or other personal digital audio recorder/player using MP3 standards). Such 'podcasting' can be done by established broadcasters, such as the BBC and NPR – National Public Radio – in the USA and also by anyone who wants to post a sound file on a website for downloading.

All three of these aspects can be viewed as a significant transfer of power to users/consumers, although we must be careful about attributing too much 'democratisation' as a result of the internet. There are such huge issues about 'the digital divide' and 'information *haves* and *have-nots*' that we cannot go into them here.

Activity 1.13

Based on your own experience of the internet, or that of your friends or family, how far do you agree with the assessment(s) of Reading 1.3 and the quotations from Castells? ■ ■ ■

Your response to Activity 1.13 will, of course, depend very much on your personal circumstances, experience and opinions. I suppose that I am what is called an 'early adopter' of the new technology, and can still remember my amazement at the power of the new Web browsers when they were introduced in the mid-1990s. But my major use of the internet is for email and simple online purchases of airline tickets and hotel bookings. And having spent my early childhood in a household without a telephone or a television (or a car), I tend to side with Winston on the 'unrevolutionary' nature of the internet – the other three technologies changed my life as much, if not more, than the internet!

It seems to me that the jury is still out on many of Castells's arguments with regard to the media. Modern 'networked society' has had comparatively little effect on my own consumption of media products. In 2005 I still go to the cinema (although the production technology has certainly changed), and I frequent 'real' as opposed to 'virtual' shops. I watch broadcast (analogue, not digital) technology; and I buy CDs rather than download MP3 files. (On the other hand, my daughter downloads movies via a broadband connection over the net!)

Where I agree with both writers is that social practice has affected media technologies just as much as media technologies have changed social practices.

7 Conclusion

So, what should you to take away from your study of this chapter? I hope you have understood that media technologies owe as much to features such as standardisation and 'systems building' as to scientific and technological discovery and invention and that you will be sceptical when people claim 'unprecedented' or 'revolutionary' characteristics for media (and other) technologies.

The key points that you should take with you as you read the rest of this book are:

■ technology and society are mutually constitutive;

■ media technologies have encouraged new social practices; have tended to 'reorganise time and space';

■ conversely, social practices have shaped the development of media technologies;

- standards and regulation are key factors in technological development;
- new technologies only rarely replace older ones. Print, film, radio, television, video, internet all currently coexist (although video tape recorders may well have been largely replaced by digital machines by the time you study this);
- the element of continuity in media technologies is just as remarkable as that of change.

Activity Answer 1.9

The original sequence codes for: MEDIA STUDIES

Adding 32 to the code for the alphabetic characters results in: media studies. ■ ■ ■

Further reading

Castells, M. (2001) *The Internet Galaxy*, Oxford, Oxford University Press.

Eisenstein, E.L. (1983) *The Printing Revolution in Early Modern Europe*, Cambridge, Cambridge University Press. This book on printing is very interesting and looks forward to themes explored in Chapter 2.

MacKenzie, D. and Wajcman, J. (eds) (1999) *The Social Shaping of Technology*, Buckingham, Open University Press. This provides a good way into debates about technological determinism and social shaping – if you read it you will also discover how the refrigerator got its hum!

Williams, R. (1974) *Television, Technology and Cultural Form*, London, Fontana.

Winston, B. (1998) *Media, Technology and Society*, London, Routledge.

Your first port of call should, almost certainly, be the full texts of the key works discussed in this chapter. There is no substitute for reading the full argument made by authors, reflecting on them yourself and drawing your own reasoned conclusions. The extraction of sections from extensive arguments – often of book length – means that authors' reasoning is sometimes abbreviated and almost always their substantiation of their arguments with evidence and examples is underrepresented. Remember, these are just suggestions for you to follow up if you are interested, you are not expected to read any or all of these books.

References

Bijker, W.E., Hughes, T.P. and Pinch, T.J. (eds) (1987) *The Social Construction of Technological Systems*, Cambridge, MA, MIT Press.

Carey, J. (1989) *Communication as Culture*, Winchester, MA, Unwin Hyman.

Castells, M. (2001) *The Internet Galaxy*, Oxford, Oxford University Press.

Chandler, D. (1998) *Personal Home Pages and the Construction of Identities on the Web*, Aberystwyth University, http://www.aber.ac.uk/media/ Documents/short/webident.html (accessed 19 January 2005).

Consumers' Association (1977) 'Inside story: video cassette recorders', *Which?*, October.

Consumers' Association (1979) 'The rival systems', *Which?*, July.

Eisenstein, E.L. (1983) *The Printing Revolution in Early Modern Europe*, Cambridge, Cambridge University Press.

Hughes, T.P. (1983) *Networks of Power: Electrification in Western Society 1880–1930*, Baltimore, CT, Johns Hopkins Press.

MacKenzie, D. and Wajcman, J. (eds) (1999) *The Social Shaping of Technology*, Buckingham, Open University Press.

Maximiser (2004) *A Short History of Messaging Services*, http://www.m-maximiser.com/news.htm (accessed 16 March 2004).

Shapin, S. (1996) *The Scientific Revolution*, Chicago, IL, University of Chicago Press.

Smith, M.R. and Marx, L. (1995) *Does Technology Drive History?*, Cambridge, MA, MIT Press.

Williams, R. (1974) *Television, Technology and Cultural Form*, London, Fontana.

Winston, B. (1998) *Media, Technology and Society*, London, Routledge.

The media, technology and social change

Richard Collins

Contents

1 Introduction

We are accustomed to talking about the power of the media. The media can, we often think, change our minds about who to vote for, how we think of people who are different from us, or even which car to buy. These seem significant powers, but in comparison with claims that changes in media and communications have changed the whole way in which we behave, the structure of human societies, and language itself, claims that the media have the power to change governments (and our taste in cars) are small claims indeed. Consider the following ideas, which we shall examine later on in this chapter.

Firstly, from Charles Barber (a British scholar in comparative and historical linguistics):

> A powerful force for standardization was the introduction of printing, and by the middle of the sixteenth century, although there was no standard system, there were quite a number of widely accepted conventions [...] the standardized spelling which became established in the late seventeenth century was already an archaic one, and broadly speaking it represented the pronunciation of English as it had been in late mediaeval times. This explains many of the oddities of present-day English spelling.
>
> Barber, 1964, p.207

Here Barber contends that a new medium of communication, printing (with moveable types), shaped and standardised the English language on the basis of medieval speech.

Secondly, from Joshua Meyrowitz (a US media scholar):

> Electronic media destroy the specialness of place and time. Television, radio and the telephone turn once private places into more public ones by making them more accessible to the outside world. And car stereos, wrist watch televisions and personal sound systems such as the Sony 'Walkman' make public spaces private.
>
> Meyrowitz, 1985, p.125

Meyrowitz's and Barber's claims are similar: new communication technologies, independent of their content, reshape the world by changing our perceptions of it and of the ways we live in it. What is important, Barber and Meyrowitz argue, is not (primarily) the content of the message (still less its veracity) but the habits and routines that arise from the interaction between the medium itself (whether newspaper, telephone or television) and its users. The philosopher Hegel referred to reading the morning newspaper as a form of morning prayer: reading the same information as others and in a similar situation (the breakfast table or the bus going to work) means participation in a shared ritual that binds the participants together and also orients them to the world. In this version of things, what counts is not the message but the regularity and patterning which follows from the medium itself rather than its content.

In short, as Marshall McLuhan (a Canadian scholar of English Literature and theorist of communications, whom you encountered in **Bennett, 2005**) put it, 'the medium is the message' (McLuhan, 1964). Seen from this point of view, the changing content of the *Six O'Clock News* is unimportant compared with the regularity of the news programme itself. The very existence of the programme tells us that the social relations and infrastructure necessary to produce and transmit the news have survived another day. All is well with the world. Or, as one of the founding fathers of US media research put it, 'the media have rendered it possible [...] For Americans from all social strata to laugh at the same joke' (Klapper, 1960, p.252). It does not matter what the joke is – what counts is that everyone is able to laugh at the same one.

What is argued above is a version of the 'technological determinism' thesis considered in Chapter 1 where you will have come across the argument that media technologies have encouraged new social practices and have tended to reorganise time and space. But, as you will have also seen, technological determinism is only one force among others. Social forces shape technology and technology shapes society, and societies can, and frequently do, make rules that determine which technologies (including media technologies) are used and what use can be made of them.

Activity 2.1

Consider the extent to which your life has been shaped by media and communications. For instance, how far is your life made different by media and communications from that of your parents and your grandparents? ■ ■ ■

You might explore these questions by talking to family members or friends of a different generation to identify how each generation communicated at a distance (for example, by personal face-to-face visit, letter, phone, internet). You might prompt those to whom you talk by asking how each generation obtained the food that they ate for breakfast. Was it by personal visits to the local producer, to a local shop or to a distant shop? Was food delivered? If so, how was the order placed – directly to the producer, or to a local, national or international retailer? You might reflect on the information your conversations yield by asking yourself what different generational experiences tell us about the relationship between technical change in communications and the organisation of daily life. You will then be well tuned in to the issues we consider in the rest of this chapter.

Societies often try to countervail, or at least mitigate, the power of media and communications by subjecting them to rules or, as it is more usually described, by regulating them. This is done either by setting limits to what the media can legitimately do (for example, by making laws that prohibit publication of offensive material) or by encouraging the media (for example, by subsidising them) to do certain things; for instance, provide regional news and religious television programmes. Regulation is an instance of the shaping of the media by social institutions and practices referred to in Chapter 1.

Regulation may operate through general law; for example, the provisions in the British Race Relations Act 1976 and the Public Order Act 1986, which make it an offence to use or publish threatening, abusive or insulting words (or behaviour) with an intention to stir up racial hatred. It may also operate through specialised regulatory institutions (for example, the US Federal Communications Commission, the UK's Ofcom and France's Conseil superior de l'audiovisuel) and through dedicated publicly funded agencies such as the British Broadcasting Corporation (BBC).

Thus the main types of media regulation are as follows:

- the law
- specialised regulatory agencies
- publicly funded bodies.

Broadly and simply put, media regulation is what governments do to shape the media in ways they think desirable. But, of course, neither governments nor citizens always agree on what is desirable and so media regulation takes different forms at different times and in different places. What happens in any particular time and place is shaped by the combination of the forces of technological change, the ideas which inform the actions of governments and citizens and the relative power of the forces in question. Of course, there is lots of room for disagreement among well informed (and not so well informed) commentators and citizens in these matters.

In this chapter we will consider two influential interpretations of the impact of the media – each of which imply different regulatory strategies for society. One is by the German philosopher Jürgen Habermas, and the other by the US scholar Ithiel de Sola Pool. Because Habermas is so important to recent debates about regulation, Section 3 then looks in greater detail at his core ideas. The rest of this chapter then examines some examples of the interrelated impacts of technological change on the media, and of the media on society and social life, and the parallels between some of the challenges posed by modern media and by media with which we have long been familiar. Section 4 looks at the impact of print on the English language, and Section 5 at television's impact on domestic and family relationships. Building upon the basis provided by the first five sections, Section 6 then examines the history of newspapers in England. Section 7 examines the impact of media technologies on conceptions of time and space, and Section 8 considers whether we might see media history as progress or decline. Our account will, we hope, enable you to better understand the complex knitting together of media and technological **power,** the forces of **change and continuity**, and the different bodies of **knowledge and belief** through which we make sense of these matters, and which have informed the actions of others to produce the media worlds in which we live.

2 Technologies of freedom?

2.1 The media and the public sphere: Jürgen Habermas

Jürgen Habermas's concept of the public sphere is one of the most influential theoretical ideas to be mobilised in contemporary media studies. For example, his arresting and complex idea of the public sphere has been taken up in influential analyses of public service broadcasting. In *Media Audiences*, David Herbert discusses the importance of the public sphere for debates about democratic legitimacy in modern media-rich societies (**Herbert, 2005**). Herbert also discussed criticisms and later modifications of Habermas's theory. Habermas defines the public sphere as 'a domain of our social life where such a thing as public opinion can be formed. Access to the public sphere is open in principle to all citizens. A portion of the public sphere is constituted in every conversation in which private persons come together to form a public [...] When the public is large, this kind of communication requires certain means of dissemination and influence; today, newspapers and periodicals, radio and television are the media of the public sphere' (Habermas, 1996, p.55 – see Reading 2.1).

Habermas's notion of the public sphere is thus one of a media space in which all of us, as individuals, can come together to collectively form an opinion. His argument implies a time (and a kind of society) where public opinion could not exist, where people, although linked together in a shared economic, social and political system, simply could not share ideas and exchange views. In the European Middle Ages, for example, it was difficult for people to communicate with each other (because of difficulties in transport, low levels of literacy, etc.) and so there was no public sphere. Later, and most notably in the eighteenth century, the interdependent growth in literacy, increase in accessibility and fall in prices of printed works, along with the growth of a powerful and relatively independent class of merchants and urban manufacturers, led, according to Habermas, to the establishment of a relatively large-scale, modern, public sphere.

True, participation in this eighteenth-century public sphere was limited to a minority of people (mostly male, mostly well off, mostly urban) but there was, Habermas argues convincingly, a change in the disposition and exercise of power. Society became more open, decision making became more evidence- and reason-based, and more people participated in the exercise of power. However, with the growth of a mass public and a mass media (high circulation newspapers, large-scale cinema-going and, especially, a socially pervasive radio and television broadcasting system), society became 'refeudalised'. Refeudalisation is a Habermasian term which refers both to Habermas's idea that contemporary society is returning to the form of organisation characteristic of the European Middle Ages (of separate power blocs, or estates, such as the church, the monarchy and the nobility) and the linked idea that power was exercised and consolidated through display and the cultivation of the rulers' images. In a feudal, and in a refeudalised, society the public sphere, a forum for collective acquisition, and for exchange of information and democratic debate and deliberation, closes down.

Habermas is not always easy to understand. The architecture of his argument is complex, he roots his propositions in a specialised philosophical frame of reference, his history is sometimes shaky and he has not always been well served by those who have translated his work into English. Nonetheless, his ideas have informed much contemporary analysis of the media. Followers of Habermas, whom we shall call the Habermasians, have argued that changes to broadcasting (notably the increase in the number of channels) since the 1980s have destroyed, or at least damaged, the modern public sphere: a public sphere that was, to condense the Habermasians' arguments, based on public service broadcasting. Public service broadcasting, for the Habermasians, had knitted together society by providing to all at an affordable price a unified image of society and of their place in it. Once, we all watched the same television news at the same time (for example, prior to 1955 the BBC was the only television news available to UK viewers), whereas now, for most of us there is a host of different television news programmes screened at different times and often espousing different values.

Commercial broadcasting, with its proliferation of channels destroyed both the equality between viewers (and listeners) characteristic of public service systems, and the national character of broadcasting, by importing programming from overseas (largely from the USA). The English scholar

Nicholas Garnham (1992, p.362), who was responsible for some of the most important effects of Habermas's ideas on media studies, puts this nicely, stating that more channels and more choice had brought:
'the creation of a two-tier market divided between the information-rich (provided with high-cost specialized information and cultural services) and the information-poor (provided with increasingly homogenized entertainment services on a mass scale): [and ...] a shift from largely national to international markets in the informational and cultural sphere'. Accordingly, Habermasians have demanded tighter regulation of commercial services and stronger public service broadcasting.

In this argument, broadcasting technology first created a national public sphere and then destroyed it as society shifted its use of broadcasting technology from using it for a single broadcaster to using it for many broadcasters. In the UK, the single television news service formerly provided by the BBC has given way to various television news services provided by the BBC, ITN, Sky, Fox, Bloomberg, al-Jazeera, and so on. You can see that we have here a theory of social change being brought about by a combination of technological change, which sets the terms for what follows, and social choices, which affect outcomes within the terms set by technology.

2.2 The media, pluralism and competition: Ithiel de Sola Pool

The American scholar Ithiel de Sola Pool makes what may seem to be a similar argument. In his *Technologies of Freedom* (1983) he contends that:

> Civil liberty functions today in a changing technological context. For five hundred years a struggle was fought, and in a few countries won, for the right of people to speak and print freely, unlicensed, uncensored and uncontrolled. But new technologies of electronic communication may now relegate old and freed media [...] to a corner of the public forum. Electronic modes of communication that enjoy lesser rights are moving to center stage. The new communication technologies have not inherited all the legal immunities that were won for the old [...] as speech increasingly flows over those electronic media, the five-century growth of an unabridged right of citizens to speak without controls may be endangered.
>
> Sola Pool, 1983, p.1

Sola Pool's argument here seems to evoke Habermas but he has introduced a new element to the argument. Sola Pool contends that the very mass media — the popular press, radio and television — which Habermas believes to have refeudalised modern societies, have had a positive, not a negative, influence. Indeed these media are the 'technologies of freedom' to which the title of his book refers. He states that the 'development of multiple technologies of communication [...] will foster [...] pluralistic and competitive communication systems. With hundred-channel cable systems, videocassettes, videodisks, ISDNs [integrated services digital network] and network links to thousands of online information services, there should be a diversity of voices far beyond anything known today' (Sola Pool, 1983, p.229).

However, the pluralisation that Sola Pool welcomes can be hostile to the public sphere advocated by Habermasians because pluralisation (fragmentation) may create a host of different, more or less private, spheres; for example, the separate spheres inhabited by those who watch Fox News and those who watch al-Jazeera. On the other hand, a Sola Pool fan might see a Habermasian public sphere as undesirable precisely because it is unified and therefore likely to exclude diverse and different currents of opinion and expression. Sola Pool welcomes pluralisation because, he believes, it fosters the diversity on which, for him, freedom and democracy depend. Whereas a Habermasian, who is likely to see dialogue as an essential characteristic of democracy, might see such pluralisation as fatal to the communality on which such a conception of democracy depends.

Sola Pool thus contends that the regulation that Habermasians advocate may threaten the pluralism which modern media technologies bring. For Sola Pool, state regulation is likely to be the enemy of freedom and he argues against governments strongly regulating electronic media – indeed, he refers to broadcasting regulation as a 'politically managed system' (Sola Pool, 1983, p.2).

These positions recall the divisions you have encountered in *Media Production*, where **John Downey (2006)** distinguished between three different perspectives on the role of the media industries in contemporary societies: the market liberal, social market and political economy perspectives. Sola Pool's views in many ways fit with the market liberal perspective, which argues that free markets are the most efficient way of allocating resources and ensuring economic vitality and prosperity; and that markets are the best way to ensure freedom and democracy as they provide a plurality of views and prevent the state from restricting the liberty of individuals in society. For those Downey calls political economists of communication, markets are altogether more problematic than this. Because Habermas is critical of certain developments associated with the market in contemporary societies, his work has often been taken up by adherents of political economy approaches which are hostile to markets. But Habermas's work has also appealed to some who take what

Downey calls the social market approach, which steers a course between market liberalism and political economy, recognising the threat that media markets might pose for pluralism, but also acknowledging a potential threat posed by state control.

Reading 2.1 Activity

Read the following extract from Habermas's work, 'The public sphere'. This will give you first-hand access to Habermas's writing – always better than believing what someone else (like us) says! Write a few lines on each of the following questions to ensure you understand the main points of Habermas's arguments.

- What does Habermas mean by a political public sphere?
- Are the newspapers that you read accurately characterised by Karl Bucher (whom Habermas quotes)?
- What about those newspapers read by your workmates or by members of your family?

Reading 2.1

Jürgen Habermas, 'The public sphere'

Concept

By 'public sphere' we mean first of all a domain of our social life in which such a thing as public opinion can be formed. Access to the public sphere is open in principle to all citizens. A portion of the public sphere is constituted in every conversation in which private persons come together to form a public. [...] When the public is large, this kind of communication requires certain means of dissemination and influence; today, newspapers and periodicals, radio and television are the media of the public sphere. We speak of a political public sphere (as distinguished from a literary one, for instance) when the public discussions concern objects connected with the practice of the state. [...] The term 'public opinion' refers to the functions of criticism and control of organized state authority that the public exercises informally, as well as formally during periodic elections. Regulations concerning the publicness (or publicity [*Publizität*] in its original meaning) of state-related activities, as, for instance, the public accessibility required of legal proceedings, are also connected with this function of public opinion. [...]

It is no accident that these concepts of the public sphere and public opinion were not formed until the eighteenth century. They derive their specific meaning from a concrete historical situation.

It was then that one learned to distinguish between opinion and public opinion, or *opinion publique*. Whereas mere opinions (things taken for granted as part of a culture, normative convictions, collective prejudices and judgments) seem to persist unchanged in their quasi-natural structure as a kind of sediment of history, public opinion, in terms of its very idea, can be formed only if a public that engages in rational discussion exists. Public discussions that are institutionally protected and that take, with critical intent, the exercise of political authority as their theme have not existed since time immemorial – they developed only in a specific phase of bourgeois society, and only by virtue of a specific constellation of interests could they be incorporated into the order of the bourgeois constitutional state.

History

It is not possible to demonstrate the existence of a public sphere in its own right, separate from the private sphere, in the European society of the High Middle Ages. At the same time, however, it is not a coincidence that the attributes of authority at that time were called 'public'. For a public representation of authority existed at that time. At all levels of the pyramid established by feudal law, the status of the feudal lord is neutral with respect to the categories 'public' and 'private'; but the person possessing that status represents it publicly; he [*sic*]displays himself, represents himself as the embodiment of a 'higher' power, in whatever degree. This concept of representation has survived into recent constitutional history. Even today the power of political authority on its highest level, however much it has become detached from its former basis, requires representation through the head of state. [...]

[...] The *bourgeois public sphere* can be understood as the sphere of private persons assembled to form a public. They soon began to make use of the public sphere of informational newspapers, which was officially regulated, against the public power itself, using those papers, along with the morally and critically oriented weeklies, to engage in debate about the general rules governing relations in their own essentially privatized but publicly relevant sphere of commodity exchange and labor.

The liberal model of the public sphere

[...]

The political daily press came to have an important role during this same period. In the second half of the eighteenth century, serious competition to the older form of news writing as the compiling of items of information arose in the form of literary journalism. Karl Bücher describes the main outlines of this development: 'From mere institutions for the publication of news, newspapers became the vehicles and guides of public opinion as well, weapons of party politics. The consequence of this for the internal organization of the newspaper enterprise was the insertion of a new function between the gathering of news and its publication: the editorial function. For the newspaper publisher, however, the significance of this development was that from a seller of new information he became a dealer in public opinion.' [...]

The public sphere in mass welfare-state democracies

[...] With the spread of the press and propaganda, the public expanded beyond the confines of the bourgeoisie. Along with its social exclusivity the public lost the cohesion given it by institutions of convivial social intercourse and by a relatively high standard of education. Accordingly, conflicts which in the past were pushed off into the private sphere now enter the public sphere. Group needs, which cannot expect satisfaction from a self-regulating market, tend toward state regulation. The public sphere, which must now mediate these demands, becomes a field for competition among interests in the cruder form of forcible confrontation. Laws that have obviously originated under the 'pressure of the streets' can scarcely continue to be understood in terms of a consensus achieved by private persons in public discussion; they correspond, in more or less undisguised form, to compromises between conflicting private interests. Today it is social organizations that act in relation to the state in the political public sphere, whether through the mediation of political parties or directly, in interplay with public administration. With the interlocking of the public and private domains, not only do political agencies take over certain functions in the sphere of commodity exchange and social labor; societal powers also take over political functions. This leads to a kind of 'refeudalization' of the public sphere. [...]

[...] Whereas at one time publicness was intended to subject persons or things to the public use of reason and to make political decisions susceptible to revision before the tribunal of public opinion, today it has often enough already been enlisted in the aid of the secret policies of interest groups; in the form of 'publicity' it now acquires public prestige for persons or things and renders them capable of acclamation in a climate of non-public opinion. The term 'public relations' itself indicates how a public sphere that formerly emerged from the structure of society must now be produced circumstantially on a case-by-case basis. The central relationship of the public, political parties, and parliament is also affected by this change in function.

Reference

Bücher, K. (1917) 'Die Anfänge des Zeitungswesens', in *Die Entstehung der Volkswirtschaft*, Tübingen, Verlag der H. Lauppschen Buchhandlung, vol.1, p.256.

Reading source

Habermas, 1996, pp.55–9 ■ ■ ■

Reading 2.2 Activity

Now read the following extract from Sola Pool's work *Technologies of Freedom*. Write a few lines on each of the following questions to ensure you understand the main points of Sola Pool's argument.

What does Sola Pool mean by 'soft technological determinism'? What changes to freedom of expression does Sola Pool see following, firstly, the introduction of printing; secondly, the introduction of broadcasting; and thirdly, the introduction of new media technologies such as those he calls 'novel video services'? In what respect are print and electronic media treated differently by regulators, and on what grounds? Finally, you might like to consider how far Sola Pool's arguments are applicable outside the USA (from where he draws most of his examples).

Reading 2.2

Ithiel de Sola Pool, 'Technologies of freedom'

What has changed in twentieth century communications is its technological base. [...] new and mostly electronic media have proliferated in the form of great oligopolistic networks of common carriers and broadcasters. Regulation was a natural response. [...] as electronics advances further, another reversal is now taking place, toward growing decentralisation and toward fragmentation of the audience of the newest media. [...]

The causal relationships between technology and culture are a matter that social scientists have long debated. Some may question how far technological trends shape the political freedom or control under which communication takes place [...] Some argue that technology is neutral, used as the culture demands; others that the technology of the medium controls the message.

The interaction over the past two centuries between the changing technologies of communication and the practice of free speech, I would argue, fits a pattern that is sometimes described as 'soft technological determinism.' Freedom is fostered when the means of communication are dispersed, decentralized, and easily available, as are printing presses or microcomputers. Central control is more likely when the means of communication are concentrated, monopolized, and scarce, as are great networks. But the relationship between technology and institutions is not simple or unidirectional, nor are the effects immediate. Institutions that evolve in response to one technological environment persist and to some degree are later imposed on what may be a changed technology. [...]

Simple versions of technological determinism fail to take account of the differences in the way things happen at different stages in the life cycle of a technology. When a new invention is made, such as the telephone or radio, its fundamental laws are usually not well understood. It is designed to suit institutions that already exist, but in its early stages if it is to be used at all, it must be used in whatever form it proved experimentally to work. Institutions for its use are thus designed around a technologically determined model. Later, when scientists have comprehended the fundamental theory, the early technological embodiment becomes simply a special case. Alternative devices can then be designed to meet human needs. Technology no longer need control. A 1920s motion picture had to be black and white, silent, pantomimic, and shown in a place of public assembly; there was no practical choice. A 1980s video can have whatever colors, sounds, and three-dimensional or synthetic effects are wanted, and can be seen in whatever location is desired. In the meantime, however, an industry has established studios, theaters, career lines, unions, funding, and advertising practices, all designed to use the technology that is in place. Change occurs, but the established institutions are a constraint on its direction and pace.

[...]

The key technological change, at the root of the social changes, is that communication, other than conversation face to face, is becoming overwhelmingly electronic. Not only is electronic communication growing faster than traditional media of publishing, but also the convergence of modes of delivery is bringing the press, journals, and books into the electronic world. One question raised by these changes is whether some social features are inherent in the electronic character of the emerging media. Is television the model of the future? Are electromagnetic pulses simply an alternative conduit to deliver whatever is wanted, or are there aspects of electronic technology that make it different from print – more centralized or more decentralized, more banal or more profound, more private or more government dependent?

[...]

[...] Europe and America entered the mass media era by the vehicle of print; the printed word and mass communication were for a while synonymous. Then in the first quarter of the twentieth century nonprint mass media came into use. [...] By 1977 broadcasting had grown to the point where, according to a census of communications flows, average Americans consumed four times as many words electronically as they read in print. [...] In the total flow of media-delivered information, the relative part carried by newspapers, magazines, and books has dropped from being virtually all of it to being only 18 percent of the words to which people expose themselves.

[...]

The declining dominance of print media is a cause for concern, for they are the media that in the United States and elsewhere in the free world enjoy autonomy from government. It matters that people are increasingly getting their news and ideas through governmentally controlled media. The fact that media enjoying the full protection of the First Amendment, or of its equivalent traditions abroad, have ceased to dominate the information marketplace is in itself troublesome.

[...]

The regulatory system

In the days of Milton, licensing was imposed on publishing by the Crown [in Britain] with a view to restricting the press. In the United States, on the contrary, the intent in imposing licensing was to promote radio expansion, though without clear understanding of the economic and technical implications of what was being done. Gradually and with reluctance both the government and the industry moved in the 1920s toward a regulated regime.

[...]

The First Amendment and the choice made

To the detriment of freedom, [...] radio and television has settled into a regime regulated by the values and judgments of public authorities. Apocalyptic prophecy might have projected a trend toward a full dictatorship of the airwaves, but life is more complicated than that. The political selection of broadcasters, when carried out in a pluralistic society with a free printed press and strong traditions of private enterprise and freedom, and governed by a radio law with explicit injunctions against censorship, has produced an uneasy compromise: a system in which political officials meddle, though with reluctance, in the activities of individual stations, and do in fact decide what type of broadcasting the American public wants and shall receive.

[...]

The coming of cable, along with videotapes and videodisks, may ameliorate the problem of narrow uniformity. There is already a nascent market for novel video services. [...]

> Now for the first time, with pay television, cassettes, and disks, those consumers who want a different product from what Madison Avenue provides and the FCC willingly licenses can exercise some choice by paying for it. Educational courses, ideological propaganda, pornography, religion, high culture, and whatever else substantial groups of people desire to watch are increasingly available [...]
>
> *Reading source*
>
> Sola Pool, 1983, pp.4–6, 20–22, 116, 149 ■ ■ ■

Sola Pool and Habermas thus share a view of the media having the power both to shape society and to look to regulation as a way for societies to control and direct their media. Sola Pool provides a good account of the way in which these two sorts of power – media and regulatory – operate together. He states:

> The causal relationships between technology and culture are a matter that social scientists have long debated. Some may question how far technological trends shape the political freedom or control under which communication takes place. [...] Some argue that technology is neutral, used as the culture demands; others that the technology of the medium controls the message.
>
> The interaction over the past two centuries between the changing technologies of communication and the practice of free speech [...] fits a pattern that is sometimes described as 'soft technological determinism' [and that] 'the relationship between technology and institutions is not simple or unidirectional, nor are the effects immediate.'
>
> Sola Pool, 1983, p.5

Sola Pool puts a different spin than Habermas on how 'soft technological determinism' affects media and communications. He believes that new communication technologies are freedom and democracy friendly, for they have the potential to pluralise sources of information and make information more easily accessible, whereas Habermas is deeply suspicious of broadcasting which, he states, disempowers its users:

> With the arrival of the new media the form of communication [...] has changed. [...] Under the pressure of the 'Don't talk back!' the conduct of the public assumes a different form. In comparison with printed communications the programs sent by the new media curtail the reactions of their recipients in a peculiar way. [...] The world fashioned by the mass media is a public sphere by appearance only.
>
> Habermas, 1989/1962, pp.170–1

3 Habermas, the public sphere, the ideal speech situation and refeudalisation

Let us look at Habermas's theories of media power more deeply. We do so because:

- Habermas gives an interesting basis for normative action in the media domain (that is, he gives us some principles on which we, and society at large, may want to act).

- He gives us a good way of understanding some of the prominent characteristics of contemporary media.

- His writing integrates, in a coherent and illuminating way, ideas about technical change, political values and the media that have proven very influential among media scholars.

We can identify three central ideas in Habermas's work that have been used fruitfully by numerous contemporary media theorists. Firstly, Habermas argued for what he called an 'ideal speech situation'. This is a communicative relationship in which the participants strive to speak (or write) the truth; to ensure that their contributions to the ideal speech situation are appropriate; and to contribute with sincerity. Habermas stated (and don't be put off by the complex language in brackets – that is the way he writes and the way his translator represents him):

> [...] an actor who is oriented to understanding in this sense must raise at least three validity claims with his utterance, namely:
>
> 1 That the statement made is true (or that the existential pre-suppositions of the propositional content mentioned are in fact satisfied);
>
> 2 That the speech act is right with respect to the existing normative context (or that the normative context that it is supposed to satisfy is itself legitimate); and
>
> 3 That the manifest intention of the speaker is meant as it is expressed.
>
> Habermas, 1984, p.99

Secondly, as we have seen above, Habermas argued for a public sphere, both historically and normatively. This means he believed that a public sphere did come into existence (at least in part) – this was his historical argument, and that a public sphere ought to exist – this was his normative argument.

Thirdly, Habermas argued that contemporary societies were experiencing a process of 'refeudalisation'. Essentially Habermas argued that contemporary societies were increasingly constituting power and authority on lines similar to those obtained in the Middle Ages. Then, Habermas argued, there was essentially no difference between the public and the private. Power was signified, and exercised, through public display. The main power blocs – monarch, nobility and church – combined to publicly legitimise each other, for example, in the public coronation of the monarch. As he said, 'the person possessing that status [that is, that of the feudal lord] represents it publicly; he displays himself, represents himself as the embodiment of a "higher" power' (Habermas, 1996, p.56). As we proposed earlier, Habermas's notion of the public sphere implies a time (and a society) in which public opinion could not exist, in which the people who were linked together in a shared economic, social and political system simply could not share the same ideas and exchange views.

Habermas contrasts the feudal practices of the Middle Ages to that of a 'new social order' (Habermas, 1989, p.14) in which the 'publicity of representation' (that is, the feudal practices of display described below) slowly gave way to 'the new domain of a public sphere whose decisive mark was the published word' (Habermas, 1989, p.16). For Habermas, feudal practices of representation, the feudal practices of power, were ones of:

> [T]he territorial ruler conven[ing] about him ecclesiastical and worldly lords, knights, prelates and cities [...] this was not a matter of an assembly of delegates that was someone else's representative. As long as the prince and the estates of his realm 'were' the country and not just its representatives [...] [t]hey represented the lordship not for but 'before' the people. The staging of the publicity involved in representation was wedded to personal attributes such as insignia (badges and arms), dress (clothing and coiffure), demeanour (form of greeting and poise) and rhetoric (form of address and formal discourse in general.
>
> Habermas, 1989, pp.7–8

You will have seen in Reading 2.1 that Habermas explains what he means by the term 'public sphere' and how he understands feudalism – on which his notion of 'refeudalisation' depends. He also distinguishes between the public and the private realms of life and experience and observes that the boundary between public and private is drawn differently at different moments in history. In consequence, the public sphere itself is something that exists only at certain historical moments and in particular circumstances, with the media playing a key role in its creation and extension.

You have also probably seen that Habermas's arguments focus attention on media content as well as on the structure and organisation of the media (the latter focus is the one that he shares with Sola Pool). Partly for this reason, modern media scholars have extensively mined

Habermas's work. Following Habermas, they have argued that the modern media, in partnership with a changed modern politics, have refeudalised the public sphere. A successful politician must now look good and actively present him (or her) self to the mass public. She or he, like the feudal monarch, must be *seen* – and the whole of his or her life must be open to the public's view. Bill Clinton's presidency, for example, is likely to be remembered more for his relations with one of his staff than for his foreign or economic policy (see Figure 2.1). (See also **Evans and Hesmondhalgh, 2005.**)

Figure 2.1 *Monica Lewinsky smiles at President Clinton as he greets well-wishers at a White House lawn party in 1996*

3.1 Refeudalisation in contemporary public life

As Habermas put it: 'Publicity loses its critical function in favour of a staged display; even arguments are transmuted into symbols to which again one cannot respond by arguing but only by identifying with them' (Habermas, 1989, p.206). For examples of this process, think of the way in which the campaign against anti-personnel mines was symbolised by one of the great media celebrities of recent times: by Princess Diana wearing a flak jacket next to a mine-warning sign (see Figure 2.2). Or think of how the US sense of success in the 2003 invasion of Iraq was symbolised by President Bush, wearing flight gear, embracing sailors

on the deck of the US aircraft carrier *USS Abraham Lincoln*
(see Figure 2.3). Politicians have become celebrities (see **Evans
and Hesmondhalgh, 2005**) in the way in which monarchs were
celebrities in the Middle Ages. Power has to be exercised publicly,
politicians who hide from the media cannot effectively exercise political
power.

Figure 2.2 *Princess Diana campaigns on behalf of The Halo Trust, a de-mining project in
Angola*

Contemporary politics lends much support to Habermas's proposition
about refeudalisation. An important criterion for contemporary political
success is looking good on television – hence the importance Tony Blair
and New Labour in the UK have placed on the appearance and
grooming of leading Labour politicians. But on 8 October 2003 an even
better example to support Habermas's refeudalisation thesis was
provided in the USA. A film star with no political experience, Arnold
Schwarzenegger, decisively won the election campaign for appointment as
Governor of California (See Figure 2.4). Schwarzenegger successfully
recruited other celebrities to support his campaign, including Rob Lowe
(who was best known at the time of the election for his role as a White
House adviser in the television drama series *The West Wing*, which was
first screened in the USA in 1999). Lowe testified to his support for
Schwarzenegger, whom he described as a natural leader, saying: 'I know
that when I'm on a set, I want to know who the director is. I don't want
to have to guess,' and 'That's what Arnold will bring to this state. He's a
leader' (Lowe, quoted in a WENN report, 2003).

Figure 2.3 *President George W Bush in May 2003 aboard the USS Abraham Lincoln where he was greeted with the message 'Mission Accomplished'*

Refeudalisation means that policy issues become personalised. For example, the division in the current UK Labour Government and Party over the UK's adoption of the euro as its currency has been constructed as an expression of a personal rivalry between Tony Blair and Gordon Brown. But politics was not always so personalised. Matheson gives a good case in point when he contrasts the 1901 report in *The Times* of the resignation of the Chancellor of the Exchequer to an implied contemporary report:

> We have this morning to make the startling announcement that the Chancellor of the Exchequer [in the UK the Minister of Finance is called the Chancellor of the Exchequer] has placed his resignation in the hands of Lord Salisbury.
>
> *The Times*, 1 January 1901, p.6, in Matheson, 2000, p.557

One hundred years ago the report was depersonalised, indirect and curiously de-dramatised – as its place on the sixth page of the newspaper exemplifies. And the report is representative, as Matheson states, of 'a newspaper style that is now long gone' (p.557).

Compare this to the front page reports from *The Financial Times* of 27 January 2004 on the efforts of Prime Minister Tony Blair and Chancellor of the Exchequer Gordon Brown to win support for the government's proposals on university funding. Here is an extract:

> It was a manic Monday in Westminster. Miserably so for Tony Blair, marvellously so for Gordon Brown his chancellor. While Mr Blair

Figure 2.4 Hasta La Victor! *Arnold Schwarzenegger's election as Governor of California.* The Daily Mirror, *9 October 2003*

was begging for every last vote in a frantic attempt to save his skin, across the road Mr Brown was basking in the adulation and reflected glory of his chums Bill Gates [Founder and Chairman of Microsoft] and Jean-Claude Trichet, the European Central Bank boss.

Newman and Crooks, 2004

Try to identify what makes these two newspaper stories (from *The Times* of 1901 and the *Financial Times* of 2004: see Figure 2.5) so different.

We found it useful to compare the length of the sentences in the two reports and to identify the subject of each sentence. (Who speaks in each? It is explicit in the 1901 report 'We have this morning ...', but who speaks in the 2004 report?)

What is the effect of the differences? How far do colloquialisms such as 'manic Monday' change readers' attitudes to the subject and personalities reported on? ■ ■ ■

If you want to explore issues like these further, we suggest you buy a contemporary tabloid and a broadsheet (or compact) newspaper and compare their reporting of the same event. You might consider issues like these: Are there differences in the way the papers handle the same event? What gets included and what is left out? Are the sentences the same length? Is the vocabulary different? And what is the effect of the differences? Why do different papers treat the same event in different ways?

To summarise Sections 2 and 3, we have seen that the influence of media and communication technologies is neither simple, unidirectional, nor immediate. We have also seen that interpretations of the power of the media can be different – those of Habermas and Sola Pool, for example – and these differences point towards different types of regulation and different applications of regulation. But what evidence do we have that media and communications do actually change our world? We should not just assume they do because others say so – even when the others are as eminent as Ithiel de Sola Pool or Jürgen Habermas.

4 Language, printing and the impact of the media

To consider these issues in another context, let us consider the evidence about the power of media and communications and the importance of technological change by returning to the issues of language and of the boundaries between public and private which we signalled at the beginning of this chapter (in the quotations from the US media scholar Joshua Meyrowitz). We will consider these issues by examining firstly the evidence presented by literary texts in English and, secondly, Meyrowitz's arguments that modern media have fundamentally altered the boundaries separating the public from the private.

Knife-edge vote to test Blair's grip on power

● Whips fear Commons showdown could still be lost
● Hutton preview adds to tension over top-up fees

By James Blitz, Christopher Adams and Ben Hall

Tony Blair's grip on power will tonight face its sternest test in a knife-edge Commons vote on the university funding proposals central to his efforts to reform the public services.

At the end of a day that saw the prime minister holding tense meetings with many key Labour rebels, Downing Street and government business managers feared Mr Blair could still lose the vote on introducing tuition fees for university students.

If Mr Blair is defeated it would be seen as the prime minister's biggest political setback since he came to power six years ago and would inflict serious damage on the Labour party. There were signs last night that more Labour rebels were moving the government's way, improving Mr Blair's chance of securing a narrow victory when the Commons votes in the second reading of the higher education bill at 7pm tonight.

Gordon Brown, the chancellor, was stepping up pressure on reb-

els to back Mr Blair in one-to-one meetings. And John Prescott, deputy prime minister, also intervened to broker talks between Mr Blair and rebel leaders.

An ally of the chancellor cautioned against being too pessimistic ahead of the vote, saying: "We are making it absolutely clear to the rebels that defeat would not be in the wider interest."

But Labour backbench critics continued to insist that the rebellion remained firm and an air of uncertainty hung over ministers.

Adding to the tension today, Mr Blair will get his first sight at noon of Lord Hutton's report into the death of David Kelly, the weapons scientist.

One Labour whip conceded last night: "As things stand, we're going to lose."

Government business managers hope that a sufficient number of rebels will abstain to ensure victory in the first big vote on legislation aimed at increasing university investment.

Some MPs argued that even if Mr Blair wins, his authority will have been damaged.

The prime minister yesterday held a string of one-to-one meetings with around 30 rebel MPs in the Commons. However, he refused to agree to the rebels' request that the right of universities to vary fees should be subject to an independent review.

The most dramatic moment came when the prime minister met George Mudie, the Labour MP widely acknowledged as the

leader of the rebellion. Mr Blair was said to have looked Mr Mudie in the eye and said: "You will be loyal, you will vote for me." Mr Mudie replied that he would not.

Some MPs were swayed by last minute concessions made by Charles Clarke, education secretary, and a fear of inflicting severe damage on the prime minister just a day before publication

of the Hutton report. One vocal critic of the bill who has now decided to support the government said: "What people have got from their constituencies at the weekend is 'Do you want to boot the prime minister in the backside the day before Hutton?'"

The Financial Times' latest analysis suggests 76 Labour MPs are planning to vote against the bill and six to abstain. Another

21 are undecided, while 41 have been won round.

Assuming all those yet to decide do support the prime minister, and a handful of opposition party abstentions are taken into account, he would win by a mere 10 votes.

Spectres of past defeats, Page 3
Position impossible, Page 5
Editorial Comment, Page 18

Tony Blair arrives at the Commons yesterday: Labour backbench critics of the university funding legislation insisted that the rebellion remained firm   Jeff Moore

Gordon shakes hands as Tony twists arms

The frantic attempts to drum up last-minute support contrasted with the chancellor's relaxed gathering for the global A-list, write **Cathy Newman** and **Ed Crooks**

It was a manic Monday in Westminster. Miserably so for Tony Blair, marvellously so for Gordon Brown, his chancellor.

While Mr Blair was begging for every last vote in a frantic attempt to save his skin, across the road Mr Brown was basking in the adulation and reflected glory of his chums Bill Gates and Jean-Claude Trichet, the European Central Bank boss.

The prime minister was forced into pleading, cajoling, strong-arming and bribing rebel MPs. Intimate *tête-à-têtes* with Labour MPs are nobody's idea of fun but after a day spent doing nothing

else Mr Blair could be forgiven for wanting to nip off to the Post Office for his pension cheque.

Mr Brown, on the other hand, was doing what he loves most, hobnobbing with the international A-list.

His "friends" Hans Eichel and Gerrit Zalm, his opposite numbers from Germany and the Netherlands, cosied up to him; "Sir Bill" shared a joke about *Monty Python*. Even his hero Alan Greenspan, chairman of the US Federal Reserve, was there in spirit, delivering a homily via video-link on one of the chancellor's pet subjects, the importance

of economic flexibility and free trade.

Mr Brown's temple might have moistened when he struggled to reach John Snow, US Treasury secretary, by videophone. But that was as nothing compared with the sweat that must have been pouring from Mr Blair's brow as he stared into what one of his cabinet ministers, in an admirable understatement, called "the abyss".

Chained to his desk in Downing Street in the morning as he pounded the phones, Mr Blair spent the afternoon imprisoned in his Commons office in the bowels of the Palace of Westminster.

Austin Mitchell, Great Grimsby MP, was in no doubt how low Mr Blair had to stoop to get *his* vote. "I will be bribed on this bill. If

they can give me something big for Grimsby, I will think Tony Blair is wonderful."

Bribery was one thing, but Mr Blair also employed hypnosis, fixing his penetrating gaze on one diehard rebel and commanding him to back the government. It didn't work. He tried supplication, beseeching another: "I need

your support." That didn't work either.

There are those who believe that for Mr Blair, yesterday was the beginning of the end. For Brown it looked more like the end of the beginning.

Chancellor's admirers, Page 2
Observer, Page 18

Hobnobbing: Gordon Brown yesterday

Figure 2.5 *From the front page of the* Financial Times, *27 January 2004*

4.1 Printing and writing in Europe

What counts as the first communication technology? Arguably it is writing. Writing makes communication possible over time and distance. Speech-based societies are by necessity small-scale societies; their ability to transmit information through time depends on fallible human memory and, indeed, the survival of the communities that use a particular form of speech. Writing permits information to survive – even if the last member of the language community from which it originates has died. The 'resurrection' of Cornish (a Celtic language spoken in Cornwall, the most westerly part of England, until the nineteenth century) was possible only because there were written Cornish texts. In 2002, after a revival of Cornish, between 30 and 500 people were estimated to be fluent Cornish speakers (see McGonagle et al., 2003, p.486). Languages both unite communities and separate them from others. But, languages are dynamic; they change over time – some die and others grow. The communities that are defined by language are, correspondingly, also dynamic. The technologies through which knowledge and information are recorded and disseminated – writing, printing, telephony, sound recording, broadcasting – have a powerful impact on the character of language and on the spatial and temporal boundaries in which particular linguistic communities exist.

Print is a communication technology that amplifies the effects of writing. It makes possible large-scale complex social organisations which can extend through time and space. Moreover, because print was a technology which dramatically lowered the marginal cost of producing additional copies of a written work (do not worry too much about the term 'marginal cost': there is an extensive consideration of communication and media economics in Chapter 3), written works quickly became much cheaper and more accessible than before. It is plausibly claimed that before Gutenberg's 'invention' of printing with moveable types around 1450 (see Eisenstein, 1979; Febvre and Martin, 1976; and Steinberg, 1955), there were only about 30,000 books on the entire continent of Europe, nearly all of them Bibles or biblical commentaries. By 1500 Gates estimates there were more than nine million books, on all sorts of topics (Gates, 1996, p.9).

Martin Luther (1483–1546), the founder of Protestantism, is said to have been 20 years old before he saw a Bible. The anecdote is plausible, for books were very scarce before the advent of printing. One hundred years after Luther saw his first Bible, the Bible was widely available in translation in many European languages; for example, in German – Luther's Bible of 1522, in English – Coverdale's Bible of 1535, in Finnish – Agricola's New Testament in 1548. In consequence, as the Dedication of the British Authorised, or King James (1611), Version of the Bible declared, 'God's holy truth […] be yet more and more known unto the people'. The explosion in accessibility of knowledge brought about by printing meant that the literate had independent access to what was claimed to be authority. Whereas before printing most people's access to authoritative information depended on intermediaries – priests controlled access to 'God's holy truth' – after printing more people could enjoy independent access, independent of priestly mediation, to the Bible.

Why was printing such a big deal? Consider how knowledge was produced and circulated before Gutenberg. In western Europe monasteries (later joined by universities) produced books by hand copying. (See Figure 2.6 for a representation of this activity taking place in a scriptorium – a room where manuscripts were written.) Not surprisingly these institutions tended to reproduce books that supported the religious, and political, status quo. Maintaining the established Roman Catholic orthodoxy was not confined to the area of religious doctrine and theological debate, but extended to all other areas of enquiry. It is important not to overstate this, for a broader range of works were produced than one might expect – classical texts, contemporary prose and poetry, and translations of works in Arabic emanating from the Islamic world. But there is no doubt that the effect of the copying system was to 'mainstream' reproduction and circulation of works that supported the Church and its view of the world. And, not coincidentally, the institutions that controlled the production of books also tended to control education.

Figure 2.6 A scribe in a scriptorium reproducing a manuscript (fifteenth century)

Written knowledge was for the most part accessible only to small, educated elites and its reproduction and dissemination was also controlled by these elites. Books were often chained, so they could not be removed, in libraries (as can still be seen in some places, for example in Hereford Cathedral in the west of England – see Figure 2.7; and Ripon Minster in the north) and only the very wealthy could own books. The increased accessibility of written works at affordable prices brought about by printing encouraged literacy. There was some point in learning to read when written works were accessible – not much reason to do so if there were no books around! Paradoxically, as well as extending communicative communities, printing also separated communicative communities from each other. National languages, and nation-based states, became more firmly established and cemented across Europe.

Figure 2.7 Chained books at Hereford Cathedral library

Activity 2.3

Write down what changes there would be in your daily life if either printing was still done by hand or there was no electronic communication (no phone, email, radio or television). ■ ■ ■

Here are examples of changes that we identified. On printing – we, the authors, would probably not be working as academics! (It would have been too costly to develop our skills and knowledge.) And you would probably not be a student! On electronic communication – our relationships, with colleagues, friends and family, would be much more limited and confined to those within easy reach of where we lived and worked.

Printing did change things but the change it stimulated was not a big bang impact. Rather, printing's impact grew as its ripples spread through established habits, structures and relationships. As Paul Lazarsfeld, a founding father of media studies, is once said to have quipped, 'if a foundation had made a grant to researchers to evaluate printing a decade or two after its invention, they would have concluded that the new device was vastly overrated' (Lazarsfeld, quoted in Sola Pool, 1983, p.13). By about 1510 around 400 book titles (many of them printed in huge numbers) had been published in England. A century later the cumulative total had risen to around 6,000, by 1710 to 21,000 and by the 1790s to 56,000 (Blanning, 2002, p.137). This trend has continued. By the late twentieth century UK book production had risen so much that in the year of 1985 52,861 separate titles were published (UNESCO, 1989, p.324). More titles were published in the UK in a single year than had been published in the first three hundred years of printing in England. Of course, this change did not go uncontested or uncontrolled. Important landmarks in the regulation of printing – that is, the attempt of authorities to countervail the influence exerted by printing – include: the 1501 Papal Bull against unlicenced printing; the Roman Catholic Church's 1559 Index of prohibited books; and, in England, the chartering in 1557 of the Stationers Company (which controlled printing and publishing).

4.2 Print and English: language in *Sir Gawain and the Green Knight* and *The Canterbury Tales*

One can see some of the effects of printing at a fine-grained level by comparing the language used in English literary works written in the fourteenth century; that is, before printing. Formerly, the language written and spoken in different parts of England differed significantly. Two works, both poems, exemplify these differences: the anonymous *Sir Gawain and the Green Knight*, generally thought to have been written in the version of English spoken in Lancashire, and *The Canterbury Tales*, a work we know to have been written by Geoffrey Chaucer (a member of the English Royal Court) in London. Compare these extracts from these two roughly contemporary English poems.

From the beginning of Sir Gawain and the Green Knight (original version)

Þis kyng lay at Camylot vpon Krystmasse

With mony luflych lorde, ledez of þe best,

Rekenly of þe Rounde Table alle þo rich breþer,

With rych reuel ory3t and rechles merþes.

Þer tournayed tulkes by tymez ful mony,

Justed ful jolilé þise gentyle kni3tes,

Syþen kayred to þe court caroles to make.

Tolkien and Gordon, 1967, p.2 of online version

From the Prologue to The Canterbury Tales by Geoffrey Chaucer, circa 1387 (original version)

Whan that Aprill, with his shoures soote

The droghte of March hath perced to the roote

And bathed every veyne in swich licour,

Of which vertu engendred is the flour;

Whan Zephirus eek with his sweete breeth

Inspired hath in every holt and heeth

The tendre croppes, and the yonge sonne

Hath in the Ram his halfe cours yronne,

And smale foweles maken melodye,

That slepen al the nyght with open eye-

(So priketh hem Nature in hir corages);

Thanne longen folk to goon on pilgrimages.

Librarius, 1997

Activity 2.4

Compare the language and comprehensibility of *Sir Gawain* with Chaucer's opening to *The Canterbury Tales*. How much of each text do you understand? Which original is closest to modern English and why? Now read the modern English versions below.

Sir Gawain and the Green Knight (modern version)
One Christmas in Camelot King Arthur sat
at ease with his lords and loyal liegemen
arranged as brothers round the Round Table.
Their reckless jokes rang about that rich hall
till they turned from the table to the tournament field
and jousted like gentlemen with lances and laughs,
then trooped to court in a carolling crowd.

Deane, 1999

From the Prologue to The Canterbury Tales (modern version)
When in April the sweet showers fall
That pierce March's drought to the root and all
And bathed every vein in liquor that has power
To generate therein and sire the flower;
When Zephyr also has with his sweet breath,
Filled again, in every holt and heath,
The tender shoots and leaves, and the young sun
His half-course in the sign of the Ram has run,
And many little birds make melody
That sleep through all the night with open eye
(So Nature pricks them on to ramp and rage)
Then folk do long to go on pilgrimage.

Librarius, 1997 ■ ■ ■

Although both poems show the characteristics of works made for oral delivery (alliteration – particularly in *Gawain*, rhyme, regularity of metre, etc.), Chaucer's English is, we think you will agree, much more accessible to us than that of the *Gawain* poet. Why, 600 years later, should one version of fourteenth-century English be so much more intelligible than another? We think that it is because Chaucer's English was the English that was printed. Technology made the difference.

It was in London that printing in Britain began and it was London's language that became the language of print. Chaucer's work was among the first English poems to be printed by William Caxton, the first English printer, who produced two separate editions of Chaucer's *Canterbury Tales*, whereas *Sir Gawain and the Green Knight* was not printed until the nineteenth century. Chaucer's work was (because in print) more widely disseminated, and the style of English that he used, rather than the *Gawain* poet's, became standardised. The unfamiliar letter characters used in *Sir Gawain* – the 'Thorn', written and printed 'Þ' (a runic symbol pronounced 'th'), and the '3', the 'yough' (pronounced either 'gh' or 'y'), fell out of use earlier in London and the English Midlands than in other parts of Britain and so, because seldom printed, they are absent in modern English.

Of course, print does not explain everything. Chaucer's work was widely known in manuscript (around 90 manuscript copies of *The Canterbury Tales* have survived compared with only one manuscript of *Sir Gawain and the Green Knight*) and his style of English was used throughout the eastern side of Britain. Compare this short extract from John Barbour's *The Brus*, the Scots' national epic poem of the same period, celebrating Robert Bruce.

Lines 225–228 from Book 1 of The Brus (original version)

A! Fredome is a noble thing

Fredome mays man to haiff liking.

Fredome all solace to man giffis,

He levys at es that frely levys.

Duncan, 2005

Lines 225–228 from Book 1 of The Brus (modern version)

Ah, Freedom is a noble thing,

Freedom lets a man have pleasure.

Freedom all solace to man gives

He lives at ease that freely lives.

Barbour, 1997, p.56

In spite of the subject of *The Brus* – Scottish resistance to England, personified in the Bruce – the language of Barbour and Chaucer has more in common, whether one calls Barbour's language Scots or English, than do the languages of Chaucer and the *Gawain* poet. This may be because of communication between the Scottish and English elites (Barbour certainly travelled to England several times and negotiated at a very high level with the English court), but is probably also due to easier communication by sea between eastern Scotland and eastern England than between London and Lancashire, whether by land or sea. Standardisation of London English would certainly have been strengthened through the circulation of printed books. London was the centre of English printing, and only the university presses of Cambridge and Oxford were licensed to print outside London.

Printing not only standardised written English spatially – London English became the norm – but it also affected the rate at which linguistic usage changed temporally. Print tends to slow down change and to fix particular linguistic usages as Barber stated in the quote at the beginning of this chapter. Although Barber does not use McLuhan's phrase, 'the medium is the message' (McLuhan, 1964), he is making the same point – it is media technology that makes the difference.

5 Joshua Meyrowitz and the media's impact on domestic and family relationships

Let us consider another example of the power of media and communications and the importance of technological change. The American scholar Joshua Meyrowitz, in his influential book *No Sense of Place* (1985), argues that electronic media (he refers to the telephone, radio and television, but now the internet is also a striking case in point) have decisively changed our behaviour. Beginning from the premise that 'Sociologists have long noted that people behave differently in different "social" situations' (Meyrowitz, 1985, p.viii), he argues that there are distinctive behaviours which apply in situations that the media determine. We behave, Meyrowitz argues, differently in unmediated situations to the way we do in 'print situations', and our print behaviour in turn is different to our behaviour in 'electronic situations'.

Meyrowitz argues that electronic media, television in particular, unavoidably bring together groups, individuals and discourses which in face-to-face relationships seldom, if ever, encounter each other. He observes that:

> When distinct social situations are combined, once-appropriate behaviour may become inappropriate [...] The combination of many different audiences is a rare occurrence in face-to-face interaction [...] Electronic media, however, have rearranged many social forums so

that most people now find themselves in contact with others in new ways. And unlike the merged situations in face-to-face interaction, the combined situations of electronic media are relatively lasting and inescapable.

Meyrowitz, 1985, pp.4–5

For example, Meyrowitz proposes that television brings new subjects into children's worlds and so erodes the barriers between the worlds of adults and children. Before television, Meyrowitz argues, 'children were [...] shielded from certain topics such as sex, money, death, crime and drugs. Even more significant, however, children were shielded from the fact that they were being shielded. Print allowed for an "adult conspiracy"'. But,

> Television discussions and warnings are as accessible to children as they are to adults. Ironically, such advice on television often cues children to which programmes they are not supposed to see and increases children's interest in what follows. Even if such warnings are heard by parents, and even if parents act to censor the program, parental control is nevertheless weakened because the control becomes overt and therefore often unpalatable to both children and parents.

Meyrowitz, 1985, pp.246–7

Think back to the arguments made in Chapter 1, that 'new forms of cultural practice emerged' with the spread of the video cassette recorder (VCR). Meyrowitz makes a similar argument – television itself has, he argues, brought the worlds of children and adults closer together.

Meyrowitz also proposes that television has eroded the distinction between public and private. He asks: 'when a reporter meets with the President and his wife before television cameras, how should the President and the First Lady behave? Is the encounter an intimate social meeting among three people or is it a public performance before the nation?' And he finds that:

> The answer is that it is both, and, therefore, that it is neither [...] To the extent that actions are shaped to fit particular social settings, this new setting leads to new actions and new social meanings. In this sense we have not only a different situation, but also a different President, and – in the long run – a different Presidency.

Meyrowitz, 1985, p.43

There is a similarity to Habermas's idea of refeudalisation here. Finally, Meyrowitz argues that:

> By merging discrete communities of discourse, television has made nearly every topic and issue a valid subject of interest and concern for virtually every member of the public. Further, many formerly

private and isolated behaviours have been brought out into the large unitary public arena. As a result, behaviours that were dependent on great distance and isolation have been undermined; performances that relied on long and careful rehearsals have been banished from the social repertoire. The widened public sphere gives nearly everyone a new (and relatively shared) perspective from which to view others and gain a reflected sense of self. We, our doctors, our police officers, our Presidents, our secret agents, our parents, our children, and our friends are all performing roles in new theaters that demand new styles of drama.

Meyrowitz, 1985, p.309

What unites these cases identified by Meyrowitz is the power of a particular communication technology – television – to restructure our social lives; distinctions between public and private that are obtained in a 'print world' are weakened and eroded in a 'television world'. The American feminist film scholar Linda Williams in her book on pornography, *Hardcore* (Williams, 1999), makes a similar argument in a somewhat different context. She argues (notably in Chapter 8 of *Hardcore*) that the general accessibility of the VCR has changed the character of pornographic moving images. Before the VCR pornography was produced for an exclusively male audience who often consumed porn in collective male situations such as stag nights. After the VCR the repertoire of moving image porn broadened to include 'couples porn' made for a heterosexual couple to watch together. 'Couples porn' mandated a consequential change in the type of sexual activity shown, a different balance between sexual and non-sexual action, and so on. But, it is not just the content of porn that changes (if Williams is right), it is also the habits of consumption of porn. Porn reaches different groups of people in different circumstances. Williams argues that technological change has been decisive and her argument is, like Meyrowitz's, technologically determinist.

Here again it is worth thinking back to Reading 1.3 in Chapter 1, in which it was argued that porn was linked to the initial success of another new technology, the internet. Williams argues somewhat differently – she contends that the VCR changed porn. But the contradiction is more apparent than real. Technology, content and social practices seem to be interdependent and mutually constitutive.

However, a different, less technology-centred, argument could be made that attributes change not principally to technological change but to a more general social change in women's status and a wider recognition of women's sexuality. One could point to the birth of a new female heterosexual public for porn – those who read *Black Lace* books, for example. Perhaps it is not (only) technology that has changed but also women's image of themselves, as well as a more pervasive social acceptance of pornography – whether video porn for couples or literary porn for women readers. This growth in the accessibility of porn is made possible by regulatory change (for example, in film certification) and mandates regulatory change (for example, liberalising lawful access to pornography).

We can see a structure of argument emerging that is shared by Meyrowitz and Habermas, Sola Pool and Barber, and which a host of examples (such as the difference in the general intelligibility of the language used in medieval English poetry) support. Communications technology changes the terms on which society functions and people live. Let us see how far this idea helps us to understand the historical development of a key mass medium – the newspaper. Our brief consideration of newspaper history will also give us a basis for seeing how useful Habermas's ideas are in understanding the mass media.

6 Printing, democracy and the public sphere in England

The impact of printing extended through both time and space. Printing not only changed the structure of society but also the form which written works took. At first printed works, books, took the form of manuscripts, but then, over time, new kinds of written works emerged – the newspaper, for example. Consider the English novelist Daniel Defoe's statement in *A Journal of the Plague Year*, written more than 250 years after Gutenberg, which gives a vivid sense of what the impact of the new communication technology had been:

> We had no such things as printed newspapers in those days to spread rumours and reports of things, and to improve them by the invention of men as I have lived to see practiced since. But such things as those were gathered from the letters of merchants and others who corresponded abroad, and from them was handed about by word of mouth only; so that things did not spread instantly over the whole nation, as they do now. But it seems the Government had a true account of it.
>
> Defoe, 1960/1723, p.11

The fictional narrator who speaks this on the first page of Defoe's book addresses imagined readers in the early 1720s and refers them to a time, circa 1665, when 'We had no such things as printed newspapers'. True, this statement comes from a fictional work and there is no necessary correspondence between the fictional world that Defoe created and how things actually were. But it alerts us to the constructed nature of something, the newspaper, which customarily we take for granted. Not only, Defoe tells us (and he was right), was there a time when there were no newspapers but there were also times when newspapers had a very different form to those we now know.

It took some time before newspapers were published daily. Widespread dissemination of printed news first took place through 'broadsides' which were printed occasionally and sold for long periods (see Figure 2.8). There was none of the instant perishability of today's newspapers. By the early seventeenth century the production and dissemination of printed news was sufficiently well established for the English playwright and poet Ben Jonson to dramatise it in his play *The Staple of News* (1625) and for one of the characters in the prologue, Gossip Tattle, to demand that 'news be new and fresh'. Up to 1641, and the intense political conflicts that culminated in the English Civil War, most of the periodicals published with some regularity in England were translations and adaptations of foreign periodicals such as the *Mercurius gallobelgicus* (The French and Belgian Mercury).

The first regular weekly newspaper in Britain seems to have been the 1622 *Currant of Generall News*. The first English daily newspaper, *The Daily Courant* (see Figure 2.9), started in London in 1702. Defoe's own *The Review* appeared every Tuesday, Thursday and Saturday from 1702 (whilst its editor was imprisoned in Newgate prison). The oldest surviving London newspaper, *The London Gazette*, started in 1666 – the year after the great plague which was the subject of Defoe's *A Journal of the Plague Year* (1960/1723). It grew out of the *Oxford Gazette*, published in 1665, doubtless by Londoners who had fled the plague to Oxford. There are thus some grounds for Defoe's narrator's contention. A major change did take place around the early eighteenth century.

The growth of the newspaper sector testifies to a democratisation of access to information. It was no longer just the government who enjoyed quasi-exclusive possession of and control over information. A new information network, based on merchants who corresponded with each other and whose pool of intelligence provided the basis for newspaper publishing (a 'technology of freedom' in Sola Pool's sense), came to supplant government control. Of course, such merchants not only corresponded, but actually met each other. London coffee houses were the classic locations for the exchange of information both in writing and face-to-face. The first London coffee house was established in the 1670s in Saint Michael's Alley, Cornhill, London, in the centre of the 'square mile'. It acted as a specialised centre for information about Jamaica. Letters were left there for delivery to Jamaica and letters from Jamaica were left there for collection. Merchants who wanted to import from or export to Jamaica met there, as did seamen, ship brokers and others who

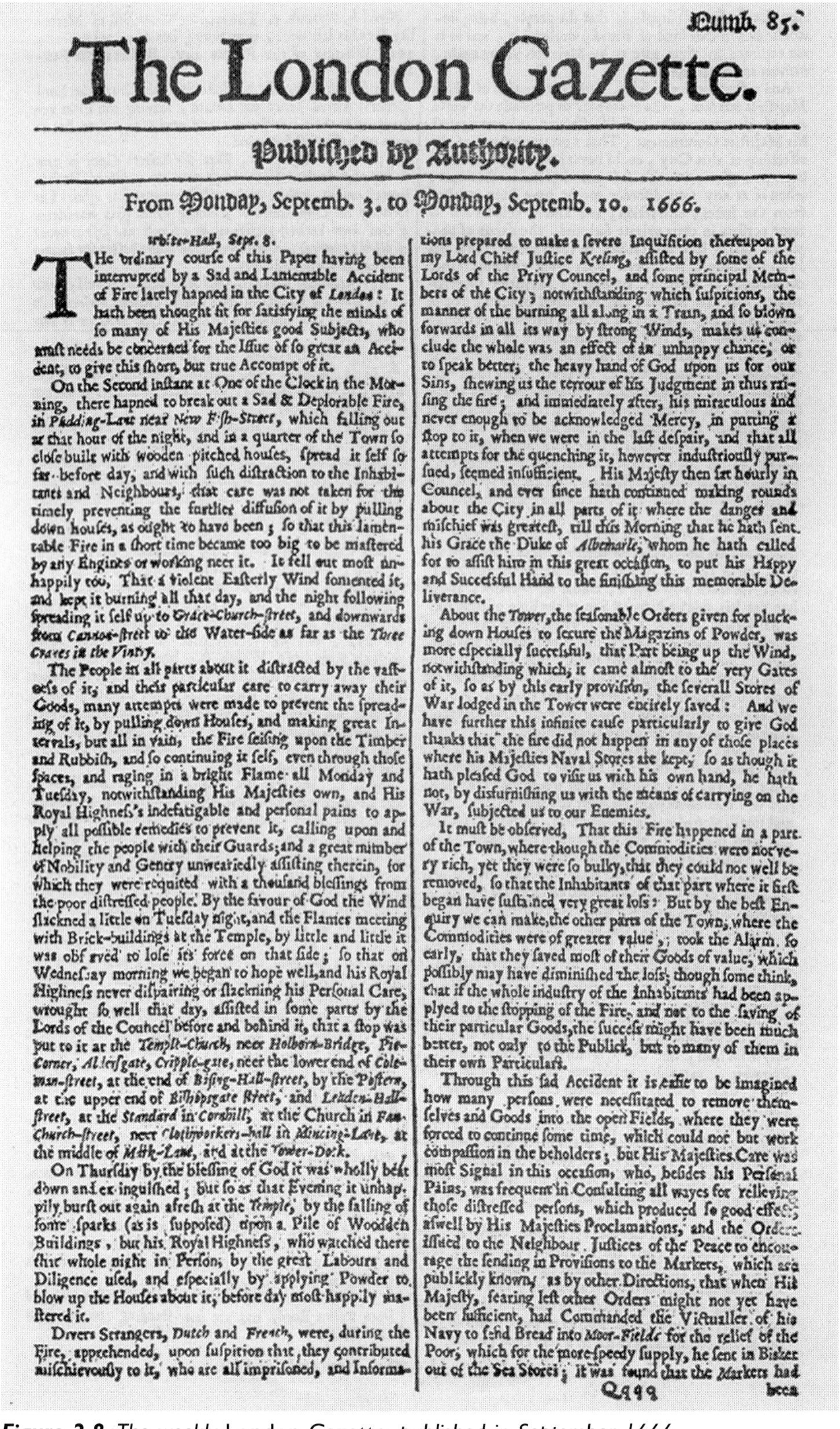

The London Gazette.

Numb. 85.

Published by Authority.

From Monday, Septemb. 3. to Monday, Septemb. 10. 1666.

Whitehall, Sept. 8.

The ordinary course of this Paper having been interrupted by a Sad and Lamentable Accident of Fire lately hapned in the City of London: It hath been thought fit for satisfying the minds of so many of His Majesties good Subjects, who must needs be concerned for the Issue of so great an Accident, to give this short, but true Accompt of it.

On the Second instant at One of the Clock in the Morning, there hapned to break out a Sad & Deplorable Fire, in Pudding-Lane near New Fish-Street, which falling out at that hour of the night, and in a quarter of the Town so close built with wooden pitched houses, spread it self so far before day, and with such distraction to the Inhabitants and Neighbours, that care was not taken for the timely preventing the further diffusion of it by pulling down houses, as ought to have been; so that this lamentable Fire in a short time became too big to be mastered by any Engines or working neer it. It fell out most unhappily too, That a violent Easterly Wind fomented it, and kept it burning all that day, and the night following spreading it self up to Grace-Church-street, and downwards from Cannon-street to the Water-side as far as the Three Cranes in the Vintry.

The People in all parts about it distracted by the vastness of it, and their particular care to carry away their Goods, many attempts were made to prevent the spreading of it, by pulling down Houses, and making great Intervals, but all in vain, the Fire seizing upon the Timber and Rubbish, and so continuing it self, even through those spaces, and raging in a bright Flame all Monday and Tuesday, notwithstanding His Majesties own, and His Royal Highness's indefatigable and personal pains to apply all possible remedies to prevent it, calling upon and helping the people with their Guards; and a great number of Nobility and Gentry unweariedly assisting therein, for which they were requited with a thousand blessings from the poor distressed people. By the favour of God the Wind slackned a little on Tuesday night, and the Flames meeting with Brick-buildings at the Temple, by little and little it was observed to lose its force on that side; so that on Wednesday morning we began to hope well, and his Royal Highness never dispairing or slackning his Personal Care, wrought so well that day, assisted in some parts by the Lords of the Council before and behind it, that a stop was put to it at the Temple-Church, near Holborn-Bridge, Pie-Corner, Aldersgate, Cripple-gate, neer the lower end of Coleman-street, at the end of Basing-Hall-street, by the Postern, at the upper end of Bishopsgate street, and Leaden-Hall-street, at the Standard in Cornhill, at the Church in Fan-Church-street, near Clothworkers-hall in Mincing-Lane, at the middle of Mark-Lane, and at the Tower-Dock.

On Thursday by the blessing of God it was wholly beat down and extinguished; but so as that Evening it unhappily burst out again afresh at the Temple, by the falling of some sparks (as is supposed) upon a Pile of Wooden Buildings, but his Royal Highness, who watched there that whole night in Person, by the great Labours and Diligence used, and especially by applying Powder to blow up the Houses about it, before day most happily mastered it.

Divers Strangers, Dutch and French, were, during the Fire, apprehended, upon suspicion that they contributed mischievously to it, who are all imprisoned, and Informa-

tions prepared to make a severe Inquisition thereupon by my Lord Chief Justice Keeling, assisted by some of the Lords of the Privy Council, and some principal Members of the City; notwithstanding which suspicions, the manner of the burning all along in a Train, and so blown forwards in all its way by strong Winds, makes us conclude the whole was an effect of an unhappy chance, or to speak better, the heavy hand of God upon us for our Sins, shewing us the terrour of his Judgment in thus raising the fire; and immediately after, his miraculous and never enough to be acknowledged Mercy, in putting a stop to it, when we were in the last despair, and that all attempts for the quenching it, however industriously pursued, seemed insufficient. His Majesty then sat hourly in Council, and ever since hath continued making rounds about the City in all parts of it, where the danger and mischief was greatest, till this Morning that he hath sent his Grace the Duke of Albemarle, whom he hath called for to assist him in this great occasion, to put his Happy and Successful Hand to the finishing this memorable Deliverance.

About the Tower, the seasonable Orders given for plucking down Houses to secure the Magazins of Powder, was more especially successful, that Part being up the Wind, notwithstanding which, it came almost to the very Gates of it, so as by this early provision, the severall Stores of War lodged in the Tower were entirely saved: And we have further this infinite cause particularly to give God thanks that the fire did not happen in any of those places where his Majesties Naval Stores are kept, so as though it hath pleased God to visit us with his own hand, he hath not, by disfurnishing us with the means of carrying on the War, subjected us to our Enemies.

It must be observed, That this Fire happened in a part of the Town, where though the Commodities were not very rich, yet they were so bulky, that they could not well be removed, so that the Inhabitants of that part where it first began have sustained very great loss: But by the best Enquiry we can make, the other parts of the Town, where the Commodities were of greater value, took the Alarm so early, that they saved most of their Goods of value, which possibly may have diminished the loss; though some think, that if the whole industry of the Inhabitants had been applyed to the stopping of the Fire, and not to the saving of their particular Goods, the success might have been much better, not only to the Publick, but to many of them in their own Particulars.

Through this sad Accident it is easie to be imagined how many persons were necessitated to remove themselves and Goods into the open Fields, where they were forced to continue some time, which could not but work compassion in the beholders; but His Majesties Care was most Signal in this occasion, who, besides his Personal Pains, was frequent in Consulting all wayes for relieving those distressed persons, which produced so good effect, aswell by His Majesties Proclamations, and the Orders issued to the Neighbour Justices of the Peace to encourage the sending in Provisions to the Markets, which are publickly known as by other Directions, that when His Majesty, fearing lest other Orders might not yet have been sufficient, had Commanded the Victualler of his Navy to send Bread into Moor-Fields for the relief of the Poor; which for the more speedy supply, he sent in Bisket out of the Sea Stores; it was found that the Markets had

bee[n]

Figure 2.8 The weekly London Gazette, published in September 1666

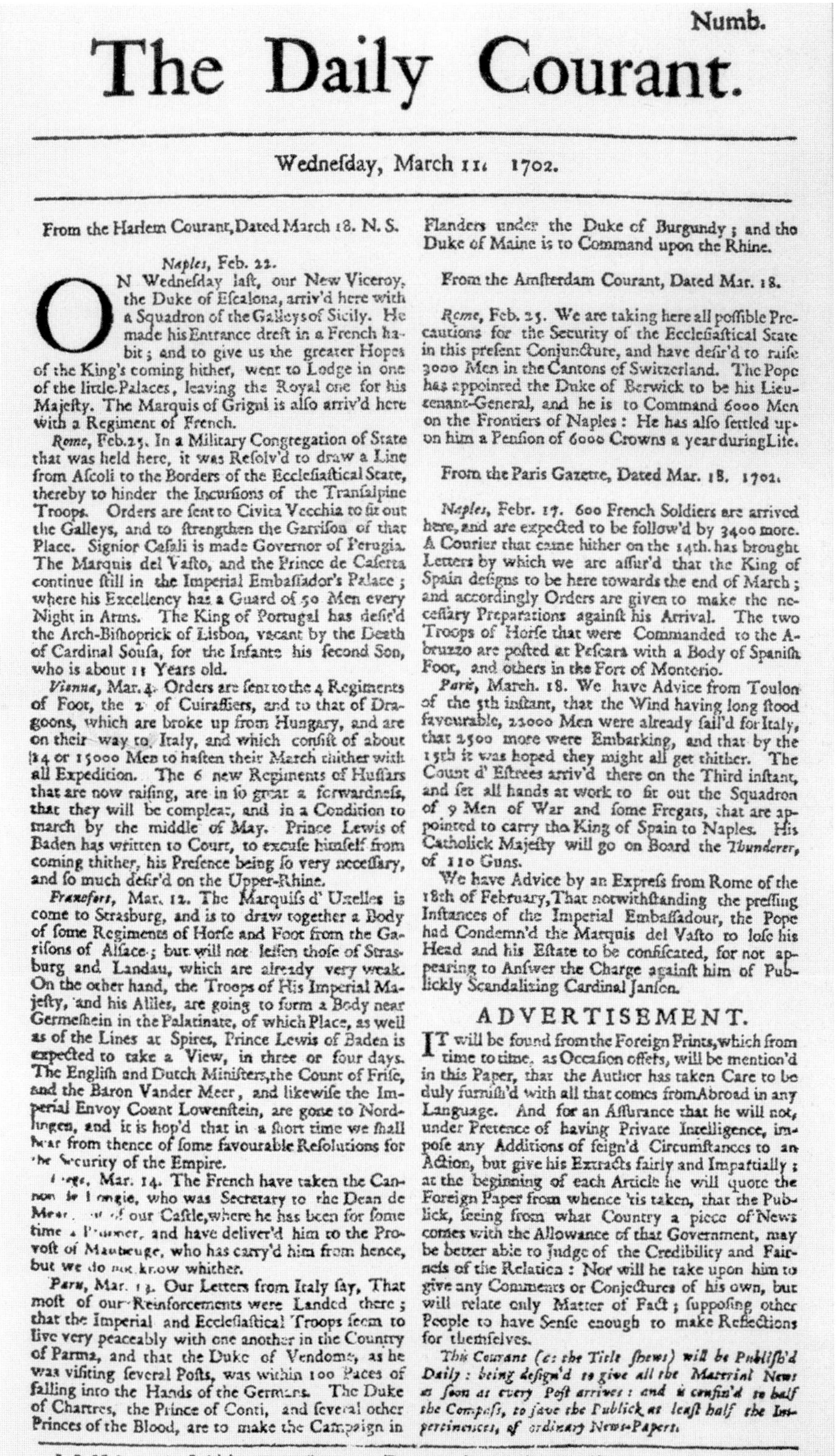

The Daily Courant.

Numb.

Wednefday, March 11, 1702.

From the Harlem Courant, Dated March 18. N. S.

Naples, Feb. 22.

ON Wednefday laft, our New Viceroy, the Duke of Efcalona, arriv'd here with a Squadron of the Galleys of Sicily. He made his Entrance dreft in a French habit; and to give us the greater Hopes of the King's coming hither, went to Lodge in one of the little Palaces, leaving the Royal one for his Majefty. The Marquis of Grigni is alfo arriv'd here with a Regiment of French.

Rome, Feb. 25. In a Military Congregation of State that was held here, it was Refolv'd to draw a Line from Afcoli to the Borders of the Ecclefiaftical State, thereby to hinder the Incurfions of the Tranfalpine Troops. Orders are fent to Civita Vecchia to fit out the Galleys, and to ftrengthen the Garrifon of that Place. Signior Cafali is made Governor of Perugia. The Marquis del Vafto, and the Prince de Caferta continue ftill in the Imperial Embaffador's Palace; where his Excellency has a Guard of 50 Men every Night in Arms. The King of Portugal has defir'd the Arch-Bifhoprick of Lisbon, vacant by the Death of Cardinal Soufa, for the Infante his fecond Son, who is about 11 Years old.

Vienna, Mar. 4. Orders are fent to the 4 Regiments of Foot, the 2 of Cuiraffiers, and to that of Dragoons, which are broke up from Hungary, and are on their way to Italy, and which confift of about 14 or 15000 Men to haften their March thither with all Expedition. The 6 new Regiments of Huffars that are now raifing, are in fo great a forwardnefs, that they will be compleat, and in a Condition to march by the middle of May. Prince Lewis of Baden has written to Court, to excufe himfelf from coming thither, his Prefence being fo very neceffary, and fo much defir'd on the Upper-Rhine.

Francfort, Mar. 12. The Marquifs d' Uxelles is come to Strasburg, and is to draw together a Body of fome Regiments of Horfe and Foot from the Garifons of Alface; but will not leffen thofe of Strasburg and Landau, which are already very weak. On the other hand, the Troops of His Imperial Majefty, and his Allies, are going to form a Body near Germefhein in the Palatinate, of which Place, as well as of the Lines at Spires, Prince Lewis of Baden is expected to take a View, in three or four days. The Englifh and Dutch Minifters, the Count of Frife, and the Baron Vander Meer, and likewife the Imperial Envoy Count Lowenftein, are gone to Nordlingen, and it is hop'd that in a fhort time we fhall hear from thence of fome favourable Refolutions for the Security of the Empire.

Liege, Mar. 14. The French have taken the Canon de Longie, who was Secretary to the Dean de Meer, out of our Caftle, where he has been for fome time a Prifoner, and have deliver'd him to the Provoft of Maubeuge, who has carry'd him from hence, but we do not know whither.

Paris, Mar. 13. Our Letters from Italy fay, That moft of our Reinforcements were Landed there; that the Imperial and Ecclefiaftical Troops feem to live very peaceably with one another in the Country of Parma, and that the Duke of Vendome, as he was vifiting feveral Pofts, was within 100 Paces of falling into the Hands of the Germans. The Duke of Chartres, the Prince of Conti, and feveral other Princes of the Blood, are to make the Campaign in Flanders under the Duke of Burgundy; and tho Duke of Maine is to Command upon the Rhine.

From the Amfterdam Courant, Dated Mar. 18.

Rome, Feb. 25. We are taking here all poffible Precautions for the Security of the Ecclefiaftical State in this prefent Conjuncture, and have defir'd to raife 3000 Men in the Cantons of Switzerland. The Pope has appointed the Duke of Berwick to be his Lieutenant-General, and he is to Command 6000 Men on the Frontiers of Naples: He has alfo fettled upon him a Penfion of 6000 Crowns a year during Life.

From the Paris Gazette, Dated Mar. 18. 1702.

Naples, Febr. 17. 600 French Soldiers are arrived here, and are expected to be follow'd by 3400 more. A Courier that came hither on the 14th. has brought Letters by which we are affur'd that the King of Spain defigns to be here towards the end of March; and accordingly Orders are given to make the neceffary Preparations againft his Arrival. The two Troops of Horfe that were Commanded to the Abruzzo are pofted at Pefcara with a Body of Spanifh Foot, and others in the Fort of Monterio.

Paris, March. 18. We have Advice from Toulon of the 5th inftant, that the Wind having long ftood favourable, 25000 Men were already fail'd for Italy, that 2500 more were Embarking, and that by the 15th it was hoped they might all get thither. The Count d' Eftrees arriv'd there on the Third inftant, and fet all hands at work to fit out the Squadron of 9 Men of War and fome Fregats, that are appointed to carry the King of Spain to Naples. His Catholick Majefty will go on Board the *Thunderer*, of 110 Guns.

We have Advice by an Exprefs from Rome of the 18th of February, That notwithftanding the preffing Inftances of the Imperial Embaffadour, the Pope had Condemn'd the Marquis del Vafto to lofe his Head and his Eftate to be confifcated, for not appearing to Anfwer the Charge againft him of Publickly Scandalifing Cardinal Janfon.

ADVERTISEMENT.

IT will be found from the Foreign Prints, which from time to time, as Occafion offers, will be mention'd in this Paper, that the Author has taken Care to be duly furnifh'd with all that comes from Abroad in any Language. And for an Affurance that he will not, under Pretence of having Private Intelligence, impofe any Additions of feign'd Circumftances to an Action, but give his Extracts fairly and Impartially; at the beginning of each Article he will quote the Foreign Paper from whence 'tis taken, that the Publick, feeing from what Country a piece of News comes with the Allowance of that Government, may be better able to Judge of the Credibility and Fairnefs of the Relation: Nor will he take upon him to give any Comments or Conjectures of his own, but will relate only Matter of Fact; fuppofing other People to have Senfe enough to make Reflections for themfelves.

This Courant (as the Title fhews) will be Publifh'd Daily: being defign'd to give all the Material News as foon as every Poft arrives: and is confin'd to half the Compafs, to fave the Publick at leaft half the Impertinences, of ordinary News-Papers.

LONDON. Sold by E. Mallet, next Door to the King's-Arms Tavern at Fleet-Bridge.

Figure 2.9 *An early English daily,* The Daily Courant, *published in March 1702*

travelled to and from Jamaica. There is now a pub on the same site whose name, the *Jamaica Wine House,* commemorates this past (see Figure 2.10).

The nascent English newspaper sector drew on the clientele of the coffee houses as sources and made them customers, either directly or, through their readership of papers supplied and purchased by the coffee house proprietors for customers' use, indirectly. An anonymous

Figure 2.10 The Jamaica Wine House, *on the reputed site of the first London coffee house*

contemporary broadside of 1674 about coffee houses gives a flavour of such places:

> First, Gentry, Tradesmen, all are welcome hither,
>
> And may without Affront sit down Together:
>
> Pre-eminence of Place, none here should Mind,
>
> But take the next fit Seat that he can find:
>
> Nor need any, if Finer persons come,
>
> Rise up for to assigne to them his Room.
>
> Quoted in Blanning, 2002, p.161

This amusing little vignette of seventeenth-century life is the central image that Habermas used to underpin his notion of the 'public sphere'. One way of looking at the idea of the public sphere is to ask: Was the eighteenth century like that? Was there ever a public sphere? Was it first found in the coffee houses where City of London merchants met, as Habermas claimed? Did reason prevail in the discussions that took place over the coffee cups and newspapers? 'Democratisation' of access to information, to which we have referred above, of course had its limits. Not everyone could read and, still less, afford coffee which was, in the seventeenth and eighteenth centuries, an exotic and expensive beverage. As the gendered nouns and pronouns 'tradesmen', 'he' and 'his' suggest, the coffee house was seldom a place for women to engage in democratic debate and participate in 'the public sphere'.

But there is evidence to support Habermas's view – coffee houses were sufficiently troubling to the authorities for King Charles II to issue a *Proclamation for the Suppression of Coffee Houses* in 1675. The Proclamation testified to 'very evil and dangerous effects', to the spreading of 'divers, false, malitious and scandalous reports [...] devised and spread abroad to the Defamation of His Majesty's Government' and to the consequential need to 'put down and suppress' coffee houses (quoted in McGee, 1997, p.220). Here, regulation steps in to countervail the power exerted by technology. In spite of the regulation or repression of print and the undoubted impact of exclusion by social class, gender and ability to read printed books and papers, the power of print technology fostered a wider public culture of informed debate and discussion. Both soft technological determinism and social shaping were at work.

7 Changing concepts of time and space

Soft technological determinism holds that technologies can also shape our mental maps. Our concepts change, as do what we mean by particular concepts. For example, what counts as 'distance' alters as communication and transportation media change. In the eighteenth century improvements to English roads reduced the journey time from Birmingham to London from two days to nine hours (Blanning, 2002, p.129). The railways progressively reduced that time to between two and three hours. Electronic communications now enable a Londoner to communicate with her colleague in Birmingham as quickly as with a fellow Londoner (whether they are in the next room, the next street or the next district). Indeed, she can communicate with her colleague in Birmingham Alabama no less quickly and, using email, no more expensively than she can with her colleague in Birmingham England.

Today it costs no more to send a message via satellite a third of the way across the Earth (for example, across the Atlantic) than it costs to send the same message by the same route to next door. Formerly cost and distance in communications were closely related – it cost more to string a telephone cable 20 kilometres than it took to string the same cable 10 kilometres. The price of a long distance call was correspondingly higher than a call over a shorter distance. Cost and distance in communications have been decoupled. What distance costs, and what counts as distance, have changed. Moreover, modern communication technologies, such as communication satellites, have reduced communication sovereignty – the ability of countries to set the terms on which communication takes place within their borders. This is because the 'footprint' (the area within which the signals can be received) of a communication satellite does not match the political boundaries between states. Broadcasting has become internationalised, to the alarm of those who fear erosion of national cultures and values and/or the lowering of standards. The power exerted by a new technology changed the power of political institutions. So too has it changed more fundamental and general relationships, including our sense of time and of space.

What changed between the European Middle Ages, when it was difficult for people to communicate with each other (due to poor transport, low levels of literacy and, often, no shared language, even among the subjects of a single monarch), and the eighteenth century when, Habermas contends, a modern public sphere first came into existence, was the greater availability of information. Printing made this possible, changed transportation, and amplified information distribution technologies. As the public sphere grew, so public discussion came to resemble more closely an ideal speech situation, and the old model of display and reproduction of power gave way to a more rational, inclusive and democratic system. Of course, printing did not do the job alone. An interdependent growth in literacy, an increase in accessibility and a fall in prices of printed works, coupled with the growth of a powerful, relatively independent class of merchants and urban manufacturers, combined to establish a relatively large-scale, modern, public sphere. But technology, and printing, counted for a lot.

True, there were limits on what could lawfully be reported. The power of print was shaped by the power of regulation. Until 1771 the printing of parliamentary speeches was unlawful in England. Indeed, the reporting of UK parliamentary affairs was not fully liberalised until the twentieth century when, in the mid-1950s, the BBC was freed from the '14 day' rule (which had provided that the BBC should refrain from broadcasting on a subject due to be discussed in parliament for the two preceding weeks), and subsequently was permitted to televise parliamentary proceedings.

8   Progress or regress?

We can see from this account of how media and communications exercise power that there is more than one way of looking at what the media do. Some see media history as a history of progress and improvement, but others dissent and see recent media history as a story of regression. For example, the British scholars James Curran and Jean Seaton, in the successive editions of their book on the UK press and broadcasting, *Power without Responsibility* (2003) (first published in 1981) have insisted on the dark side of the UK's media history – the measures the state has taken to suppress information and inhibit its circulation and the failures of the market to provide full, free and fair media representation.

But what of media content? Habermas's account of the development of a public sphere is representative in leaving unnoticed the scurrilous, scandalous, lubricious staples of the mass media. It leads us to focus on news and current affairs, on democratic debate and the links between politics and the media. Media history tends to foreground the earnest, the responsible and the serious in its account of events; but much gets left out in such a story. Scandal, scurrility and celebrity have been media staples since the beginnings of printing, as the dust cover of Jeremy Black's *The English Press 1621–1861* reminds us with its invocation of 'Deaths, executions, and discoveries of the most audacious and unheard of villainies' available in *Mist's Weekly Journal* of 14 May 1726 (quoted in Black, 2001). In this historical context there is nothing new or surprising in the US *National Inquirer*, Canada's *Journal de Montréal* or the UK's *The News of the World* and *The Daily Star*. Even the UK's *Sunday Sport*, with unforgettable headlines such as 'World War II bomber found on moon' (24 April 1988) or 'Man from Atlantis found in pub brawl' (17 July 1988) (see Figure 2.11), had ample precedents in the early British press.

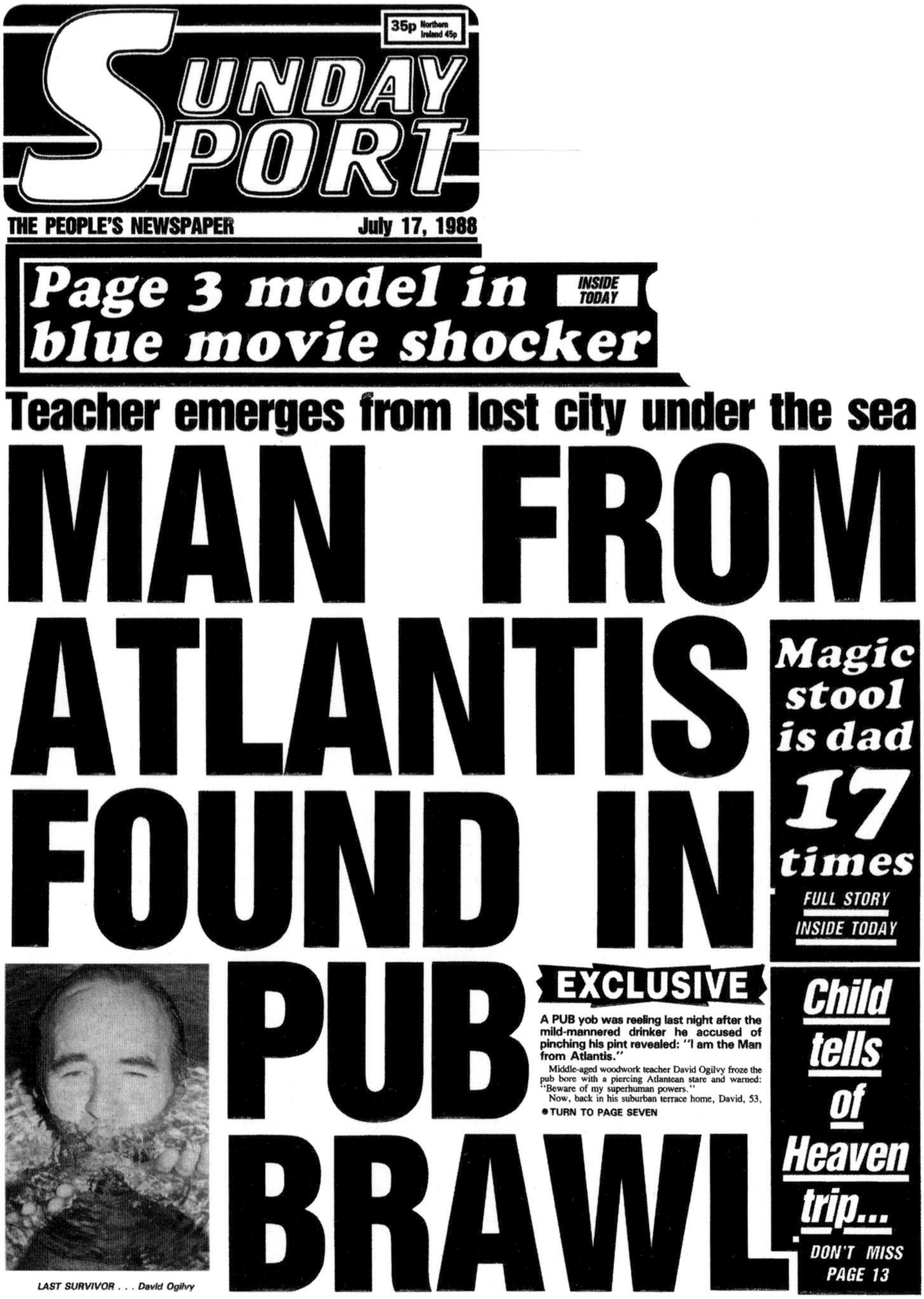

SUNDAY SPORT

35p Northern Ireland 45p

THE PEOPLE'S NEWSPAPER July 17, 1988

Page 3 model in blue movie shocker INSIDE TODAY

Teacher emerges from lost city under the sea

MAN FROM ATLANTIS FOUND IN PUB BRAWL

EXCLUSIVE

A PUB yob was reeling last night after the mild-mannered drinker he accused of pinching his pint revealed: "I am the Man from Atlantis."

Middle-aged woodwork teacher David Ogilvy froze the pub bore with a piercing Atlantean stare and warned: "Beware of my superhuman powers."

Now, back in his suburban terrace home, David, 53,

● TURN TO PAGE SEVEN

LAST SURVIVOR . . . David Ogilvy

Magic stool is dad 17 times

FULL STORY INSIDE TODAY

Child tells of Heaven trip...

DON'T MISS PAGE 13

Figure 2.11 Sunday Sport *front page*

9 Conclusion

What can we conclude from the ideas and examples that we have considered in this chapter? Firstly, that one's view of media history (and media content) will tend to influence one's view of media policy (what governments ought to do in respect of the media). As argued in Chapter 1, there are important parallels to be drawn between established and emerging communication technologies. See, for example, Bill Gates's comparison of printing and the internet (to which we referred earlier):

> The single shift that has had the greatest effect on the history of communication took place about 1450, when Johann Gutenberg [...] invented moveable type and introduced the first printing press to Europe [...] That event changed Western culture forever [...] The printing press did more than just give the West a faster way to reproduce a book. Until it came on the scene, life had been communal and nearly unchanging despite the passing generations. Most people knew only what they had seen themselves or had been told [...] The printed word changed all that. It was the first mass medium [...] Before Gutenberg there were only about 30,000 books on the entire continent of Europe, nearly all of them Bibles or biblical commentaries. By 1500 there were more than 9 million books, on all sorts of topics [...] The global interactive network will transform our culture as dramatically as Gutenberg's press did the Middle Ages.
>
> Gates, 1996, pp.8–9

Secondly, Habermas and Sola Pool provide us with different ways to interpret and understand technological change and the influence of the media on society. Each also points towards a different sort of media regulation. Our choice between the rival paradigms offered by Habermas and Sola Pool will depend, in part, on the extent to which we believe the past will be a model for the future. For example, how far there is a public sphere in modern mass societies; whether newspapers, radio and television provide a forum in which a modern public sphere can come into being; whether Bill Gates is right about the parallels between printing and the internet.

So, the arguments that we have put forward propose that technology counts for a lot and that the concepts developed by modern media theorists help us understand the contemporary mass media. But there is another sense in which such ideas are important. They provide (and here the notion of a public sphere has been particularly influential) a kind of ideal, a baseline against which actual media environments can be evaluated. They enable us to ask, for example, how far television news in a particular country constitutes a well functioning public sphere in which all can be well informed, all can deliberate and share views with each other, and do so through the exchange of well reasoned and well founded viewpoints? How far do the newspapers available in a particular market provide the conditions in which a well functioning public sphere can thrive? Has the internet helped or hindered the establishment of a public sphere? How far do modern media markets provide the diversity and pluralism which Sola Pool thought so important?

It may seem a long way from *Sir Gawain and the Green Knight* to Bill Gates's vision of the future but we hope, after reading this chapter, that you can see a connection. The argument is based on the view of 'soft technological determinism' put forward in Chapter 1. Technology counts – but it does not count for everything. History counts too as we can see that one's view of history is not only likely to shape one's view of the future, but also how one acts to produce the future. If you broadly agree with Habermas, you are likely to favour strong regulation of commercial media and a powerful role for public service broadcasting. If you favour Sola Pool's vision and his ideal of diversity and pluralism you may well take the opposite position. Reasonable people – for example, Habermas and Sola Pool – can reasonably reach very different conclusions about the desirability of the effects that follow from the unfolding of technological change. Their conclusions are rooted in the authors' broader schemes of values: Sola Pool, for example, appears to believe more strongly than Habermas in the importance of pluralism and diversity for freedom and democracy (and of course there are many people who do not believe that freedom and democracy are ultimate, universal or absolute values), while Habermas, on the other hand, believes more strongly in the importance of an integrated public sphere. From these different versions of history, different values and different understandings of media and communications come, naturally enough, different ideas about what should be done, about how the media should be organised and regulated. And that brings us neatly on to the next two chapters in this book.

Further reading

We suggest that you go to Ithiel de Sola Pool's *Technologies of Freedom* (1983) and Jürgen Habermas's *The Public Sphere* (1996). After these you might find Meyrowitz's *No Sense of Place* rewarding and/or one of the histories of printing referenced below (either Eisenstein, Febvre and Martin, or Steinberg, whichever comes most conveniently to hand). For an account of the press and broadcasting in the UK see the latest edition of Curran and Seaton's *Power without Responsibility* (at the time of writing this was the 2003 edition).

References

Barber, C. (1964) *The Story of Language*, London, Pan.

Barbour, J. (1997) *The Bruce* (trans. A. Duncan), Edinburgh, Canongate Books.

Bennett, T. (2005) 'The media sensorium: cultural technologies, the senses and society' in Gillespie, M. (ed.) *Media Audiences*, Maidenhead, Open University Press/The Open University (Book 2 in this series).

Black, J. (2001) *The English Press 1621–1861*, Stroud, Sutton.

Blanning, T. (2002) *The Culture of Power and the Power of Culture*, Oxford, Oxford University Press.

Curran, J. and Seaton, J. (2003) *Power without Responsibility*, London, Routledge.

Deane, P. (1999) 'Historical prologue, *Sir Gawain and the Green Knight*', *A Treasury of Alliterative and Accentual Poetry*, http://alliteration.net/Pearl.htm (accessed 26 October 2004).

Defoe, D. (1960/1723) *A Journal of the Plague Year*, New York, Signet.

Downey, J. (2006) 'The media industries: do ownership, size and internationalisation matter?' in Hesmondhalgh, D. (ed.) *Media Production*, Maidenhead, Open University Press/The Open University (Book 3 in this series).

Duncan, A.A.M. (ed.) (2005) 'Book 1, *The Brus* by John Barbour', STARN, www2.arts.gla.ac.uk/SESLL/STELLA/STARN/poetry/BRUS/text01.htm (accessed 27 November 2005).

Eisenstein, E. (1979) *The Printing Press as an Agent of Change: Communications and Cultural Transformations in Early Modern Europe*, New York, Cambridge University Press.

Evans, J. and Hesmondhalgh, D. (eds) (2005) *Understanding Media: Inside Celebrity*, Maidenhead, Open University Press/The Open University.

Febvre, L. and Martin, H. (1976) *The Coming of the Book*, London, New Left Books.

The Financial Times, 27 January 2004.

Garnham, N. (1992) 'The media and the public sphere' in Calhoun, C. (ed.) *Habermas and the Public Sphere*, Cambridge, MA, MIT Press.

Gates, B. (1996) *The Road Ahead*, London, Penguin.

Habermas, J. (1984) *The Theory of Communicative Action Vol 1*, London, Heinemann Educational Books.

Habermas, J. (1989) *The Structural Transformation of the Public Sphere*, Cambridge, Polity.

Habermas, J. (1996) 'The public sphere' in Marris, P. and Thornham S. (eds) *Media Studies: A Reader*, Edinburgh, Edinburgh University Press.

Herbert, D. (2005) 'Media publics, culture and democracy' in Gillespie, M. (ed.) *Media Audiences*, Maidenhead, Open University Press/The Open University (Book 2 in this series).

Klapper, J. (1960) *The Effects of Mass Communication*, New York, The Free Press.

Librarius (1997) 'General prologue, *The Canterbury Tales*', Librarius, www.librarius.com/canttran/genpro/genpro001-042.htm (accessed 2 February 2004).

Lowe, R. (2003) 'Rob Lowe joins Arnie' *Internet Movie Database WENN*, www.imdb.com/news/wenn/2003-08-19#celeb4 (accessed 27 November 2005).

Matheson, D. (2000) 'The birth of news discourse; changes in news language in British newspapers, 1800–1930', *Media, Culture and Society*, vol.22, no.5, pp.557–73.

McGee, H. (1997) *On Food and Cooking*, New York, Fireside.

McGonagle, T., Noll, B. and Price, M. (eds) (2003) *Minority-Language Related Broadcasting and Legislation in the OSCE*, study commissioned by the OSCE High Commissioner on National Minorities, Programme in Comparative Law and Politics, Wolfson College, Oxford University and Institute for Information Law, Universiteit van Amsterdam.

McLuhan, M. (1964) *Understanding Media*, London, Routledge.

Meyrowitz, J. (1985) *No Sense of Place*, New York, Oxford University Press.

Newman, C. and Crooks, E. (2004) 'Gordon shakes hands as Tony twists arms', *The Financial Times*, 27 January, p1.

Sola Pool, I. de (1983) *Technologies of Freedom*, Cambridge, MA, Harvard University Press.

Steinberg, S. (1955) *Five Hundred Years of Printing*, Harmondsworth, Penguin.

Tolkien, J.R.R. and Gordon, E. (eds) (1967) *Sir Gawain and the Grene Knyghte*, Oxford, Clarendon Press; also available online at http://etext.lib. virginia.edu/etcbin/toccer-new2?id=AnoGawa.sgm&images=images/ modeng&data=/lv1/Archive/mideng-parsed&tag=public&part= 1&division=div1 (accessed 27 November 2005).

UNESCO (1989) *World Communication Report*, Paris, UNESCO.

Williams, L. (1999) *Hardcore. Power, Pleasure and the 'Frenzy of the Visible'*, Berkeley and Los Angeles, CA, University of California Press.

The economics of the media and the media in economics

Nick Wells

Contents

1 Introduction

The media industries today are big business and among societies' most important institutions, commanding enormous economic resources in the production and distribution of products and services. This being so, in this chapter we consider:

- the particular economic and social characteristics of the media industries and their role in shaping our societies;

- why governments have regulated media, and whether they should continue to do so;

- whether there is something particularly special or distinct about media products or media enterprises.

We begin with how the media industries are organised as a market. Markets enable people to exchange goods, or money and goods, so that all, ideally, are better off by doing so. The farmer takes cabbages to market because she or he would rather have money than cabbages. Cabbage eaters buy cabbage because they would rather have cabbage than retain the money equivalent of the price of a cabbage. Most media and communications goods and services are transferred from producers to consumers in market relationships.

Because the media are such a prominent source of many different kinds of information, and are one of the primary ways in which we learn about the world and our political and social spheres, some immediate questions arise. What is the role of government and regulation for the media sector? Is the market alone a good way for deciding what television, radio, newspapers, internet content, etc., is on offer, just as it is for other goods? These enquiries take us to the heart of issues of media *power* and lead us to ask how far media and communications should be regulated.

We can start by identifying some of the most important characteristics of media industries. One is that they tend to be highly concentrated – in other words, a relatively small number of giant organisations dominate supply (see also the discussion in **Downey, 2006**). This is true of television, radio broadcasting, cable, telecommunications (telecom), and sometimes even newspapers at local and/or national levels. Concentration of media ownership and control is not a new phenomenon. This was the case even 130 years ago when a media cartel consisting of three European news agencies – Reuters (Britain), Wolff (Germany) and Havas (France) – signed an agreement dividing the world news market among them, enabling them to eliminate competition. Their cartel remained in place until 1920, when it was challenged by the Associated Press from the USA (Moore, 2005).

The global media industries today are dominated by giant conglomerate firms operating across many countries: the 'five sisters', as they are called by some media analysts. These groupings are:

1   The Rupert Murdoch empire, News Corporation, which includes, among others, the BSkyB and Direct TV satellite broadcast networks, the Fox TV network (USA), HarperCollins Publishing, *The Australian, New York Post,* the *Sun* and *The Times* newspapers, as well as shares in important televison content, especially football teams;

2   Time Warner (publishing, film), CNN (television news), AOL (internet services), among others;

3   General Electric, NBC (US television network), Universal Studios (film), Vivendi (multimedia operations in many countries), among others;

4   Disney, ABC (US television network), ESPN (sports television network), among others;

5   Viacom (multimedia), CBS (US television network), MTV (music network), among others.

Each of the individual companies listed here for each conglomerate is a dominant player in its own industry, and each one is involved in other media activities as well. They also own some of the largest internet companies. So this listing actually understates the breadth of media activities covered by these global media conglomerates. At the time of writing (in 2004) Comcast, the world's largest cable company, was bidding to buy Disney, which would launch it to the number one position over Murdoch. In Philadelphia, Comcast owns the basketball team, the stadium, the cable sports channel televising the games and the cable company delivering the signal.

This tendency of the media industry to become concentrated follows some basic economic characteristics of media and communications – what we will call economies of scope and scale. So, if we want to understand why the media are as they are (and if we want to devise robust and effective measures to redress some of the undesirable consequences of concentration), we need to understand their basic economics. Media conglomerates argue that their continuing accumulation of media companies enables them to take advantage of *economies of scale*. This means that the average cost of producing and distributing each unit (a newspaper, television show, etc.) is reduced by creating a larger number of copies.

Sometimes people in the media industries (for example, those working in the printing industry) refer to this idea of economies of scale by using the terms 'first copy' and 'second and subsequent copy' costs. To give a simplified account of this, the first copy cost of a newspaper includes the capital costs of setting up the newspaper company, the journalists' salaries, fees to photographers, as well as the cost of the paper and ink used in printing the first copy. Clearly these costs exceed the price likely to be charged for the first copy of the newspaper (which in the UK is often less than 50p). But second and subsequent copy costs are little more than the cost of the paper and ink. There is likely to be a significant surplus left from the sale of each of the second and subsequent copies once the cost of paper and ink has been paid. Thus, if first copy costs can be spread across a large number of subsequent copies, then costs can be covered and, if enough are sold, profits can be high. Or, put another way, there are big potential returns to economies of scale in such a business.

Economies of scope also lower unit costs by providing the same content across different media (for example, television, radio, cable, press). The BBC, for instance, is able to reversion reports from its journalists for transmission as radio, television and internet services. The cost of these reports is paid for once, but the reports may be used more than once in different media. It is cheaper for each medium to draw on and reversion common source material than to originate its own news coverage from scratch. There are, we say, strong returns to economies of scope in such a situation. New media technologies, such as satellites, digital recording and the internet, have amplified the potential to realise high returns from economies of scope and scale.

The combination of scale and scope economies tends to make the media industries highly concentrated. Critics such as those who follow the political economy perspective outlined elsewhere in this course (for example, **Hesmondhalgh, 2005**; **Downey, 2006**) or the social market approach outlined by **Downey** (**2006**) may claim that companies that exploit scope and scale economies are thereby likely to accumulate monopoly power. According to these critics, economies of scope and scale lead to a few companies deciding most of what we will see, hear and read as news and entertainment. Because they can shut out different opinions and perspectives, media monopolies may be a threat to an informed citizenry, and therefore to democracy. For example, political candidates become beholden to the media monopolies and to their often far-flung economic interests; and those that criticise the media and propose to take steps to reduce the power and influence of the media monopolies are unlikely to get much coverage in the media themselves.

Critics of the concentration of ownership and control are not just academics. Ted Turner, founder of CNN and chairman of Turner Enterprises wrote recently about how he started out with a small company. He asked:

> What will programming be like when it's produced for no other purpose than profit? What will news be like when there are no independent news organizations to go after stories the big corporations avoid? Who really wants to find out? Safeguarding

the welfare of the public cannot be the first concern of a large publicly traded media company. Its job is to seek profits.

Turner, 2004, p.30

A further problem with media market concentration is that media conglomerates tend to depend heavily on advertising revenues, so criticism of advertisers is unlikely. We see many examples of programme content, as well as advertising, being designed to promote the economic interests of advertisers and the media conglomerates. Shortly after *Ms.* magazine started up in 1972, the publication became embroiled in a dispute with Clairol (a dominant advertiser) over the editorial policies and practices that Clairol sought to influence. The magazine decided that the only way to be free of advertisers' influence was to publish without advertising (see Steinem, 1990). For most media, this is not the path taken. Fees charged to advertisers, as well as to viewers/consumers of their products and services (for example, pay- television), are not subject to effective competition, so prices can be charged that are much higher than costs, and the consequential high profits may be used to buy up even more media companies.

Media giants can use their enormous market power to block the entry of new independent competitors to the media market. In a *New York Times* article written in 2004, a US journalist, William Safire, asked 'where will all this end?' He stated:

If one huge corporation controlled both the production and the distribution of most of our news and entertainment, couldn't it rule the world? ... You don't have to be a populist to want to stop this rush by ever-fewer entities to dominate both the content and the conduit of what we see and hear and write and say.

Safire, 2004, p.19

This article was not published widely across the media outlets of these conglomerates – but it was published in one of the world's leading newspapers and did get some syndication. The power of the media giants is not complete, not least because they compete against each other.

One can see similar tendencies towards increasing concentration of the media within most countries. In 2003, the UK government approved a merger that effectively integrated the ITV network (formerly made up of 13 separate companies) so that it became dominated by a single company with more than 90 per cent of ITV. The merger was justified primarily on the grounds of creating a network strong enough to compete with international rivals and the BBC and BSkyB. In the USA and Canada, the media industries are dominated by a few television and cable networks, and the vast majority of cities and towns have only one local newspaper.

The trend toward increasing concentration in the media is similar in most other democratic countries, and under authoritarian regimes, of course, it is even greater. Although one can identify many smaller media firms serving niche markets of relatively small numbers of special viewers, readers and consumers, these seldom influence the mass media messages and, if they show signs of becoming significant, they are likely to be bought by a media conglomerate.

The following sections examine the distinctive economic characteristics of the media industries. Understanding media economics will help you to better understand why the problems of media power that we have identified above arise and why economic factors are so important in determining the shape of the media (Sections 2 and 3). To understand how media industries came to be structured the way they are, we must also examine how the development of the economy and new technologies have influenced media development, and look at the role of the media in influencing the development of the economy (Section 4). These concerns have implications for broader issues of change and continuity: that is, for the roles of the media and of media technologies in shaping, or inhibiting, change. The final section (Section 5) examines a number of recent changes in the media.

Activity 3.1

Use your media diary to list the media that you use on a regular basis. List the alternatives available to you.

- Do you know who owns them?
- Do you know the other financial or economic interests of the media owners?
- Can you easily find out?
- For example, can you tell by visiting their websites?
- Try using a search engine to secure this information. ■ ■ ■

2 Tension in the relations between government and markets

Many governments have been concerned about the type and extent of independent, private economic power in the economy, and the possible need for the application of political power – for example, through government control or regulation – to limit the accumulation of private economic power outside government. This concern has been manifested in all kinds of areas, ranging from aircraft production to water supply, and is not confined to media and communications. However, media industries have grown to become a major sector of the economy, and government concerns have been especially acute in these industries (television, radio, press, telecommunications, post) because of their pervasive influence over the channels of communication in society, and thereby over the marketplace of ideas.

Governments may respond to such kinds of media power in different ways: some may go along with it (and establish a cosy, mutually supportive relationship between political and media power); others may seek to countervail media power (perhaps through fostering competition, through regulation and/or by promoting countervailing media institutions).

We use the term 'marketplace of ideas' frequently. The term has attractive connotations, such as freedom from state interference and robust competition between many alternative viewpoints. But 'marketplace of ideas' can be a misleading term for, as we will see, the distinctive economics of the media mean that when media markets operate free of state regulation (or 'interference'), a very unfree marketplace of ideas is often the result. So what do we mean by markets and how do media markets work?

2.1 Markets and market failures

Markets are where buyers and sellers exchange goods and services. These people may or may not meet physically, or even know one another, depending upon the product and the circumstances. With the modern electronic media, more and more market exchanges take place without face-to-face meetings of buyers and sellers. Amazon.com and eBay are examples of electronic commerce, or online markets, where individuals can purchase goods without meeting (see Figure 3.1). Many large businesses are using improved media and transport, and the boundaries of markets are being expanded to such a degree that for many goods and services there is a now a global market. The expansion of the media has been a major factor contributing to the expansion of economic markets to regional and global levels. In fact, one of those global markets is the media themselves, as illustrated by the media conglomerates identified in the previous section.

There has been a tension between markets and government, and the appropriate roles for each, since the earliest days of capitalism and the development of what we now call the social science of economics. In his classic work *An Inquiry into the Nature and Causes of the Wealth of Nations* (1776), one of the first and finest of political economists, Adam Smith (1723–1790) (see Figure 3.2), argued that growth in the economy would be stimulated by freeing the population to produce and exchange goods

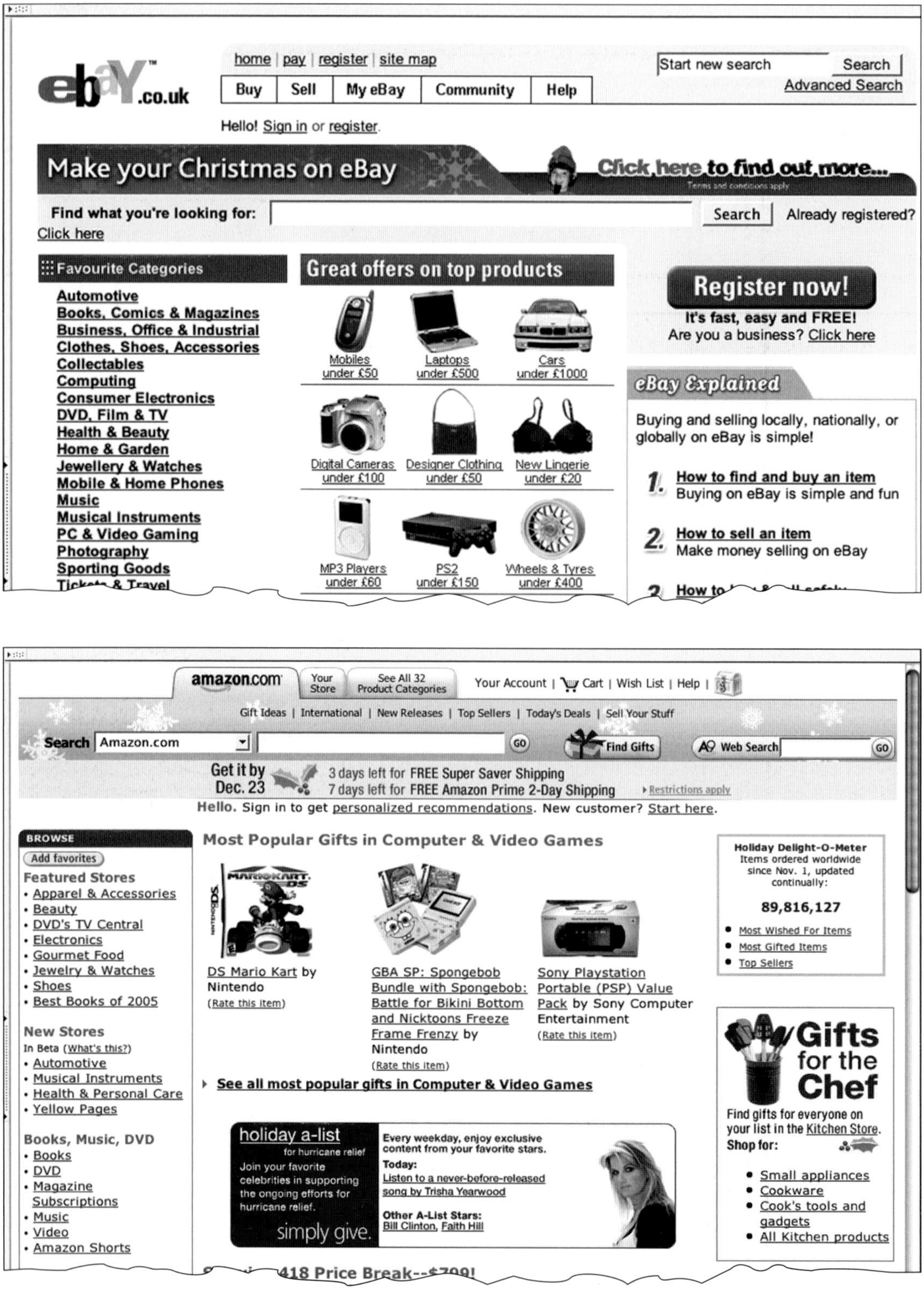

Figure 3.1 Amazon and eBay web pages. Two examples of the modern 'virtual' marketplace
Source: www.ebay.co.uk and www.amazon.com

in local and regional markets, and enabling them to shift their labour freely among employers and locations. This freedom would lead to a progressive division of labour that would foster the cultivation of specialised skills, increase productivity, reduce unit costs, increase production and sales, and provide greater wealth for the country, and possibly even for the state treasury. The greater the possibilities of production for exchange in open markets, the greater the benefits that are possible from the division of labour. The extent of the division of labour is limited by the extent of the market: that is, where the cost of transport becomes so high that trade becomes uneconomic. Additional benefits can be realised by developments that widen the market, such as the removal of restraints on trade, and improvements in transport and communications.

The following quotation is from Adam Smith's *An Inquiry into the Nature and Causes of the Wealth of Nations* (usually known as *The Wealth of Nations*) where he sets out his argument for the division of labour:

> To take an example, therefore, from a very trifling manufacture; but one in which the division of labour has been very often taken notice of, the trade of the pin-maker; a workman not educated to this business [...] nor acquainted with the use of the machinery employed in it [...] could scarce [...] make one pin in a day, and certainly could not make twenty. But in the way in which this business is now carried on, not only the whole work is a peculiar trade, but it is divided into a number of branches, of which the greater part are likewise peculiar trades. One man draws out the wire, another straightens it, a third cuts it, a fourth points it, a fifth grinds it at the top for receiving the head [...] I have seen a small manufactory of this kind where ten men [...] could make among them upwards of forty-eight thousand pins in a day.
>
> Smith, 1904/1776, Book 1, Chapter 1, Paragraph 3

Figure 3.2 *The economist, Adam Smith (1723–1790)*

Smith's analysis of the harmful effects on economic growth of restrictions on production, labour and trade was not limited only to restrictions imposed by the state. Restrictions that were imposed by private monopolies and conspiracies of private suppliers to restrain trade and charge monopoly prices were also seen as harmful. Smith argued that the economy would be more productive if what he called the 'invisible hand' of a freely competitive market ordered affairs. A monopoly in economic affairs, whether by the state or private suppliers, was seen as an inefficient allocation of society's resources, restricting the opportunities of others and forcing an unnecessary and unjustified transfer of wealth from consumers to the monopolists via exploitive monopoly prices.

The following quotation is from another famous section of *The Wealth of Nations*, in which Adam Smith very cannily shows his awareness that proprietors of firms do not always work in the public's interest. Hence his interest in arguing for an economic system, one of well-functioning markets and effective competition, that minimises the opportunities for proprietors to conspire against the public:

> People of the same trade seldom meet together, even for merriment and diversion, but the conversation ends in a conspiracy against the public, or in some contrivance to raise prices. It is impossible indeed to prevent such meetings, by any law that either could be executed, or would be consistent with liberty and justice. But though the law cannot hinder people of the same trade from sometimes assembling together, it ought to do nothing to facilitate such assemblies.
>
> Smith, 1904/1776, Book 1, Chapter 10, Paragraph 82

Smith and the economists who followed him recognised that, even if 'people of the same trade' were not able to conspire against the public and raise prices, some kinds of economic activity were inherently prone to problems of private monopoly power, even after all government restrictions were removed. A competitive market was unlikely to develop or be sustainable for activities such as building and maintaining roads, bridges, or canals in Smith's time. For these kinds of infrastructure services there would be a potential role for the state in providing services directly or by the government regulating private monopolies. During most of the twentieth century the state either regulated the media industries or was the provider of them – for example, in post, telecom, radio and television broadcasting – and sometimes did both. In contrast, publishing and the press have, for the most part, been viewed as part of business in general and thus subject to the general laws, such as those on competition, libel, indecency, and so on, rather than to special media laws. Commentators differ as to whether the distinction between state provision for one set of communications and media services (for example, broadcasting and telecommunications) and market provision for another (for example, newspapers and books) is intrinsically valid. But for our purposes it is enough to acknowledge a widespread recognition that neither state nor market provision is likely to be desirable (or possible) in all circumstances.

Coincidentally, 1776 was both the year of publication of *The Wealth of Nations* and of the United States Declaration of Independence, from which followed the United States of America and a constitution that declared both a minimal role for the government in economic affairs, and a commitment to open markets in the exchange of both goods and ideas. The so-called 'First Amendment' to the United States' Constitution in the US Bill of Rights has been enormously influential and its prohibition of state action to limit freedom of speech and the press echoes the non-interventionist emphasis of the US Constitution as a whole. The first clause of the Bill of Rights prescribes that:

> Congress shall make no law respecting an establishment of religion, or prohibiting the free exercise thereof; or abridging the freedom of speech, or of the press; or the right of the people peaceably to assemble, and to petition the government for a redress of grievances.
>
> United States Department of State, 2005

The Bill of Rights thus constrains the US government's exercise of lawful power over the press and (because of the mention of freedom of speech) over the media as a whole. Competitive markets came to be associated with the widespread availability of information, opportunities for communication and participation in economic activity. This doctrine of market liberalism, or versions of it, has become very pervasive.

The failure of the Soviet Union to move away from an economy based on state planning and towards one based on markets significantly discredited the main twentieth-century rival economic model – communism. Moreover, the complementary influences of the European Union's pro-competition regulations and national governments' liberalisation of national economies and privatisation of state monopolies (such as electricity and gas supply, telecoms and broadcasting, airlines and railways) have also shifted European countries strongly towards this model. In the UK, examples of this trend are the privatisation of British Telecom (BT), the establishment of satellite and cable television, and the end of the Royal Mail's postal monopoly.

Competition was seen not only as economically efficient but also as a significant step towards democratisation. As we mentioned in the previous section, monopoly practices tend to restrict information flows, diversity of opinion and opportunities to communicate and participate in markets. In contrast, markets that have many buyers and sellers in which no provider dominates the market are called 'workably competitive'. However, many media markets are far from 'workably competitive'.

There is therefore an important gap between the *theoretical* benefits of competitive markets and the *actual* structure of many media and communications markets. For example, even after 20 years of privatisation and competition in UK telecoms, the former state monopoly, British Telecom, still controls about 80 per cent of telephone lines. Markets that have only a few very large suppliers dominating the market are called 'oligopolies', and those that are assessed as possessing a significant degree of monopoly may require regulation by the state. Nevertheless, even in this general framework favouring free competitive markets and minimal government regulation to address market failures, it has often been considered, in spite of 'First Amendment' considerations, essential for government to play a special role in owning, operating and/or regulating most of the media industries.

2.2 Characteristics of well-functioning markets

Economists following Smith have refined the analysis of markets considerably, defining more precisely the essential elements that are necessary for markets to be fully competitive and documenting the range of benefits that competitive markets can provide. They have defined the necessary conditions for markets to be effectively competitive and the possible roles for government when markets are not competitive or cannot be expected to become so.

In theory, a competitive market will provide powerful economic incentives towards:

- the efficient allocation and use of existing economic resources by firms supplying goods and services;
- innovation by existing and new firms;
- wide consumer choice and comparatively low market prices that reflect the cost of efficient production.

We will briefly review the essential characteristics of effectively competitive markets, so that we can then examine the extent to which they exist in the media industries. For many economists the most important attributes of well-functioning competitive markets are as follows:

- widespread availability of information;
- absence of significant monopoly power;
- ease of market entry and exit;
- absence of market externalities;
- achievement of public interest objectives.

Widespread availability of information

Markets are themselves a specialised medium of communication. Markets exist in the communication of information between buyers and sellers, and from this information the market generates new information, notably market prices. In many cases the extent of the market is determined by the availability of information. All parties in the market, or potentially in the market, including firms and consumers, must be well informed in order to be able to make effective decisions. Timely and relevant information must be easily accessible and readily communicated. Barriers to information weaken the ability of markets to function efficiently.

Absence of significant monopoly power

In a well-functioning competitive market, no firm has power to dominate the market. The existence of significant monopoly power in a market restricts the participation opportunities of smaller competitors and potential new market entrants. The market pressure for competitive efficiency and innovation is reduced, consumer choice is restricted and prices are higher than they need to be.

Ease of market entry and exit

Free entry and exit help markets function efficiently. Firms with new ideas and products enter. Inefficient firms leave. Barriers to entry (such as governments giving operating permissions – licences – to some firms and not to others, very large investment requirements, etc.) reduce possibilities for participation in the market and limit competition (and market efficiency).

Absence of market externalities

There can be positive or negative externalities. If all the costs of producing a particular good or service are not borne by the firm supplying it, the additional costs (for example, of pollution, or of too many people accessing the internet at the same time causing connections to slow down) are social costs *external* to the market, and are imposed on others who may not be party to the transaction at all. These social costs are called *negative market externalities*. On the other hand, if the benefits to society are not all captured in the prices that individual consumers pay and the revenues the firms collect, the additional benefits are social benefits external to the market and received by others (for example, defence, public health and safety). By being healthy, you make life better for those around you by not missing work, needing medical attention or spreading illness. Thus you create *positive market externalities*. In a well-functioning market, all the social costs and benefits are fully captured in the firm's costs of production and the market prices. There are no externality spill-over effects of consequence. Of course, externalities are seldom absent in any actual real world case.

Achievement of public interest objectives

In theory, the market will achieve public interest objectives as it achieves its goals of efficiency in the allocation of economic resources, innovation and consumer protection. But there are cases in which, although markets are working well, key public interest objectives are not achieved. For example, some rural areas may not receive services (perhaps the population is too small to make it profitable to serve these areas), and if society thinks it important that they should, then the state often steps in to ensure universal accessibility of the goods or services in question. Again, media and communications are striking cases in point.

2.3 Policy and regulation to reduce market failure

When particular markets do not do what they are supposed to do and effective competition does not develop, governments may attempt to redress the specific failings that block the achievement of competitive market objectives. Common areas of market failure, and the typical government policy responses to them, include monopoly power, market externalities and natural monopoly:

Monopoly power

For general industry, governments in most countries have established competition authorities to monitor the state of competition in industries across the economy. Where an effective competitive market can be established, competition policy and regulation may prohibit mergers, force firms to sell assets or lines of business, require the licensing of patents to potential competitors, prohibit specific forms of anti-competitive behaviour (e.g. charging different prices to different customers), impose fines and, in some countries, apply criminal penalties (e.g. for price fixing). In extreme cases, large firms can be broken up into smaller ones, as happened in the USA in 1984 when the telecom monopoly AT&T (American Telephone and Telegraph) was broken up into eight companies, all of which were still large companies.

Market externalities

Economists often use the term 'externality' to refer to a cost or benefit that is not accounted for in the price of something – 'externality' is a useful concept and the term is increasingly used. As mentioned in Section 2.2, a 'negative externality' is something undesirable but which is not reflected in the price of a product or service (pollution is often given as an example) whereas a 'positive externality' is something desirable which is not reflected in the price (such as the benefits to people in general if someone is immunised against a disease: the person immunised benefits but so does everyone else because the overall chance of infection, even for those not immunised, is reduced). If an industry produces significant market negative externality social costs (such as pollution), government regulations typically set acceptable standards to minimise the social costs, and/or impose the social costs on polluters through taxes, fines and/or clean-up requirements. When significant social benefits from positive market externalities exist, or there are extra-market and public interest objectives to be achieved (for example, defence, education, universal access and public information), governments typically play a dominant role in service provision to ensure these social benefits are achieved.

Natural monopoly

For a few industries, competitive markets are inherently unsustainable. The economies of scale and scope in a single supplier, the enormous investment requirements of entering the market, and the very high costs of competitive duplication of facilities are so great that the market is considered to be a *natural monopoly*. The role for government, then, is either to provide the service itself or to regulate a private monopoly supplier.

For most of the twentieth century the postal, telegraph and telephone (PTT) and broadcast media, as well as electricity, rail, highways, gas, water and other infrastructure sectors of the economy, were viewed as natural monopolies. Not only has it been thought that competition would be economically inefficient but in these industries there are important extra-market objectives, such as universal access and public information. Under these conditions, either direct government provision or direct regulation is required. You will probably have recognised that in the twenty-first century many of these services are no longer provided by monopolies – one reason for this is technological change, which has made competition cost effective in sectors such as telecommunications where, formerly, this was not (or thought not to be) the case.

Activity 3.2

We shall be exploring the economic characteristics of the media industries in more detail later in this chapter, but it would be useful here for you to jot down your impressions of the relationship between government and the media. Do you think there is any reason for the government to own or regulate the media today? Why, or why not? List the pros and cons and revisit your list after completing your work on this chapter. ■ ■ ■

There are many pros and cons to the relationship between government and the media. Examples of the 'pros' of government ownership might be greater public control of media than under private ownership; greater potential equality (for example, between urban and rural areas and/or between rich and poor) in provision; more social stability; less likelihood of a 'race to the bottom' in standards. Examples of the 'cons' of government ownership of the media might be greater innovation and change under private ownership; dispersal of power between government, business and civil society; greater democratic accountability of government; competition lowers prices and better provides services and products that people want. Try to think of your own reasons and, when doing so, assess the validity of the reasons I have suggested.

3 How market conditions shape media products and services

In this section we move beyond basic economic concepts and examine the particular aspects of the media in economic terms. Who gets to own the media? Who has access to the media? And who and what shapes and influences the answers to these questions? As noted above, because of some of the economic characteristics of media markets, the government has a role to play in making sure that, when media markets do not work properly, citizens still have access to services and information.

3.1 Ownership

The economic development of the media industries has been very much influenced by new technological possibilities and economic opportunities (in Section 1, we examined this in terms of economies of scale and scope). Governments also have recognised the media as a special class of industry requiring special policies and regulation. This has stimulated a debate about whether the particular treatment of the media by government is to protect the public interest for citizens to be informed and to be able to communicate, or rather to protect and preserve the privileged interests of the government itself.

Here we focus on the underlying economic conditions that purportedly justify special treatment of the media by government and the key issues in the policy debates that arise because of these factors. We will begin by reviewing some key concepts of market theory and the policy debates it has stimulated historically, before examining the economics of the media industries in the early twenty-first century.

The relationship between government and markets is determined primarily by who owns the production facilities or otherwise controls the capital investment in the operation. For example, the UK satellite television broadcaster BSkyB is owned by private investors who have supplied the investment capital and determine the terms and conditions of production and distribution of the firm within the general laws that apply to any normal business. It earns its revenue primarily from payment by viewers for specific content (such as football games and films) and also from advertisers. When BSkyB expands, the investment funds to do so are provided either by the profits it has made from the business or additional funds from private investors. The government may establish special policies and regulations for private media operators (see Chapter 4), which may limit what BSkyB can do (for example, by limiting the advertising or prohibiting obscenity), but BSkyB operates as a private player in media markets.

The BBC is owned by the UK state, but is significantly influenced by economic considerations and partially (and increasingly) by market conditions. The BBC receives enormous resources to manage its operations and provide a wide range of media services – £3.8 billion (thousand million) or about 5.5 billion euros in 2004–2005; close to one day's UK annual GDP. The government funds the BBC by charging all UK television viewers a licence fee and by making it an offence to watch television without one. The licence fee has increased over time as the BBC has expanded its activities. At the time of writing, the licence fee costs £126.50 a year. The BBC is also expected to earn some of its revenue by charging fees for activities: for example, selling programmes to other countries and renting out its production studios when it is not using them. But for its mass market broadcasting services, the BBC does not charge viewers for access to specific programmes and does not accept advertising.

Periodically the government assesses the licence fee for the BBC (at the time of writing the UK was going through an intense debate about the terms on which the BBC's charter should be renewed in 2006), and when it does it looks at audience ratings to see how well the BBC is attracting viewers. So in this sense the BBC is in market competition with private broadcasters in the UK, including BSkyB.

The BBC is a major player in the UK and international media markets, but its participation is determined by its very different economic structure and the major role of the state as its owner. The government justifies this arrangement on the grounds that the BBC provides UK citizens with a universal public interest information, education and entertainment service that facilitates an informed democracy. To preserve the independence of the BBC, the government has established an independent Board of Governors (see Figure 3.3). Nevertheless, economic critics would argue that the owner calls the tune to which the organisation dances – whether the organisation is privately owned (like BSkyB) or publicly owned (like the BBC). Ownership means power.

BBC GOVERNORS

ABOUT THE GOVERNORS
As Governors of the BBC, we're here to represent your interests. You pay £126.50 every year for BBC services; it's our job to make sure you get quality programmes and services in return.

Michael Grade, Chairman · Anthony Salz, Vice-Chairman · Deborah Bull · Andrew Burns · Ruth Deech · Dermot Gleeson

Merfyn Jones · Fabian Monds · Jeremy Peat · Angela Sarkis · Ranjit Sondhi · Richard Tait

We do this by laying down long term strategies for the BBC, keeping track of progress to make sure they deliver on their defined objectives, and, if they don't, asking management to make changes on your behalf.

There are twelve Governors of the BBC. All of us are part-time, and we come from a variety of backgrounds, bringing a wide range of experience. We're appointed by the Queen on advice from ministers following an open appointments procedure in accordance with Nolan principles, and we include National Governors for Scotland, Wales and Northern Ireland, and another with special responsibility for the English regions. We also have an International Governor who helps set the framework for the BBC's international role and responsibilities.

Related links

The Department for Culture, Media and Sport

Ofcom

DCMS Charter Review Website

How Your Licence Fee is spent

Figure 3.3 *The BBC Board of Governors from the BBC Governors' website at the end of 2005*
Source: http://www.bbcgovernors.co.uk/about/index.html

3.2 The different media market models

A central concept in the economic analysis of markets is that the consumers who purchase goods and services pay directly for their purchases. But for radio and television broadcasting this has not usually been the case. Listeners and viewers have not been buying programmes or even channels. Thus programming decisions have not directly reflected consumer choice as they would if customers were actually choosing and buying programmes. The revenue for programming comes from other sources, from either advertising or government.

There are some very important differences in the market implications of the various economic models for providing media services. Economists argue that markets work best when buyers know what they are buying and pay directly for precisely what is being purchased. Purchasing a specific book, newspaper or pay-per-programme television fits this market model. Pay-per-channel television is less efficient at matching supply to demand because viewers have to buy a larger product (a subscription) that may include programmes in which they have no interest. Pay-per-service (for example, via the licence fee for all the BBC's radio and television services) is even less efficient.

Advertiser-supported 'free' television further shifts the market incentive and priorities away from the viewer's interest. The customer in this model is no longer the viewer; it is the advertiser. The programmes become the bait by which viewers (or as some analysts say, 'eyeballs') are herded in front of television sets for delivery to advertisers. Programming content is designed to attract large (or particular groupings – for example, teenage boys or sports fans) viewing audiences for particular advertisers.

If all programmes in the market are advertiser funded, then viewer options are likely to be both restricted and inferior to those that would be provided in a market where programme providers were trying to satisfy viewer, rather than advertiser, priorities. Economists call this an 'imperfect market' because of this market distortion. In addition, when there are only a few (say three or four) broadcasters of programmes, consumer choice is limited further. This is another market imperfection in comparison with what a fully competitive market would provide. When pay-TV with advertising is provided, viewers may have to both pay and be subjected to advertising, but the programmes are likely to be closer to those that they want to watch than in the advertising-based 'free' television model.

Thus, there seem to be some good reasons for state intervention in media markets. But how good are the actual instruments used when governments intervene? Let us consider the case of public service broadcasting (PSB).

The public service model

The public service model is a poor model in some very important ways. The government in authoritarian countries may use its ownership of the national public broadcaster as a propaganda machine. And even when this is not the case, paying a licence fee (the most common means of funding PSB) means that viewers are required to pay without much information about the specific programmes that will be provided. Moreover, television viewers pay whether or not they actually use PSB and are charged the same licence fee whether they are rich or poor. In a sense this might be considered as pay-per-broadcast network television, except that the payment is not optional for viewers (although private broadcasters lobby the government that it should be). In some countries, such as Canada, the government funds the public service broadcaster from the state budget and does not charge a licence fee to viewers.

However, as explained above, the justification for a national public broadcaster in a democratic country is to provide universal access to independent programming and information that inform the public in ways that will not be provided in private media markets. Precisely because it is not constrained by the market requirements of advertisers, or direct pay-TV, or by an owner concerned about profits or propaganda control, in theory the public broadcaster is free from the pressures of the marketplace so that it can apply public service criteria to meet its public interest mandate.

However, critics argue that public broadcasters can do pretty much what they please with the public's money. Indicators for assessing the public broadcaster's performance are imprecise and hard to measure. This is why there is an ongoing debate in many countries about public broadcasting, its funding and its programming. Although there is potential for beneficial programming that meets a public interest mandate, there is also the possibility for enormous waste. Some public broadcast programming, it is argued, is not really all that different from the programmes provided by private networks, and there is also the risk of undue political influence.

Market theory does, however, provide a case for public broadcasting in media markets. Any of the individual models for financing programmes will result in an imperfect market and not be fully responsive to the full range and diversity of viewer interests. Therefore, competition among media providers operating under the different market models, and their different sources of financing (including public funding), is likely to bring a greater diversity and responsiveness to the needs and interests of a diverse population, far greater than increased competition within any single financing model.

3.3 Programme content

The production of mass media content is characterised by substantial up-front investments in production of the 'first copy', and very low costs of producing additional copies or viewings. For example, the first copy of a film includes the costs of renting or owning all the necessary technical equipment (such as lighting and cameras); the salaries of the stars, writers, editors, and so on; legal advice; payment of copyright to use specific songs, and much more. The high investment needed to produce the first copy provides a barrier to entry that restricts opportunities to engage in production. But once the first copy is made, the relatively low costs of producing additional copies and viewings mean that the market can be extended almost indefinitely at very low additional cost. However, unless there is an opportunity to cover the high investment costs of the initial production, the incentive to create content will be dramatically reduced.

These are not conditions in which a free market can be expected to promote opportunities for the most efficient production and distribution of mass media content. High prices based on first copy production costs reflect monopoly power. Low prices based on distribution costs in a competitive market would achieve wide distribution but would not necessarily cover the costs of initial production. This leads to concentration of ownership and control, as shown by the 'five sisters' phenomenon discussed in Section 1.

Once programmes are produced and distributed to viewers, the added or marginal cost of expanding the number of viewers for programmes is very low. The added receivers will get benefits greater than the added costs. So from the standpoint of achieving the greatest benefits for the whole of society (social benefit), the additional viewers should have access to these programmes and services.

Economics also recognises that there is a special class of economic production called public goods. These are activities that benefit society as a whole, but cannot be provided efficiently individually or through private markets. Obvious examples of this are national defence, police and fire protection, as is emergency information about approaching bad weather, warnings about polluted lakes and the spread of contagious diseases. The canals and bridges to which we referred earlier when considering Adam Smith are further cases in point. There is a wide range of information that is important to people's lives that is included in the public good category.

The concept of the public good could be expanded to include information that goes beyond emergency and potentially dangerous situations. What about information that is important to being an informed citizen in one's local community, country and the world, and the special information needs of children, disabled people, older people and others to participate more fully in society? Although, in some countries, government regulation requires that private broadcasters provide a certain amount of local news, children's programming, public service announcements, and so forth, PSB can be expected to be more responsive to these needs and to do a far better job in fulfilling the public good information needs of a democratic society.

The following two extracts, between them, indicate the terms of the main debate in UK broadcasting policy (and that in many other countries) over the last 20 years or so. The key issues are: How far has technology changed the terms on which broadcasting services can be provided? What is the balance of advantages and disadvantages in following the flow of technological possibilities? Can broadcasting markets work as efficient markets? And if they can, will such markets work in the public interest? If not, what sort of regulatory intervention (including public service broadcasting) is required?

The first reading comes from the Peacock Committee's Report of 1986, which had a massive impact on changing the terms of the broadcasting debate in the UK and making discussion of the efficiency of broadcasting markets almost unavoidable in serious policy debates. The Committee, named after its chair, the eminent UK economist Sir Alan Peacock, argued that technological change meant that broadcasting could become much more like other markets (and, in particular, much more like the print media market), and that consequently much less intervention (notably through PSB) was required.

The second reading, commissioned by the BBC from a further two eminent British economists (one of whom subsequently became chair of the BBC Governors and the other Master of Balliol College, University of Oxford), argues that, in spite of the claims made by Peacock, broadcasting markets still fail sufficiently for intervention to be required. The carefully qualified and nuanced arguments of both sets of authors have been simplified and compressed in these extracts. To fully appreciate the authors' arguments you should read the originals.

Reading 3.1 Activity

Now read the following extract from the report of the Peacock Committee. As you read, note the key arguments made in the report with the intention of comparing them with the arguments made by Graham and Davies in Reading 3.2.

- How far do they share a view of what the problems are?
- What evidence does each adduce to support his views?
- How far are the arguments made in each reading economic arguments?

Consider how far the writers step outside the framework of economics in making their arguments. What do they say about the limits of economic analysis in considering the role of public service broadcasting?

Reading 3.1

Alan Peacock, 'Report of the committee on financing the BBC'

The fundamental aim of broadcasting policy should in our view be to enlarge both the freedom of choice of the consumer and the opportunities available to programme makers to offer alternative wares to the public. [...]

Our goal is of course derived from aims much wider than any applying to broadcasting alone. They are embedded, for example, in the First Amendment to the US Constitution (15 December 1791).
[...]

Hitherto it has been very hard either to avoid prepublication censorship in broadcasting, or apply the spirit of the First Amendment, because of spectrum scarcity and the difficulties of charging viewers and listeners directly. Intervention and regulation have been required not only to secure public service broadcasting in our sense of the term, but even to simulate the effects of a functioning consumer market. [...]

Technological developments hold promise, however, of liberation from these constraints. There is at least a chance of creating a genuine consumer market in broadcasting combined with a continuation of public service, in the positive sense of secure funding of programmes of a demanding or innovative kind.
[...]

The Committee's view of the aim of broadcasting, with its emphasis on reflection of the tastes and preferences of consumers must not be confused with what may be termed the 'commercial *laissez-faire*' system. Such a system would simply require that all broadcasting channels should be privatised and that the whole of broadcasting should be de-regulated without worrying about whether channels are financed by advertising or in other ways.
[...]

Our own conclusion is that British broadcasting should move towards a sophisticated market system based on consumer sovereignty. That is a system that recognises that viewers and listeners are the best ultimate judges of their own interests, which they can best satisfy if they have the option of purchasing the broadcasting services they require from as many alternative sources of supply as possible. There will always be a need to supplement the direct consumer market by public finance for programmes of a public service kind [...] supported by people in their capacity as citizens and voters but unlikely to be commercially self-supporting in the view of broadcasting entrepreneurs.
[...]

What we do expect to disappear or much diminish is the need for negative censorious controls. If the right conditions are established, there will be little need for 'regulation' apart from the general law of the land to cover matters such as public decency, defamation, sedition, blasphemy and most of the other matters of concern in broadcasting.

We emphasise these legal constraints on Free Speech that exist even in countries most attached to the principle of the First Amendment. Whether or not it comes within our terms of reference, we can hardly fail to be aware of public concern about excesses of violence and sex on television. Our main point is that the recourse for people concerned about these areas should lie with the normal remedies of the law. To the extent that legislation lifts some of the legal constraints in return for specific regulation, these exemptions need to be removed, as we move along the deregulation route. [...]

It follows from our concept of consumer sovereignty that we reject the commercial laissez-faire model, which is based on a small number of broadcasters competing to sell audiences to advertisers. Such a system neither achieves the important welfare benefits theoretically associated with a fully functioning market, nor meets British standards of public accountability for the private use of public assets. Furthermore, so long as the number of television channels is limited, and there is no direct consumer payment, collective provision and regulation of programmes does provide a better simulation of a market designed to reflect consumer preferences than a policy of laissez-faire. But this justification for the maintenance of regulation for the time being is only available if policy makers permit and encourage technological development which may eventually make a genuine market possible.

Reading source

Peacock, 1986, pp.125–6, 129, 133 ■ ■ ■

Reading 3.2 Activity

Now read the following extract from Andrew Graham and Gavyn Davies's work 'The public funding of broadcasting'. Compare their arguments to those made in the report of the Peacock Committee and try to answer the questions put to you in Reading 3.1 Activity.

Reading 3.2

Andrew Graham and Gavyn Davies, 'The public funding of broadcasting'

Much recent argument has focused on the extent to which new technology affecting both transmission and reception is making a purely market-based organization of broadcasting far more possible. In the case of transmission there is, or soon will be, no longer 'spectrum scarcity' and thus no need for a monopoly to exist. The range of broadcasting frequencies that is becoming available means that competition could, at least in principle, exist amongst a spread of private broadcasters. Similarly in the case of reception the new technology makes it possible in principle to charge each consumer for each broadcast. [...]

The fact that a market-based solution is technically *feasible* does not, however, make it necessarily *desirable*. In the case of broadcasting it will be shown that there are four areas in which the market, left to itself, would not produce what is desired. First, economic analysis suggests good grounds for thinking that while the market will undoubtedly produce some excellent programmes, it will, overall and taken over the longer term, provide lower quality broadcasting than consumers either individually or collectively would desire. Second, the market, being by definition the mere aggregation of individual decisions, takes no account of the community and of the complex relations between citizenship, culture and community – all of these being areas where the form that broadcasting takes is of great concern. Third, it can be argued that broadcasting has a special role to play in a democratic society – a role which cannot be left just to the market. Fourth, there is the particular context of the UK which has bequeathed us the BBC, widely regarded as the best public service broadcaster in the world. This has not been a market outcome and is not one which the market could now reproduce. [...]

The main reason that even a so-called 'perfect' market is unlikely to produce high quality television is that the broadcasting market would be characterized by what economists call 'market failures'. [...]

Market failure in consumption

There are three main causes of possible market failure in the consumption of broadcasting. First, there are 'externalities'. These are the effects of one person's purchase on someone else, but which the market ignores. The effects may be either harmful as in the case of traffic congestion arising from private car use or beneficial as in the case of vaccinations – everyone benefits from the fact that *other* people are vaccinated. The existence of externalities means that left to itself the market produces too many car journeys and too few vaccinations (which is one reason why petrol is taxed particularly heavily and why there are public health programmes for vaccinations).

The 'externalities' of broadcasting are less immediately obvious, but may be even more important. [...]

[...] An elderly person may become more fearful of walking down the street at night if he or she believes that the portrayal of large amounts of irrational violence on television encourages such behaviour, irrespective of whether in fact it does or not – the possible falseness of the belief does not alter the genuineness of the fear. In other words the television that is broadcast ought to reflect the preferences not only of those who watch it but also those affected by it indirectly – yet the market cannot do this. It follows that, if left just to the market, more 'bad' television (bad in the sense of being judged to have harmful side effects) and less 'good' television will be purchased than consumers in aggregate would have wished if they could have acted collectively.

[...]

Second, the market does not work well where what is being sold is information or experience. [...] People do not know what they are 'buying' until they have experienced it, yet once they have experienced it they no longer need to buy it! [...] If the right long run choices are to be made, the cost of the initial experiments should only be the marginal cost of disseminating the information, and in the case of broadcasting this is zero.[1]

Third, and most important, in the particular case of broadcasting, consumers may be unavoidably myopic about their own long term interests. [...] if all television is elicited by the market, there is a very real danger that consumers will under-invest in the *development* of their *own* tastes, their *own* experience and their *own* capacity to comprehend. This is not because consumers are stupid but because it is only in retrospect that the benefits of such investment become apparent. [...]

Market failure in production

Market failure can also arise in the production of broadcasting. Two potential problems exist. First, there is the danger that, if the industry were to be fully privatized, the outcome would not be a competitive one, but be dominated by a few large broadcasters. [...]

Second, and in the long run more important, there is the question of whether a purely private broadcasting industry would carry out the necessary research and development. What is required is investment in technology, in people and in good programmes. [...]

Sustaining good quality broadcasting therefore faces a number of sharply conflicting concerns which it is difficult to meet simultaneously within a purely commercial structure. The economies of scale and scope which characterize much of the industry produce strong pressures towards concentration. Such concentration is desirable to the extent that it produces the profits to finance investment, and because it allows firms to capture some of the benefits of their own investment. In a democratic society undue concentration of media ownership is, however, highly undesirable. [...]

[...] these conflicting considerations have been reconciled, at least to some extent, by the existence of the BBC. [...]

The argument, so far, has been that there is a case for public service broadcasting so as to make good the deficiencies of the market in providing what well-informed *consumers*, acting either individually or in aggregate, would wish to buy over the longer term. A quite separate argument arises from the fact that there are parts of our lives to which the market is simply not relevant. [...]

The crucial importance of broadcasting in this context is that for the great majority of people it is today their major source of information about the world, beyond that of family, friends and acquaintances. [...] It is therefore part not just of how we see ourselves in relation to the community, or communities, within which we are embedded, but also part of how we understand the community – indeed part of where the very idea of community arises and is given meaning.

Notes

1   It should be noted that the usual economic argument for charging for something (whether this is a 'price' or a 'subscription') does *not* apply to broadcasting because there is no question of anything being *scarce*. Broadcasts are a public good because one person's consumption does not compete with another person's consumption. It would therefore be perverse to insist that broadcasts become 'narrowcasts'.

Reading source

Graham and Davies, 1992, pp.170–6, 181   ■ ■ ■

In responding to the questions posed in Reading 3.1 Activity and Reading 3.2 Activity you might refer to the Peacock Report's comments on censorship (is this an *economic* issue?) and the arguments of Graham and Davies about feasibility and desirability. You might also consider how far the key propositions in each extract are supported by evidence and examples.

3.4 Transmission and distribution networks

All communications media require transmission and distribution networks to provide their services – for example, to deliver programming onto your television. These networks include infrastructure such as satellites, the radio spectrum and cables, depending on the mode of transmission (see Figure 3.4). The reach of these networks determines the extent of the market. The potential markets for the post, wired and wireless telephone networks, over the air broadcasting and cable television are determined by their respective facility networks.

Figure 3.4 A 'dish farm' for sending signals to, and receiving them from, communications satellites

The value of their respective networks depends upon the number of people each network can reach. In any network industry, competitors often realise that by interconnecting their networks and co-ordinating the provision of services over the larger interconnected network, they can improve service to all consumers and viewers and enhance the value of the overall larger network. This weakens competition; however, in a network industry the benefits of co-operation are likely to exceed those of competition. Nevertheless, these benefits may be distributed unequally and some players may not experience sufficient incentives to co-operate.

A larger network also has a powerful incentive to refuse to interconnect with smaller networks. If one competitor has a network of 1,000 customers/viewers and another has a network of 100, by interconnecting the larger competitor has access to 100 new customers/ viewers – a 10 per cent increase in its market. It makes its 1,000 customers available to the smaller competitor so that it can compete for 100 possible new customers/viewers. The smaller firm has access to 1,000 new customers/viewers, a 1,000 per cent increase in potential market size, by allowing competition for its existing 100 customers/ viewers. These inequalities in benefits to firms mean that regulation is usually required to secure the benefits to the public of *interconnection*. Interconnection is a major issue in the telecommunications and postal industries (as well as in electricity, gas and water supply) and requires the ongoing attention of regulators who act to ensure large network firms interconnect reasonably with smaller ones.

Most facility networks require very large investments in facilities that are characterised by high fixed costs, relatively low marginal costs of adding customers/viewers to the network, and significant economies of scale and scope as the network becomes larger (scale) and takes on related services (scope). The combination of these characteristics is commonly referred to as a 'natural monopoly'. This means that the most efficient industry structure for providing the network will be a monopoly. For broadcasting and telecoms this has been reinforced by the fact that national networks have been dependent on radio spectrum technologies to transmit communications signals through the air. The spectrum has limited capacity and requires co-ordinated management for it to be used efficiently.

A further consideration is that communications networks are typically characterised by significant positive externalities (social benefits that cannot be captured in the market prices of competitive service suppliers – see Section 2 above). Extending the network to customers/viewers who do not purchase any service enhances the value of the network (by making the 'receiving' network larger), often by amounts greater than the marginal cost of adding them to the network. A competitive market cannot be expected to capture the network externalities that justify the provision of universal network coverage.

3.5 Policy implications of market failures in the media industries

The characteristics of media markets described above have played a major role in influencing government policy and regulation in the different media industries. The significant barriers to entry to newspaper publishing and distribution often led to oligopolies (a few suppliers) dominating markets with content protected by copyright. Sometimes, new entrants do appear in major newspaper markets, but relatively infrequently. With the growth of press-holding companies owning major papers in many cities and countries, ownership and control in the industry is becoming more concentrated on an international basis, with power exercised by fewer owners.

The perceived experience and potential for market failure in post, telegraph, telephone, radio and television broadcasting led the UK and most other governments to conclude that there were natural monopolies in these services, all of which had significant public interest implications and could therefore best be supplied as public services. These monopoly structures, which have prevailed since the early days of development in these industries, have now been challenged and modified as it now appears they are inappropriate for twenty-first century economies and societies. This change in sentiment has been strongly influenced by changes in communications technologies that have opened more possibilities for competition than were available before.

We see, therefore, that there are structural tendencies to produce high returns to economies of scope and scale in contemporary media and communications markets and these make a genuinely well-functioning marketplace of ideas very hard to achieve. What then can be done to countervail this? What power can be exerted by states to countervail the power of media markets?

Public service broadcasting has been discussed above as one approach to mitigating failures in the media market, by providing comprehensive broadcasting services for the whole population. The justification for public broadcasting is the guarantee of a wider range of programming to all, ensuring a multiplicity of different viewpoints and supporting the nation's culture and identity. The Office of Communications's (Ofcom; see below) chief executive, Stephen Carter, asserted in a 2004 speech:

> Even a perfectly functioning market will not produce sufficient output to meet the goals that we as a society believe we want from television:
>
> - the information we need for effective participation in democracy
> - strengthening our British cultural identity

- stimulating our knowledge of science, history, the arts: education by stealth
- and supporting an inclusive and tolerant society

These four purposes need to be taken together. In sum, the social goal of public service broadcasting going forward has to be more than just 'good telly'.

Carter, 2004

As we have seen throughout this chapter, regulation in the media sector is often undertaken by specialised regulators setting rules under which firms (whether public or private) must operate. Public service broadcasting regulation, for example, usually includes access stipulations that can include geographical extension of transmission services as well as obligations on others to carry the signals. Regulation for universal service obligations serves the role of extending economic and social opportunities offered by telecommunications and broadcasting services to rural areas and to disadvantaged social groups. Universal service obligations (USOs) are justified both on grounds of equity and generally to provide access to the public realm (we look more closely at USOs in Section 5.2). The broadcasting sector's use of the radio spectrum is relevant here since it is a public resource.

Activity 3.3

In this section we have put forward the argument that a pay-per-programme model of providing television programmes would be the best in terms of competitive market efficiency. Would you prefer this? Write brief notes on the reasons why you would or would not support it. ■ ■ ■

In terms of competitive market efficiency, one might argue that a pay-per-programme model would ensure that individuals' expenditure on broadcasting was better matched to consumption (those who used most would pay most), and would provide strong signals to broadcasters about what viewers wanted and how much they wanted it. But, if you did not support this type of provision, you might argue that some people would be excluded from viewing because they could not afford to watch (even if the costs to the broadcaster would not rise if they did so), and that this would be both wasteful and unfair; that programming would tend to reflect the tastes and interests of those who could pay most rather than those of society as a whole, and that an important source of social solidarity (everyone being able to watch the same programmes) had been lost. And of course there are other potential reasons, both for and against.

4 The interplay among technologies, markets and government policies

4.1 Major forces driving change

After reading the explanation above that market failure has justified state provision or direct regulation in the media industries throughout most of the twentieth century, a perceptive reader might observe, *that is not the way it is now.* How does one square this with the introduction to this chapter describing global private media conglomerates? In the UK, the BBC and British Telecom are no longer government-protected monopolies. What brought about the changes to the current state of affairs? What is the current relation between the media industries and government?

To answer these questions, we must examine the interrelations between changing technologies, markets and government policies. Changes in each of these elements have had a major impact upon the industries and upon the other elements in a complex, but identifiable manner. This is illustrated in Figure 3.5. Note that the arrows connect each element – technologies, markets and government policies – to the media sectors, not to each other. This illustrates that, in respect of the media, the *primary* influences of technologies, markets and government policies have not been directly upon one another, but rather that they continue to shape the development of the media industries (an argument also made in Chapter 1). They do so, of course, in conjunction with other factors such as changing social, cultural, political and even ideological practices. But here we focus on the primary economic determinants – technologies, markets and the government – and regulatory policies formulated in response to these determinants.

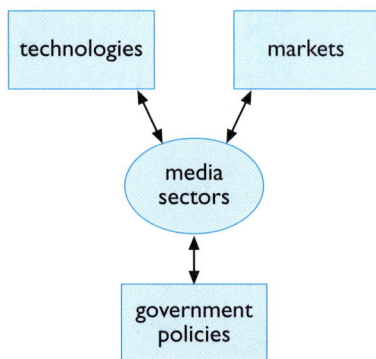

Figure 3.5 *Changes in technologies, markets and government policies have a major impact upon the media industries and upon each other*

Note also that the arrows in Figure 3.5 run both ways. Each element influences developments in the media sectors and in turn is influenced by them. In a dynamic environment, as is the one we are examining, there are no simple, direct cause-and-effect relationships. There are schools of thought that claim industry development is driven primarily by technological change, economic structures or government policies. For example, *technological determinists* often suggest a linear and sequential model of change. You will remember Chris Bissell's treatment of this issue in Chapter 1. They argue that changes in technology drive industry and market changes, which in turn require changes in government policies that have become obsolete. But they neglect to ask *what stimulated the technology changes?* A little research generally shows that it was sometimes changes in government policies, sometimes changes in industry markets and sometimes independent inventions and innovations. Here, we could argue that technology has been socially shaped as well as having determined social outcomes. In previous chapters we have seen consistently that technology can be a very powerful source of change. But change cannot be understood as a product of technology alone. Technology is itself shaped by social processes, and both regulation and user demand shape the character, rate and pervasiveness of technological change.

Activity 3.4

Do you use modern information and communications technologies (ICTs) – say, products or services that use digital technical standards – in your daily working, social or personal life? If you do, make a list of them. Are there any you cannot afford, but would like to have? Should any of these be made available to everyone because they are essential in modern society? If so, which ones would you identify as essential, and why? ■ ■ ■

You might have identified the internet and, possibly SMS (text) services on mobile telephones as examples of modern digital ICTs. Some of you may also have identified digital radio (especially likely in your car) and/or television. DVD players are becoming increasingly pervasive too. But you may also have identified ordinary wired telephone service or satellite television because in many countries these too are now digital services.

The second part of the activity asked you to reflect on the social importance of media and communications services, on what services are now essential and should be available at affordable prices to everyone. You might argue that the internet, telephone and television services all fall into this category – if so, try to reflect on why you think so (or why not).

5 Media liberalisation and convergence

5.1 The breakdown of national monopolies in the media

During the last three decades of the twentieth century, the media monopoly policies in telecom, broadcasting and post have been increasingly criticised as outdated and for creating major barriers to the application of new technologies and services by new market players. Market liberal and social market critics (see **Downey, 2006**) have argued that what may have been established as government regulation to ensure universal access to media services in the early stages of the industrial economy, had become a current example of the problem that Adam Smith and the classical economists attacked – regulation that preserved privileges for the establishment and that prevented entrepreneurs from stimulating new economic activity. Rather than appropriate change, such policies have created an undesirable continuity. According to this view, policy and regulatory failures had become a much bigger problem than the industry market failures. This has led to a partial liberalisation in media markets and a reassessment of the traditionally accepted market failures as a basis for determining the form and structure of future regulation.

The liberalisation of media regulation was influenced significantly by an increasing recognition of the changing role of the media in the economy. Earlier in the twentieth century, telecom, post, radio and television were viewed as public services, not as key industries driving economic growth (see Figure 3.6, which illustrates the perceived public service role of the public telephone system). But as they grew, other industries became more dependent on them for their own efficiency and growth. Likewise, new technologies opened up new opportunities and the pressure to allow others to participate in these industries also continued to build.

Equipment manufacturers began producing a variety of different terminal equipment they wanted to sell directly to business and residential customers, rather than only the telecom monopoly, which often made its own. Firms wanted to lease capacity from the telecom monopolies wholesale so that they could sell 'value-added' services at the retail level. By applying computer industry technologies, data communication could be provided over voice lines. Landline radio microwave technology made it possible for new firms to enter the market (if they could get licensed). Leaders in the development of satellite communication and coaxial cable (for cable TV) resisted handing over these technologies to the monopoly telephone and broadcast operators. Improved spectrum management made it possible to give out more radio and television broadcast licences, as well as permit competition in the new mobile phone (cell phone) market.

The steps towards liberalisation have varied in different countries, some countries moving more quickly than others on the path to more liberalised media markets. The liberalising movement began in the USA in the late 1960s with the licensing of new operators in telecom and for cable television. After more than a decade of slow development because of extreme resistance and anti-competitive behaviour, the US competition authority brought charges against the major US telecommunications company, AT&T that led to it being broken up in 1984. In 1996, a new US Telecommunications Act was passed, liberalising most of the communications sector, although a host of deregulatory issues remain

Figure 3.6 'Burglar conscious'
Source: 1946 Joseph Lee cartoon. BT Archive: Acc 94/0045.

to be resolved and there is little evidence that government regulation will fade away completely in this new environment.

Liberalisation in the UK is often attributed to the ideological drive of the Thatcher government in the 1980s, but there was much more to it than that. Private broadcasters in radio and television had been licensed long before, in response to demands from industry for opportunities to advertise their products and services in the media, and for greater diversity of content. In addition, the same economic and technologically based pressures for change existed in the UK and other countries. In the UK another significant factor was the inefficiency of telecom services under the British Post Office, which had prompted the banking and finance industry to threaten to move its global headquarters from London to another country. In 1984, British Telecom was privatised and the Office of Telecommunications (Oftel), an independent regulator, was established.

In 1987, the European Union (EU) issued a Green Paper (a discussion paper) as the first step in an 11-year process of liberalising European telecom markets, and, in 1989, the EU issued an important pan-European broadcast policy, *Television Without Frontiers* (European Communities, 2000). These policies were part of the EU programme to promote common markets in all industries, including the media. Liberalisation has been a headline goal for the EU for the last 20 years or so, and the EU's embrace of this agenda illustrates how pervasive the liberalisation philosophy has become.

5.2 Universal service obligations and social inclusion

Justifications for societal regulation of the media stem from the liberal democratic tradition in which a small number are elected by everyone to make decisions on their behalf. The ultimate success of a liberal democracy is determined by whether the public has ongoing access to information on the reasoning and circumstances of decisions taken by those vested with such power, and the public's capacity to understand and articulate views and beliefs on them.

In much the same vein as regulating the media for diversity, the media and telecom sectors must also be regulated for access. Providing and subsidising access to these networks and services to all of the population at affordable prices is a key policy objective in most countries. Here we see regulation being used to enable rather than inhibit. Areas that are difficult to reach, rural areas with low population density, and marginalised groups in society, are seen as economically unattractive markets. It is precisely because of this market failure that regulation must create conditions that provide opportunities for the social, political and economic participation of these groups.

As will be discussed in the following section, convergence poses significant challenges for regulators. Regulation has historically treated different technologies, and hence distribution networks, as separate entities. The primary distinction has been between broadcasting and telecoms. Telecom service providers were regulated as common carriers, meaning that distribution rather than content was the focus of the regulation, and the primary goals were to ensure access to the network and to co-ordinate the market and commercial practices of providing a service at reasonable prices. Broadcasting regulation has focused on requirements for fairness, national content, and other social objectives being justified on the basis that the radio frequencies they use are a scarce public resource. However, technological developments and changes within the industries have challenged all this – indeed, they have changed the way in which we access information and participate in society.

5.3 Media convergence in information economies

The changes taking place in the media industries in the early twenty-first century are being driven primarily by the interrelations among new media technologies, the changing structure of the economy, and changes in economic and media policy. The creation of the EU and the drive to create a European common market, and parallel developments in other regions of the world, meant that the monopoly preserves of national media operators have been gradually eroded.

New technologies are playing a significant role. Advanced communication satellites, for example, do not recognise national borders, and are especially suited to beaming broadcast signals down anywhere. BSkyB is a major player in the UK and many other national broadcast markets. During the past 20 years, mobile voice communication has grown so rapidly that it now exceeds fixed network service in many countries.

The integration of computer-based digital technologies into telecom networks has transformed their capabilities from the provision of voice telephone signals to the provision of any form of communication – voice, data, music, film, television. Government policy changes have liberalised access to the telecom network so that most services can be provided by companies other than the national telecom monopoly. Business and residential users are now permitted to purchase and connect their own telephones and other terminal devices, including personal computers (PCs). This has helped spawn the internet, which is simply the diverse array of digital services being provided by many service providers over the facility networks of telecom operators.

The digitalisation of communication networks is having other effects as well. Digitalised radio and television broadcast signals can be provided over the radio spectrum with far greater efficiency than the older analogue signals, permitting the allocation of many more licences and more competition using the same radio spectrum. Moreover, the conversion of all forms of communication to digital standards is in the process of destroying the traditional technological barriers among the different media. BT has established a broadcast service division. The BBC provides internet services. Some cable television companies are now making more money from their telephone services than from their television distribution. The mobile communications sector is planning to provide television reception on mobile phones in the future. In this environment of dynamic technological change and new services development, clearly the role of government policy and regulation must be reassessed.

These changes are often referred to as the convergence of all forms of communication on the telecommunications networks of the future. The internet is foreseen as the new model of communications networks that will have the capability to deliver all kinds of services, including broadcast television and telephone.

The convergence process is illustrated in Figure 3.7. Not too long ago, the telecom, computing and content industries were quite distinct and separate in terms of the technologies they used, their capabilities, their industry economics and their government policies and regulations. If another industry – say, banking or transport – wanted to apply these services to improve their own businesses, these would have to be separate and distinct applications that they developed themselves or with consultants.

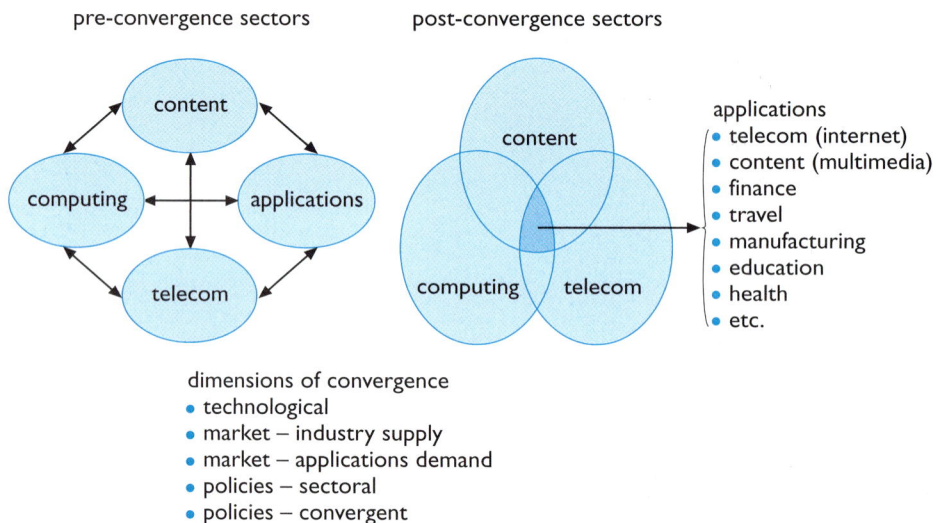

Figure 3.7 *The major dimensions of media convergence*

Convergence, as illustrated on the right-hand side of Figure 3.7, involves a series of changes in technologies, the industries, the nature of their services, and government policies and regulations, which have permitted innovative applications of new converged media services in many other industries, government agencies and other organisations, as well as for families and individuals. The increasing application of digital communication standards from the computing industry in recording and playing media content (for example, CDs for music, books and documents of all kinds) has brought convergence between computing and content. The gradual adoption of digital standards in the telecom network has brought convergence between computing and telecom. The development of digital communication terminals with appropriate software permits digital content to be sent over the digital telecom network. The personal computer connected to the telecom network to send email, reports, pictures, music and videos is a good example. It reflects convergence among computing, telecom and content.

Achieving full technical convergence is much more complex than suggested by these illustrations. It involves continuing technological improvement within each of the industries and among them. In the early twenty-first century, priority areas of attention for further technical improvement include increasing the capacity of local connections to the network from narrowband (telephone) to broadband (video); improving the capability of mobile networks to handle data, provide broadband connections and easy access to the internet; and providing voice telephone calls over the internet. The ultimate goal is to be able to provide any form of communication, delivering any form of content, from any location, seamlessly over the telecom network. Instead of the continuance of a series of separate electronic media and communications sectors (such as telephony, television, radio, internet), we may see a change to a single, integrated, digital converged electronic communications sector.

Convergence involves much more than technical issues. Technological improvements only get implemented if they also pass an economic test. They must be capable of providing services or products that people want that are affordable. New services based on converged technologies must be developed and marketed. Since these bring together firms from each of the converging industries as well as outsiders, they must adapt to the changing environment and reposition themselves in a new converged information communications technologies and services industry sector. This requires experimentation and is risky. It is a period described as 'creative destruction' by the economist Joseph Schumpeter (1975/1942). Some firms go out of business, and mergers and acquisitions are common, as we have seen with the giant conglomerate companies.

 A period of industry adjustment is underway and there is no indication that the markets will be stabilising soon. This industry and market convergence process is indicated at the bottom of Figure 3.7.

Convergence also raises issues for policy and regulation. Clearly the appropriate policies and regulations applied independently to computing (basically competitive production of hardware and software), telecom (reasonable access to telephony) and content (programming and access to information) must be reassessed in the new environment. Policies and regulations that are becoming obsolete must be removed as they may cause barriers to progress. Revised policies and regulations in light of the movement towards convergence can facilitate and prepare the ground for a converged future communications environment.

This convergence trend is seen by many people as a basis for the development of what is often called *information economies* and *information societies*. Virtually all government leaders and international agencies make glowing visionary statements regularly about the future information society and its potential for improving economic and social conditions. Although it is undoubtedly premature to draw conclusions about what future information societies will be like, it is clear that the media industries will play an even more important role in the future economy than in the past.

It will be even more important that people have access to electronic communications and information services than they have had in the industrial economy. The matter of universal access to communications opportunities and to information is likely to become more important if people are to be able to participate effectively in society. Concerns have already been highlighted about 'digital divides' both within and between countries. Fashioning policies and regulations that will respond to the specific market failures and extra-market public interest goals of states in the new media economy will be a challenging task.

5.4 The new BBC

In the new environment of twenty-first century communications markets, the traditional former monopolies – such as the BBC and BT in the UK – must reposition themselves as the major players in their respective but increasingly overlapping markets. The BBC has responded aggressively in the new communications sector markets and is now a major commercial operator – some three times bigger than the commercial television broadcaster five (Channel 5). During 2004–2005, more than 20% of the BBC's income came from commercial services and the remaining public funding – mostly from the licence fee – came to about £3.2 billion (4.6 billion euros). The BBC claimed a 38% share in the UK TV market and 53% in the UK radio market. The proportion of commercial revenue in the BBC budget is increasing annually.

The BBC is the largest television programme exporter in Europe and the third largest magazine publisher. It provides an extensive list of books, videos, DVDs, audio, music and multimedia products. It provides a range of services on a leading internet site with partners Real Networks and AOL, and is planning to make its archive of programmes available on its website for viewing on PCs. It has launched nine new digital television channels. It provides broadcast technology and web-hosting and design services, as well as sports scores to mobile phone users.

The BBC also franchises toys, such as the Tweenies (see Figure 3.8), and other products related to its popular television programmes; rents out its broadcast facilities and services; and devises branding for television stations in other countries. It does production work for other companies, including commercials. It has developed a lightweight digital wireless camera that will be sold in the security provision market. BBC World, its international television news service, was started in 1995, and now reaches 273 million homes in more than 200 countries, but so far does not cover its costs. In 1998, BBC America was launched. By 2003 it was available in 37 million US homes and growing rapidly.

Figure 3.8 *Three of the Tweenies – and their furry friend Doodles*

5.5 The evolving media market structure

Continuing in the same direction as the trends in privatisation, media concentration and convergence already identified in this chapter, there is an emerging trend involving the massive restructuring of media institutions and of the ways in which media products and services are produced, distributed and consumed. As described in terms of the 'five sisters' in the introduction to this chapter, but as also shown by the activities of the new BBC described earlier in this section, globalisation of media markets and cross-over between industries is evidenced by including increased foreign ownership of national media, the rise of global multimedia giants, and the increasing permeability of national boundaries to media products and channels. Global media products now have immediate unregulated access to national audiences via direct satellite broadcasting and the internet.

Although a significant amount of new competition has developed in the media industries, many of the conditions for market failure remain. The primary change in market structure so far has been a shift from monopoly dominance in media markets to oligopoly dominance that, in turn, has led to complaints against dominant firms for anti-competitive behaviour.

Yet, the UK government's policy objective of ensuring universal access to information and communications services in the new economy is considered by many people to be even more important for the future than it was in the past. In an information society, access to media services may be essential to participation in society. The universal access issue of the past is now being examined as an issue of a potential digital divide for the future.

In response to the changing conditions in the media industries, the UK government in 2003 merged five regulating agencies (the Broadcasting Standards Commission, Independent Television Commission (ITC), Office of Telecommunications (Oftel), Radio Authority, Radio Communications Agency) into one Office of Communications – Ofcom. The government made this change to facilitate the application of a co-ordinated regulation across the converging media industries. There is currently debate as to whether Ofcom's regulatory powers should be extended to the BBC. The government has already begun its process of consultation with respect to the BBC's charter renewal in 2006, as mentioned in Section 3.1. Fashioning the appropriate balance between market forces and government regulation, and pinpointing regulation to the market failures in the new information economy, will be a formidable challenge.

Activity 3.5

Would you say you live in an information/communications society today? Use your media diary to identify what you have done on a particular day that depends on modern communications. Which activities could you get along without and which are essential to your day-to-day living? In the new 'information society', what do you see as the market failures in the media industries, and the extra-market public interest requirements, to which government policy and regulation should attend? ■■■

You might identify activities such as using the telephone or internet to order groceries or other products to be delivered, internet banking, online booking of travel tickets, e-dating and consolidation of social networks (for example, through 'Friends Reunited'). To be sure, many (perhaps all?) of these activities could be (and were) done without the mediation of electronic communications services and networks, but you may feel that you could do fewer of them (and less conveniently) in these non-electronic ways. You might want to consider how far your participation in a modern information society would be different if you lived in a different country or were of a different generation. When considering 'market failure' issues, try considering both the technical economic market failures (such as public goods, monopolies, under-provision of merit goods) and the social aspects of market failure (for example, the inability of all to afford such services or to develop the skills needed to use them).

You will have seen in this chapter that the economics of the media potentially exert a formidable influence. How far the intrinsic economic characteristics of media and communications are realised depends on a number of factors: notably on the state of technology and of regulation. Technological change affects how far media and communications markets fail and how far regulation can, in varying degrees, redress the effects of market failure – by ensuring that the positive effects of media and communications are maximised and their negative consequences minimised.

Further reading

Fairness and Accuracy in Reporting (2005) *Fairness and Accuracy in Reporting*, http://www.fair.org/ (accessed 2 December 2005).

Free Speech Network (2005) 'What democracy looks like', Free Speech Network, http://www.freespeech.org (accessed 2 December 2005). This is the first audio/video hub on the web created and defined by the people who use it.

Goldberg, D., Prosser, T. and Verhulst, S. (1998) *Regulating the Changing Media: A Comparative Study*, Oxford, Clarendon Press.

Hamelink, C. (1999) *Preserving Media Independence: Regulatory Frameworks*, Paris, UNESCO.

Herman, E. and McChesney, R. (1997) *The Global Media: The New Missionaries of Global Capitalism*, London and Washington, DC, Cassell.

Lessig, L. (2004) *Free Culture: How Big Media Uses Technology and the Law to Lock Down Culture and Control Creativity*, New York, Penguin.

McQuail, D. and Siune, K. (eds) (1998) *Media Policy: Convergence, Concentration and Commerce*, London, Sage.

MediaChannel (2005) 'Mediachannel: a global vision new media production', *MediaChannel*, http://www.mediachannel.org/ (accessed 2 December 2005).

Moore, A. (2005) 'Who owns what?', *Columbia Journalism Review*, http://www.cjr.org/owners/ (accessed 2 December 2005).

References

Carter, S. (2004) 'Speech to the *Voice of the Listener and Viewer Spring Conference*, 29 April', Ofcom, http://www.ofcom.org.uk/media/speeches/2004/04/carter_voice_20040429 (accessed 21 June 2005).

Downey, J. (2006) 'The media industries: do ownership, size and internationalization matter?' in Hesmondhalgh, D. (ed.) *Media Production,* Maidenhead, Open University Press/ The Open University.

European Communities (2000) 'The new "Television Without Frontiers" directive', *Europa*, http://europa.eu.int/comm/avpolicy/regul/twf/newint_en.htm (accessed 21 June 2005).

Graham, A. and Davies, G. (1992) 'The public funding of broadcasting' in Congdon, T., Sturgess, B. Shew, W.B., Graham, A. and Davies, G., *Paying for Broadcasting: The Handbook*, London and New York, Routledge.

Hesmondhalgh, D. (2005) 'The production of celebrity' in Evans, J. and Hesmondhalgh, D. (eds) *Understanding Media: Inside Celebrity*, Maidenhead, Open University Press/The Open University.

Moore, A. (2005) 'Who owns what?', *Columbia Journalism Review*, http://www.cjr.org/owners/ (accessed 2 December 2005)

Peacock, A. (Chair) (1986) *Report of the Committee on Financing the BBC*, Cmnd 9824, London, HMSO.

Safire, W. (2004) 'The five sisters', *New York Times*, 16 February, Section A, p.19, www.globalpolicy.org/empire/media/2004/0216fivesisters.htm (accessed 21 June 2005).

Schumpeter, J. (1975/1942) *Capitalism, Socialism and Democracy*, New York, Harper.

Smith, A. (1904/1776) 'An inquiry into the nature and causes of the wealth of nations', *The Library of Economics and Liberty*, http://www.econlib.org/library/Smith/smWN.html (accessed 31 November 2005).

Steinem, G. (1990) 'Sex, lies & advertising', *The Publishing Business Group*, www.publishingbiz.com/html/articlebysteinem.html (accessed 21 June 2005).

Turner, T. (2004) 'My beef with big media. How government protects big media – and shuts out upstarts like me', *Washington Monthly*, www.washingtonmonthly.com/features/2004/0407.turner.html (accessed 21 June 2005).

United States Department of State (2005) *The Bill of Rights*, http://usinfo.state.gov/usa/infousa/facts/funddocs/billeng.htm (accessed 1 December 2005).

Rights, values and regulation

Chapter 4

Richard Collins

Contents

1   Introduction

In Chapter 3 we saw that information is essential if markets are to work well. If there is an imbalance of information between buyer and seller, the one with the best information is potentially able to set prices and possibly disadvantage the other. A similar argument is often made in respect of government: without information citizens and voters cannot make good civic decisions and democracy and good government both suffer. The mass media can be important sources of both types of information. But some information is judged to be either offensive or socially harmful, or both – pornography, hate speech and defamation are cases in point. So, to ensure that media help markets work well, that readers, viewers and listeners get the information they need, and that the vulnerable are protected from harm, media and communications are *regulated*. Regulation concerns both reduction of harm and increase of good.

In this chapter we shall consider:

- ideas about what should be regulated and what should be left to the market and the private sphere to decide;
- the different levels or institutions used for regulation – the law, self-regulation and statutory regulation;
- the values – rights and the principle of utility – that underpin regulatory decisions.

All of these issues are contested. All are involved when we confront real-world issues such as, to take an example that we will consider later, whether or not the private lives of celebrities are 'fair game' for the media. Firstly, should this be the subject of regulation at all? Why should it not be for the market to decide? Secondly, if we believe that the market might not always be the best decider, how should we make rules and create institutions to govern representation of celebrities' lives? Thirdly, what are the roots of our beliefs on these matters? Do people have a right to privacy? And, if so, how is that right to be reconciled with other rights (such as the public's right to know)?

You will see that running through these issues are the themes of *power* (who decides and how do they enforce decisions?), *change and continuity* (do different societies all make the same sorts of decisions on these matters, and do they stick to these decisions over the long term?), and *values* (what are the roots of our beliefs and actions in these domains?), which are the key themes of this study of the media.

2   Freedom of expression

What should be regulated? The boundaries between what should be influenced by the state and what should be left, and between the private sector and the public sector, are often highly contested. This is doubly so in media and communications because many believe in a right of 'freedom of speech and expression', and therefore tend to be opposed to state intervention in the provision of information and the practice of communication. Such people are often called 'liberals' though this term can have a variety of definitions and its meaning has changed over time. For example, someone who is described as a 'liberal' within the context of US politics might well be described differently in the UK or other European countries. However, if we follow the *Encyclopaedia of the Social Sciences* in identifying the core of liberalism as the belief in the foundational value of 'a free individual conscious of his capacity for unfettered development and self-expression' (Ruggiero, 1933, p.435), then we can understand why those who value highly freedom of speech and expression are called liberals.

The idea of a right to freedom of expression derives from the seventeenth- and eighteenth-century European Enlightenment struggle against the power of absolutist rulers. It is enshrined in canonical documents such as the United States' Bill of Rights and the French Republic's Declaration of the Rights of Man and of the Citizen. France's Declaration of the Rights of Man and of the Citizen, for example, states in Article 11 that '*The free communication of ideas and opinions* [emphasis added] is one of the most precious of the rights of man. Every citizen may, accordingly, speak, write, and print with freedom' (National Assembly of France, 1789). Similarly, the celebrated "First Amendment" to the Constitution of the United States of America, the Bill of Rights, states that 'Congress shall make no law respecting an establishment of religion, or prohibiting the free exercise thereof; *or abridging the freedom of speech, or of the press* [emphasis added], or the right of the people peaceably to assemble, and to petition the government for a redress of grievances' (Senate and House of Representatives of the United States of America, 1787). This provision is also known as the First Amendment to the Constitution of the United States.

Documents and doctrines such as these tend to give primacy to markets by stating explicitly, or at least implying strongly, that the state has no business to meddle with information. All this seems to point to the need to minimise state regulation. However, given the tendency of media markets to produce concentrated patterns of private ownership and control (as discussed in Chapter 3), there are good reasons to suppose that freedom of expression can be secured only if the state does intervene and regulate.

This may seem paradoxical. How can freedom be secured by stopping people doing things? The British/Russian philosopher Isaiah Berlin had a good response to such a question: 'Freedom for the pike is death for the minnows!' Berlin (1969) pointed to a need to restrain behaviour that reduced overall freedom – pikes should be regulated! He also argued for regulation on other grounds, proposing that we can only be fully free when we have realised our potential and that this requires more than a simple clearing away of obstacles. To achieve this kind of freedom (which Berlin called 'positive freedom'), we need to be able to develop ourselves, and this requires education, learning and (usually) co-operation with others. In turn, this means regulation to foster collective institutions (such as universities, museums and public broadcasters) even when this reduces individuals' freedom. For example, when the state spends money on schools and universities, it raises taxes and thus reduces individuals' freedom to spend. But, arguably, we are freer as a consequence because education helps us realise our potential. Or, to make the same sort of argument in the context of media regulation, the state should support public service broadcasting even though to do so is to reduce individuals' control over their own resources (for example, by requiring them to pay a licence fee to support public service broadcasting).

2.1 The state

What is the state? What is this body that we call upon when we want regulation? We know what we mean in a common-sense way when we use the term 'state' – it is a country or a government, some sort of bounded but comprehensive political authority. However, there are probably almost as many definitions of the term 'state' as there are political scientists. In the introduction to a useful collection of essays, *States and Societies*, David Held (a contemporary UK political scientist) wrote that 'the state is often linked to the notion of an impersonal and privileged legal or constitutional order with the capability of administering and controlling a given territory' (Held, 1983, p.1). This definition points to the *coercive* role of the state. But is this what we think of first when we use the term 'state'? Though coercion is certainly part of what a country or government may do, it is not the whole (or, if we are lucky, even the main part) of what they do. In many societies, the 'state' also embodies what we might call 'enabling', or 'positive freedom', institutions, such as those used to provide public goods (services such as lighthouses and navigation aids, health and education services); as well as the coercive or 'negative freedom' institutions of public order and the administration of justice (those that keep the pike from getting among the minnows). Indeed, these 'enabling' functions are in many cases more important than the coercive functions of the state. Most modern states (at least in peacetime) spend more on 'enabling' than on coercion.

3   The state and the media

A historically strong state presence in media and communications – for example, in postal and telecommunication monopolies, public service broadcasting, state news agencies and newspapers – may thus seem to conflict with 'First Amendment' presumptions that freedom of expression is incompatible with state control. How, then, do we account for a historical (and, in some countries, enduring) state presence in the media and communications sectors in democratic societies? There are two sorts of explanation: firstly, state presence in media and communications is symptomatic of something wrong – the state is acting improperly. This is the kind of argument proponents of 'negative freedom' might make. Secondly, in spite of the importance of 'First Amendment' values, state involvement is required if freedom of speech and communication is to be achieved; a 'positive freedom' sort of argument.

Few of us are proponents of simply either 'negative' or 'positive' freedom. Most of us, to varying degrees, think both kinds of freedom are important, but we often differ in our views of how much emphasis one or other conception of freedom should receive. Our views are likely to be shaped by our experience and traditions and these may be strikingly different. There are few places where there is absolutely no state intervention in media and communication markets. So though we differentiate between states and markets, in most societies a mixed system operates, with the balance between states and markets, and negative and positive freedom, changing from time to time. What is inside and what is outside the remit of the state changes. Only a few decades ago, much of the economy of the UK was run by the state – gas and electricity generation and distribution, coal mining and steel production and the entire telecommunications sector were publicly run. Now these sectors are almost completely in the private sector but, as you will see, activities and institutions move in and out of the public and private sectors over time (see Figure 4.1).

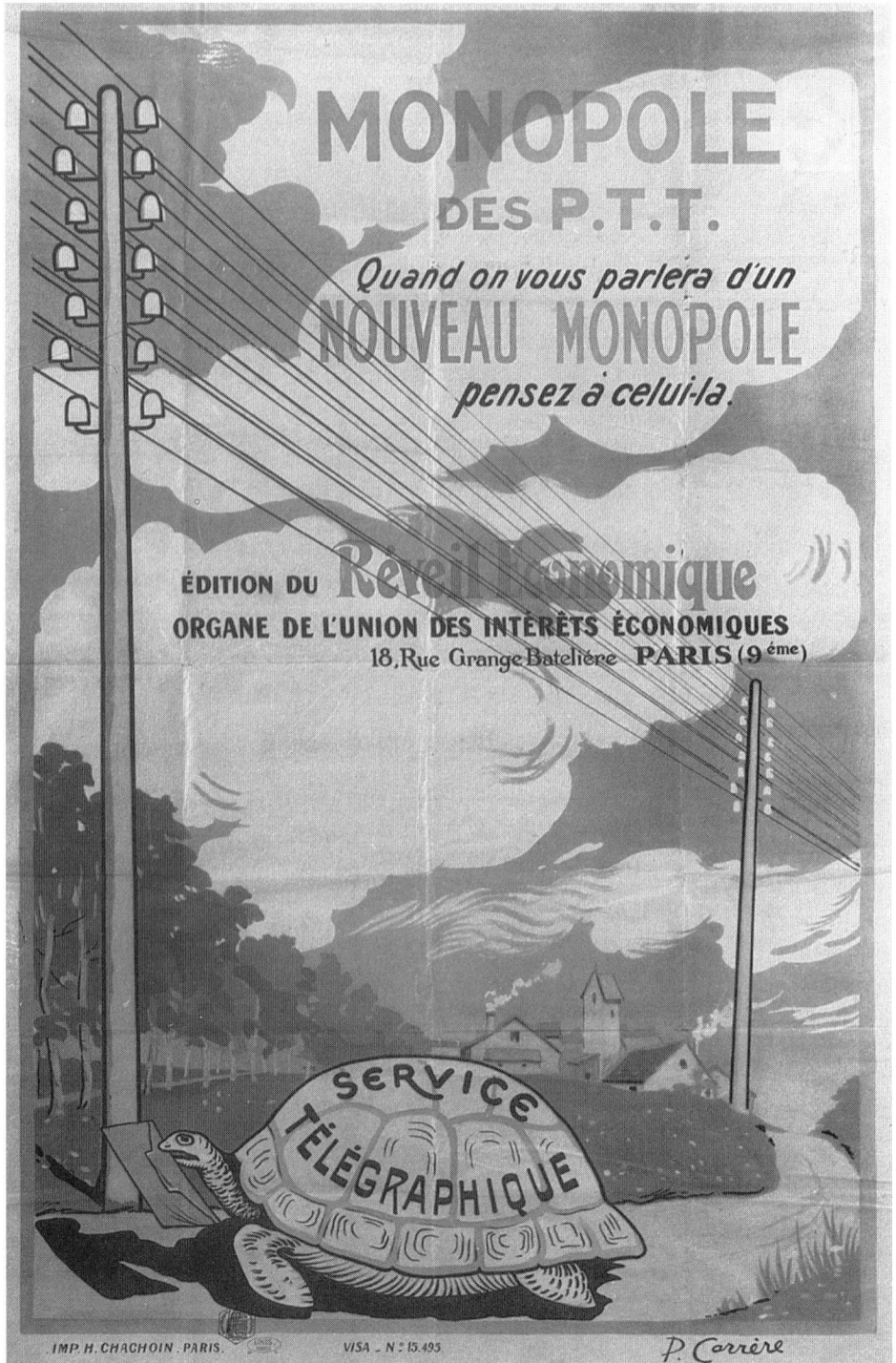

Figure 4.1 *A French poster against a public monopoly in post, telegraph and telephone (PTT)*

Activity 4.1

Use your media diary to identify the media you have used over a week. Which of these are in the public and which in the private sector? Which body regulates each of the media you have used?

You might be surprised to find how many media you use and how varied they are. You might find that classifying them into 'public' and 'private' is also a bit more difficult than it may seem at first (for example, the state may be a substantial shareholder in private companies, and public bodies may engage in significant commercial activities). Identifying who regulates what can also be challenging. Do not worry if you cannot tie up all the loose ends – the important thing is to recognise that these factors may make an important difference to the media you use.

Here is a sketch of how we, living in the UK, might answer:

■   television – private (for example, Sky, ITV, five) and public (S4C, Channel 4, BBC) – BBC Governors, Ofcom;

■   newspapers – private – Press Complaints Commission;

■   film at the cinema – private – British Board of Film Classification, Film Council (the Film Council subsidises UK film production and distribution).   ■ ■ ■

3.1   The changing balance between state and market in UK telecommunications

Consider the changing balance between public and private provision of telecommunications (literally, communication at a distance, and now the term conventionally used for telegraphy, voice telephony, fax and data transmission) in the UK. Electric telegraphy (literally, writing at a distance, the transmission and reception of electric pulses over wires – the pulses being coded to signify written letters) was first established in the first half of the nineteenth century. In the UK, telegraphy was in the private sector until 1870 when the state-owned Post Office took control of it. UK telephony (sound at a distance) also began as a private-sector business run principally by companies owned by the chief North American telephony patent holders, Bell and Edison. In 1880 these companies merged to form the privately owned United Telephone Company (subsequently the National Telephone Company). The Post Office began to establish its own networks (as did a number of municipalities including Glasgow and Hull; see Figure 4.2) and in 1911 took over the assets of the National Telephone Company. Telephony shifted from the private to the public (state) sector, where it remained until the early 1980s when the national telecommunications monopoly,

British Telecom (the successor to Post Office Telephones) was privatised and competition introduced (except in Hull, where a surviving publicly owned local monopoly provided service; subsequently the Hull system was also privatised). Now there are several hundred private companies providing telecommunications services in the UK and these are regulated by Ofcom. Other countries also saw their telephone systems moving between the public and private sectors (see Figure 4.1).

Figure 4.2 *Promotional material for the Glasgow municipal telephone company*

Thus the role of the state and the boundaries between public and private provision in media and communications are not fixed. As we have seen, the UK state directly provided communication services for long periods. Latterly it has withdrawn substantially from direct provision (though a large state sector remains in broadcasting) and has sought to achieve public policy goals in a different way – by regulating private (and, in broadcasting, also public) provision. In the following sections we will consider what is meant by regulation in the context of media and communications and consider some of the principles that underpin media regulation. We will also consider some of the different institutions used in media regulation: notably, the courts and statutory and self-regulatory agencies, which act as intermediaries between state and market.

Box 4.1 Key dates in the evolution of telecommunications in the UK

1839 – first commercial electric telegraph, enabling the public to send telegrams, opened using the system established by the Great Western Railway Company

1846 – formation of the Electric Telegraph Company

1851 – first international telegraph connection (with France)

1866 – transatlantic telegraph connection

1868 – Telegraph Act nationalised the private telegraph companies under the Post Office, aiming to extend the service across the UK and establish an affordable universal service

1870 – Post Office took over UK telegraphy

1876 – Bell's patent granted in the UK

1879 – first telephone service started in London

1880 – courts ruled that the telegraph monopoly (established under the Telegraph Act) applied to telephony

1881 – government licensed private telephone companies for 31 years and initially limited their scope to a five-mile radius to protect the Post Office's telegraph monopoly. The Post Office then began establishing its telephone service

1889 – private telephone companies merge into the National Telephone Company

1896 – nationalisation of the long-distance telephone network (private companies continued to provide local service until 1912). Marconi demonstrates radio, 'telegraphy without wires', to the Post Office

1899 – Telegraph Act empowered local municipalities to establish telephone services (13 licences granted; six networks opened, the first in Glasgow in 1901; one – in Hull – survived as a separate company)

1901 – Marconi established transatlantic wireless telegraphy link

1902 – completion of the Pacific cable (linking Canada, Australia and New Zealand) sponsored by the four governments under the Pacific Cable Act of 1901

1907 – Marconi established commercial transatlantic wireless telegraph service

1926–27 – Post Office wireless service established between UK, Australia, Canada and South Africa

1929 – government creates public/private partnership of UK-owned international cable and radio communications initially named Imperial and International Communications Ltd, renamed Cable and Wireless in 1934

1949 – Cable and Wireless nationalised

1981 – privatisation of Cable and Wireless
1984 – privatisation of British Telecom. Competition permitted (at first only by Mercury, a subsidiary of Cable and Wireless; full competition from 1991). Establishment of Oftel
1987 – privatisation of Hull Telephones as Kingston Communications
2003 – establishment of Ofcom.

Figure 4.3 *The promotion of telephony using motorcycles*

3.2 The balance between state and market in UK broadcasting

A different series of moves between the state and the market took place in UK broadcasting which began in the early 1920s. The BBC was established in 1922 as the privately owned British Broadcasting *Company* and in 1927 became publicly owned and was renamed the British Broadcasting *Corporation* (see Figure 4.4). The BBC had a monopoly of UK radio and television until 1955 when the (heavily state regulated) privately owned ITV began transmissions. The private sector grew, with

This Prospectus is sent only to bona-fide British Manufacturers of Wireless Apparatus who alone are eligible to apply for Shares.

The Subscription List will open on Monday, the 5th February, 1923, and will close on or before Monday, the 12th February, 1923.

A copy of this Prospectus has been filed with the Registrar of Joint Stock Companies.

THE BRITISH BROADCASTING COMPANY, LIMITED.

(Incorporated under the Companies Acts 1908 to 1917.)

CAPITAL - - £100,000.

Divided into 100,000 Cumulative Ordinary Shares of £1 each.

ISSUE OF

99,993 Cumulative Ordinary Shares of £1 each at par payable in full on application.

The holders of the Cumulative Ordinary Shares are entitled to receive out of the profits of the Company a fixed Cumulative Dividend at the rate of $7\frac{1}{2}$% per annum on the capital for the time being paid up or credited as paid up thereon but are not entitled to any further or other participation in profits.

DIRECTORS.

THE RT. HON LORD GAINFORD, Headlam Hall, Gainford, Durham (*Chairman*).

GODFREY C. ISAACS, Marconi House, Strand, W.C.2 (Managing Director Marconi's Wireless Telegraph Co., Ltd.).

ARCHIBALD McKINSTRY, The Red Lodge, Southill Avenue, Harrow-on-the-Hill (Joint Managing Director of Metropolitan-Vickers Electrical Export Company, Limited).

MAJOR BASIL BINYON, "Hawthorndene," Hayes, Kent (Managing Director of Radio Communication Company, Limited).

JOHN GRAY, "Beaulieu," Park Farm Road, Bromley, Kent (Chairman of the Hotpoint Electric Appliance Company, Limited).

SIR WILLIAM NOBLE, Magnet House, Kingsway, W.C.2, (Director of The General Electric Company, Limited).

HENRY MARK PEASE, 18, Kensington Court Mansions, W.8. (Managing Director of Western Electric Company, Limited).

BANKERS.

BARCLAYS BANK LIMITED, Charing Cross Branch, W.C.2.

SOLICITORS.

STEADMAN, VAN PRAAGH & GAYLOR, 4, Old Burlington Street, W.1.

AUDITORS.

DELOITTE, PLENDER, GRIFFITHS & CO., 5, London Wall Buildings, E.C.

SECRETARY AND REGISTERED OFFICE.

MAJOR P. F. ANDERSON, F.I.S.A., 15, Savoy Street, W.C.2.

17. The Company's Prospectus

Figure 4.4 *A share prospectus dating from the formation of the BBC in 1922*

commercial radio beginning in 1972, balanced by expansion of the public sector with the publicly owned (but advertising financed) Channel 4 (and S4C in Wales) in 1982. Throughout the 1980s and 1990s the private sector expanded substantially (notably with Sky television, Channel 5 and various cable services). But in 2002 the government gave the BBC a major role in digital terrestrial television, following which the BBC established several new television (and radio) channels.

We can see that, in broadcasting as in telecommunications, over time the UK has shifted the balance between private market and public state provision. Overall, at the time of writing (2004), the UK balance is tilted towards the market, but a large state presence remains in broadcasting in contrast to newspapers and telecommunications. This pattern of provision is similar in many other countries.

Box 4.2 Key dates in the evolution of broadcasting in the UK

1921 – Post Office licensed 150 radio transmitting stations (and 4,000 receiving stations)

1922 – Marconi Company starts to broadcast radio services and subsequently joins a consortium of radio manufacturers to establish the British Broadcasting Company (BBC)

1927 – British Broadcasting Company becomes the publicly owned British Broadcasting Corporation (BBC)

1931 – English language advertising-financed services begin from Radio Normandy

1933 – English language advertising-financed services begin from Radio Luxembourg

1936 – first television broadcasts by the BBC

1954 – ITA (Independent Television Authority) established

1955 – ITV (Channel 3) begins service

1964 – advertising-financed 'pirate radio' (often transmitting from ships and platforms offshore from the UK – for example, 'Radio Caroline', 'Radio Scotland') begins

1964 – BBC 2, the first UK colour television service, begins

1967 – Marine Broadcasting (Offences) Act makes offshore pirate radio unlawful. First BBC local radio station (Leicester) began service

1972 – Sound Broadcasting Act establishes commercial local radio and adds radio to the ITA's responsibilities with a consequential change of name to the IBA (Independent Broadcasting Authority)

1982 – Channel 4 begins. First pan-European satellite to cable television services

1984 – Cable Authority established
1988 – Broadcasting Standards Council (later Broadcasting Standards Commission) established
1990 – Sky Television begins direct to home satellite service. ITC (Independent Television Commission) established, merging the Cable Authority and the IBA and divesting radio regulation to the newly established Radio Authority
1997 – Channel 5 begins
2003 – Ofcom established, merging the ITC, Oftel, Broadcasting Standards Commission, Radio Authority and Radiocommunications Agency

Activity 4.2

Draw up a table showing the different balance between state and market provision of media and communications in your country at different times – say at 25-year intervals. You may find it useful to look up the names of the companies that provide media and communications on the internet and see if you can discover whether the company is state owned or private and how its history has developed. National histories of communications provide another possible source of information, as do encyclopaedias whether online or in book form. For example, a partial table for the UK would look like that given in Table 4.1:

Table 4.1

Date	State	Market
1840–1865	Post	Telegraph Newspapers
1866–1890	Telegraph (from 1870) and some telephones Post	Some telephones Telegraphs (to 1870) Newspapers
1891–1915	Telegraph and telephones (all from 1912) Post	Some telephones (to 1912) Newspapers
1916–1940	Telegraph and telephones Radio (from 1926) Post	Newspapers Radio (to 1926)

4 Regulatory institutions

Many modern states include institutions that fall somewhere between government bodies (UK examples include the Department of Culture, Media and Sport, responsible for broadcasting, and the Department of Trade and Industry, responsible for telecommunications) and institutions, such as those of law and justice (notably the courts), which have a clear degree of independence from government. Intermediate institutions that fall between the independence of the courts and the direct control experienced by government departments include a host of statutory regulators (that is, bodies established by laws and statutes passed by Parliament). In the UK these include bodies such as Ofgem (Office of Gas and Electricity Markets), Ofwat (Office of Water Services), the nicely acronymed OPRA (Occupational Pensions Regulatory Authority) and Ofcom (Office of Communications). These regulators exercise independent expert judgement within a legal and financial framework set by government.

Media and communication regulators do two important classes of tasks. They regulate content, ensuring that there is enough 'good' content and trying to minimise the amount of 'bad' content. And they regulate 'carriage', trying to ensure that provision of and access to services – whether broadcasting, telephony, letter post or the internet – is sufficiently pervasive (in geographical and financial accessibility) to meet key economic and social objectives. Carriage regulation is more often done by statutory regulators (for example, Ofcom's duties include securing the availability throughout the United Kingdom of 'a wide range of electronic communication services' and 'a wide range of television and radio services', Ofcom, 2005), but content regulation is done by both statutory and self-regulatory bodies (see below).

4.1 Ofcom

The UK's Ofcom is a good example of a statutory media regulator. Established in 2003, Ofcom is responsible for the regulation of the electronic media of communication (notably radio, television and telecommunications). Its duties are defined in the UK's Communications Act 2003, but since the Act identifies (by most counts) 263 separate duties for Ofcom, it is easy to see that it has considerable discretion in setting priorities for regulatory action. It is not simply a transmission belt for the implementation of government policy.

Ofcom replaced several long-established specialised regulators (including the Independent Television Commission, formerly responsible for commercial television; the Radio Authority, formerly responsible for commercial radio; and Oftel, formerly responsible for telecommunications). Statutory regulators exist so that specialised expertise can be brought to bear on a sector where governance beyond the extent of the general laws applying to all businesses is required. Such regulators also help ensure that governance may be independent of government. Independent regulation of media and communications is thought necessary both because media and communication markets tend to fail (see Chapter 2) and because of the presumption that media should not be directly controlled by government.

However, as we have seen, statutory regulation is not the only kind of media regulation. Self-regulatory bodies, such as (to take some UK examples) the Press Complaints Commission (PCC), the British Board of Film Classification (BBFC), the Advertising Standards Authority (ASA), and the Independent Committee for the Supervision of Standards of Telephone Information Services (ICSTIS), complement the work of statutory regulators. Self-regulatory bodies such as these usually operate by publishing codes of conduct. These are supposedly binding on their members, and self-regulatory bodies usually also handle complaints and provide some form of redress for complainants whose grievances are upheld. Customarily, these bodies are established by their respective industries to increase public confidence (and ward off statutory regulation) by guiding, and sometimes punishing, the behaviour of firms in the sector.

4.2 Other communications regulators

Other countries have similar statutory and self-regulatory bodies to those in the UK. These bodies can be thought of as agencies exerting a particular kind of power in media and communications. They do not set the terms on which the media operate, but they can and do affect the conduct of particular businesses and sectors by influencing conduct. State involvement in media and communications can be seen as either (or both) benevolent (ensuring provision of desirable services that would not otherwise be available and/or suppressing undesirable services that would otherwise be only too widely available) or malign (suppressing access to information and commentary in the interests of preserving and/or extending existing structures and relationships of power). How power is exercised by government, regulator or media business may be evaluated differently depending on the values held by whoever does the evaluation.

Activity 4.3

To get a sense of the scale of communications regulation, *either* read two newspapers today choosing from different market segments (for example, one tabloid and one broadsheet or 'compact') and count how many references to communications regulation you find; *or* go to the websites of two media regulators (such as your own country's main media regulator – for example, Ofcom in the UK; and one self-regulatory body – in the UK you might choose the Press Complaints Commission or the Advertising Standards Authority).

See how many cases and public complaints these regulators dealt with in the last year. How many were unresolved? See http://paintedcows.com/international.html for an interesting set of links to the advertising standards regulatory agencies of many countries.

Do not spend too much time trying to count exactly. The point of this activity is to prompt you to use material at hand to establish the salience of communications regulation (and, if you choose to look at newspapers, to explore whether there is a difference in the attention given to it by different segments of the newspaper market), and to encourage you to consider its appropriateness and effectiveness. For example, do you think a high level of complaint suggests good performance by the regulator? Or would a good regulator run the sector so effectively that there would be no complaints? On the other hand, would people complain at all to a regulator in whom they had no confidence – suggesting that a high level of complaints indicates public confidence? Again, do not spend too much time on this. The point of the activity is to stimulate you to explore how regulation works in your country and to get you thinking about how well it works.

(Note that the terms 'tabloid' and 'broadsheet' have traditionally referred to the size of the paper on which UK newspapers are printed. Tabloids, like the *Sun*, were smaller than broadsheets, such as the *Daily Telegraph*. In the UK, the newspaper market is segmented and tabloids have tended to have less hard news than broadsheets. But in 2003 this time-honoured distinction started to erode. Led by the *Independent*, some broadsheets started to publish tabloid or 'compact' editions.) ■ ■ ■

5 Rights

We referred earlier to the 'right' to freedom of expression. Those who exercise state power often present themselves as acting to secure rights: for example, the right to communicate; the right to be heard; the right not to be offended; the right not to be misrepresented; the right to privacy; the right to services in one's language of choice. But are these 'rights'? If rights are a claim on others, there are no 'absolute' rights. Rather, 'rights' are socially constituted and situated and embody the values of society which designates some, but not all, claims as 'claims of right'. Moreover, claims on others are meaningless unless those on whom the claims are made recognise their obligation to respond to the claims in question. Rights, therefore, go hand in hand with obligations.

The ability of a society to deliver 'rights' to its members depends on the particular society's levels of development and prosperity. Some societies do not have the power or wealth to meet or enforce legitimate rights claims. Sometimes the pike (or the shark as Michael Grade states in Reading 4.2) gets the minnows. And few of us, even in the most prosperous and peaceful of societies, ever realise our full potential. Moreover, 'rights' (and/or the values in which rights claims are rooted) may pull in contradictory directions. For example, the 'right' to freedom of speech and expression may conflict with a 'right' not to be offended or feel disrespected by the expressions of others. Realising the 'rights' of a minority may necessitate a claim on the resources of the majority and/or other minorities – a claim that may be resisted or rejected by those on whom it is made. So 'rights' that are recognised as legitimate depend on a social consensus about values.

Technology (see Chapter 1) also acts as a significant variable. Technological change alters the extent to which states (whether through law, regulation or public intervention) can exercise power and thereby enforce rights claims. For example, the last quarter of the twentieth century saw intense technological change in communications, and this cycle of change is continuing into the twenty-first century. One striking feature of this technological change is the extent to which national sovereignty in communications has diminished. Communication satellites make it possible to transmit and receive television signals across national borders, and the internet makes information from the other side of the world as accessible as that from next door. These technologies of communication mean that information regulated by the rules and values of one society is available pervasively in societies with quite different values. States do still have considerable power over media and communications within their territories, but are more and more dependent on agreement with other states, inevitably necessitating some compromises on values and objectives, to achieve public policy goals.

5.1 Positive and negative regulation

We have started to explore *what* regulators do and *why* they do it, and we have briefly identified some of the institutions, notably the statutory and self-regulatory bodies, which are used to exercise regulatory power in media and communications. But *how* do regulators actually regulate? Most regulation falls into one of two categories – *positive* or *negative* regulation. Broadly, negative regulation is regulation to stop things: for example, to prohibit or inhibit the publication of material offensive to some (such as pornography, blasphemy, group defamation, hate speech, information that infringes privacy, and anti-competitive behaviour by dominant firms). Positive regulation strives for things to happen which otherwise might not (for example, religious programmes on television, communication services – such as the letter post, voice telephony and public service radio and television), at constant and affordable prices throughout a particular territory. As you might expect, the extent and desirability of both negative and positive regulation is fiercely contested in most democratic societies. People take different (sometimes very different) views on where the appropriate balance lies between negative regulation of content: for example, over the suppression of publication of certain information and freedom of expression. So, too, with positive regulation. People disagree about whether it is right to require everyone (even those who do not watch any or much BBC) to pay the BBC licence fee. They disagree about how far services for minorities (whether ethnic, cultural or linguistic) should be a charge on the majority. And if one grants the right of some minorities to subsidy by the majority, should all minorities enjoy equal treatment? We can see that these questions of how power should be exercised are questions of *value* as well as questions of *power*. Some groups and individuals have the power to ensure it is their values that underpin policy rather than the values of others.

6   Conflicts between values

Consider the arguments of Michael Grade and Clare Short, made in the context of a discussion on restricting access to pornography. Firstly, Michael Grade (formerly Chief Executive of Channel 4 and latterly Chairman of the Governors of the BBC) pointed to the conflict between majority and minority rights in broadcasting content regulation. Grade wrote:

> Should the rules and conventions which govern content be framed to satisfy a simple majority of the population? Or should they prevent broadcasters from risking offence to the most sensitive 10 per cent of viewers? If so, you might as well argue that all swimming pools should be no more than three feet deep, because a tenth of the population can't swim.

Grade, 1996, p.44

Grade pitches his argument in terms of offence rather than harm (though one might argue that to give offence is to inflict a kind of harm): a prudent choice given the danger to his libertarian argument if harm could be shown in even a small number of cases (see **Livingstone, 2005**). The positive value, which Grade invokes, is the right of the many to have unrestricted access to information. He also offers a subsidiary argument concerning proportionality: that is, that avoiding all possibility of harm (for example, drowning in a swimming pool) involves disproportionately restricting the opportunities of most people.

Consider now this statement by Clare Short (then an MP and later also a New Labour Cabinet Minister), made at the same meeting as that to which Grade contributed:

A jungle ruled by the free market is ugly and debases humanity. The suggestion that the free market in porn or in gratuitous violence is freedom and that people like us trying to use the limited power of democracy to impose some restrictions and principles on these media barons is censorship, seems to me to distort the meaning of language. Everything that is fine and precious needs nurturing and protecting. Any culture that celebrates unrestricted freedom for pornography and gratuitous violence is destroying itself.

Short, 1996, p.41

Short argues that the libertarianism advocated by Grade is potentially destructive and that the risk of harm as well as the desirability of support for positive values justifies some limits on freedom of expression. We can see that the exercise of regulatory power, whether by the state or by others, is often based on a choice between rival 'rights' claims.

Reading 4.1 Activity

Now read the following extract in which Clare Short reflects on rights and regulation. Make notes as you read and compare Short's views to those of Michael Grade, after you have read Reading 4.2 (which follows), to see how they develop their arguments.

Reading 4.1

Clare Short, 'Page three, indecent display and the roots of concern'

I was sitting in the House of Commons one Friday, when I would rather have been in Birmingham, when Winston Churchill's 'laundry list' Bill was on. It was a Mary Whitehouse bill, which proposed a list of visual images that should always be obscene. It was a ridiculous and outrageous bill, which would have outlawed most war reporting. I remember we had letters from people, who provided sex education to young people with learning disabilities, saying it would have outlawed the pictures that they used.

[...]

I heard a series of speeches about how women in Britain were deeply concerned about rape and sexual assault and how the people of Britain, particularly the women of Britain, would never forgive the House of Commons if we didn't pass this bill. [...]

I [...] said that I agreed that there were lots of women in Britain who were outraged by both the levels of pornography that circulated in our society and the degree of sexual crime and rape, and that my own view was that one of the things that we could do to push back the tide was to remove the Page 3 phenomenon from our newspapers. I said I thought it didn't belong there, that newspapers circulating on buses and sitting on kitchen tables shouldn't have pornographic images of women within them. We have in our law a principle [...] which is that things which are legal in magazines you might buy and take home cannot be on hoardings in the street, that we have some right to be protected from things bearing down on us without our consent, and that the only alternative isn't absolutely illegality: there is a space in between which seeks to restrict the circulation of such images. [...]

There is a law called the Indecent Displays Act that entrenches in law this principle, and I was simply trying to extend that principle to newspapers, so that we could wipe out this phenomenon of half-naked women in our newspapers. As I got carried along in my little speech, I said, "In fact I think I might introduce my own Bill on this". I sat down and thought now I'll have to do it.

[...] I went away and did a little bit of work and applied for my slot for a ten-minute rule bill and introduced my bill [...] [T]here was a phenomenal reaction from women in Britain. I received 10,000 – 15,000 letters, passionate letters, from women up and down this land saying things like 'I'm not a feminist, or I didn't think I was, but I've hated all this stuff all my life and I've never dared to say so because everyone said I was screwed up, and it's so wonderful to know other people think like me – thank you, thank you, thank you'.

These women were pouring out views that no-one had given any legitimacy to. [...] There was an absolute tide [...]

You can't ignore such a powerful, passionate, moving voice that no-one was organising – this was no campaign, this was just women up and down Britain writing these eloquent, moving and powerful letters. Then there was a little bit somewhere in a *Guardian* diary item saying that I'd received lots of letters from women. Then I got hundreds of letters from men apologising profusely for not having written before, that they didn't realise that it was only women that were writing and they actually hated pornography too. Lots of decent, detailed letters of a different kind, seeing it as degrading to them and their sexuality but not quite as personal, as hurt and as passionate as the letters from women.

That was my experience from individual citizens on the one hand. On the other hand, a number of Murdoch papers and others, set out to silence and to try to destroy me. [...]

[...] *The News of the World* then put a lot of resources into crawling through my life since I was 16 years old, trying to find anyone that I had ever had any friendship or relationship with, finding a former husband who was offered lots of money to try and damage me.

I think that the passion, emotion and irrationality of the attacks on me demonstrate the strength of the feminist critique of pornography. Part of the reason for the emotion is that it goes right to the heart of what women are seeking in sexual relationships. Most women are seeking a mutuality and a mutual respect around sexuality and find the separation of sex from emotion quite frightening. They fear a culture of masculinity that seeks to separate sex from relationships. The pornography industry in Britain is, I'm told, bigger than the whole of our film and music industry combined. I think that when we look at what our culture is and we look at those figures, this is deeply depressing. It's also true that in our country and across the world the prostitution industry is massive. So there are lots and lots of men consuming pornography that separates depictions of women and their availability to be used and disposed of from any relationship with any real woman, and prostitution is another version of that sexuality without relationship.

[...] We should consider the very interesting and important distinction between soft pornography that is supposedly all right but constantly shows the woman as there to be used, disposed of and thrown away, and hard-core pornography that depicts normal acts of sexual intercourse and also lots of violence and sadomasochism and Nazi regalia and all sorts of horrible add-ons that degrade sexuality in the way that women find so frightening.

I think it's important to have that discussion quite apart from, and separate from, a question of legislative proposals. It is liberating in itself for some of those thousands of women to find out that other women feel like them, that they're not screwed up about sex because they hate pornography, that we're allowed to talk about what we think is lovely about sex and what we think is horrible about it. I think that debate enlarges freedom, and that there are an awful lot of forces with vested interests who want to silence the debate. [...]

[...] I profoundly disagree with those who say if you make any restriction you legitimise censorship therefore you can't control anything, therefore anything goes, because then you give the whole of this to the right in a most dangerous way. [...]

[...] It is as if we have two worlds – one is called freedom and the other is when some people like me come along and propose some censorship. Such an argument rests on the assumption that if Mr Murdoch and whoever else might monopolise our media outlets do exactly what they want and publish exactly what they want, and distribute exactly what they want, that is freedom. [...]

So I am arguing that there is no such thing as censorship or not censorship. There are going to be some who own our media outlets, some who decide what is portrayed, and we have to decide whether we allow concentrations of media ownership, whether we have public service broadcasting, whether we require programming aimed at children, how much religious broadcasting, where do we draw the lines, because everyone who commissions a play about sexuality, love, passion or any hurt, will have to draw some lines about how that is depicted and what is tasteful and what is not. So all the time there are people making these judgements. We have to make the judgements. It's an unavoidable discussion. There is no such thing as the freedom people on one side and then some other horrible censorship people on the other. Being a human being means that you are part of this discussion: having standards and taste is part of being a human being.

Having said that we have, of course, to carry on and re-regulate and look at the changes in new forms of media and whether we allow cross-media ownership between press and television. None of these questions are ever answered for all time, they are part of the questions of what is our culture and what is our taste. So when we admit that these are questions that are unavoidable and that everyone must engage with, we then have to say it's all a question of who draws the lines and where they are drawn, and how can we do this as well as possible to enlarge what is good and to allow freedom to all who want to experiment.

I think first of all we have to admit that child pornography is absolutely objectionable and it should always be restricted and should always be a criminal offence. [...]

There is room for argument about whether we should control adult pornography. Clearly child pornography is in a totally different category and I think there is hardly any human being in our society who would say there should be no restriction of any kind around that. In our country we have a law that says it's an offence to incite racial hatred – we should have that law, it's about decency, it's about not allowing some people to be belittled and humiliated by racist comments and racial depictions of Jewish people or black people as inferior. I think it's an enlargement of freedom to have that law. We must recognise that this law is part of this whole debate.

[...]

Then there is the question of how you categorise what is suitable for children, what is suitable for adults, and what is suitable for parental guidance. We might have to argue about who does it, who appoints the boards, have they got the principles right. We should also address what the principles should be, what kind of depiction of women should have. [...]

[...]

Much more complicated is the question of that material which is deeply and passionately offensive to lots of women and damaging to children, but which lots of men want to consume and want to spend lots of money on. That's where the really hard question arises. I think the principle behind the Indecent Displays Act and the principle that I was putting forward about the Page 3 phenomenon is that that kind of material can be made available for those who seek it out, but it must not be displayed to and imposed on those who do not want it. Underpinning that is a judgement that it is undesirable and offensive. You could rest on the principle that it is simply offensive, but I go back to what I call the feminist analysis of pornography, that it is offensive, that it is degrading, that it does degrade human sexuality. That is my judgement. I accept that there are many men who want this kind of material. I think it's one of our problems and I think it's one of the reasons why men and women hurt each other so often, but that is a slightly different discussion. My conclusion is that such material must be kept in a separate place, never displayed, never imposed; it can be bought and read in private but not imposed on those of us who do not want it.

When we look at new media outlets such as the Internet, we should separate getting the principles right and the technical difficulties of applying those principles to a new outlet. It's very important not to jumble up those arguments and say, oh dear, we've got the Internet, there's nothing we can do about it. I think there are suggestions of libel actions involving the Internet, involving copyright and libel which will start to create rules. How people are going to work this out technically, I don't know, but I'm sure it can be done. If we can frame what we require according to our principles, then we can say to those who know "Help us with this, we're trying to apply these principles", in order to preserve freedom and decency.

A jungle ruled by the free market is ugly and debases humanity. The suggestion that the free market in porn or in gratuitous violence is freedom and that people like us trying to use the limited power of democracy to impose some restrictions and principles on these media barons is censorship, seems to me to distort the meaning of language. Everything that is fine and precious needs nurturing and protecting. Any culture that celebrates unrestricted freedom for pornography and gratuitous violence is destroying itself.

Reading source

Short, 1996, pp.33–41 ■ ■ ■

Now read the following extract written by Michael Grade. As you read, compare his arguments on regulation with those of Clare Short in Reading 4.1.

Michael Grade, 'Free and fair communication and the regulation of media content'

Broadcasting regulation in the UK over the past 50 years has been based on three significant factors. The first is that broadcasting has been a highly restricted activity, government-licensed, with very few players compared with other forms of mass communication. [...] The limits of technology – spectrum shortage in the jargon – made television a very special activity indeed.

The second factor shaping the regulatory environment has been the almost universal perception that television is a uniquely influential medium. Politicians in particular have tended to view it as a powerful, mind-changing medium. They have sought both to use it, and to curb it, according to this sometimes over-exaggerated belief. And they are quick, too quick, to blame television for a whole catalogue of social ills from the distressing triviality of popular culture through to the rising crime rate. [...]

And thirdly, combining the fact of restricted access to television with its perceived social and political impact, it has been viewed generally as a medium quite different in kind to print. It is therefore deemed to need a much greater degree of regulation. Unlike print, its operation is not simply left to the laws of the land. Extra rules and structures have been deemed appropriate to achieve impartiality, and to monitor standards of 'taste and decency. [...]

[...]

The press, of course, runs on different tracks. Print escaped from government control in the 18th and 19th centuries and has fully exercised its democratic right to editorialise in the 20th century. A free press is held to be a vital symbol of democracy, even when, as in this country, it has resulted overall in a right-of-centre bias. No one suggests altering that. But compare it with the effective neutrality of broadcasting, which has been built on the early foundations laid by the BBC, and which is widely recognised as valuable and necessary in a mature democracy. Some of the legislative attempts to prescribe impartiality in greater detail have of course been risible, but the principle is sound. It isn't seen as censorship, but public welfare. It is an interesting and probably a necessary paradox that the freedom to editorialise in print is essential to free speech, whilst the requirement for television to be unbiased is a necessary service to democracy.

The regulation of taste and decency has, however, always been a much more difficult and contentious area. Let me make clear that in this instance I'm not talking about the outer fringes of exploitation and pornography, or the demeaning and dehumanising material which all but the most debased minds would reject out of hand. The problem lies in the middle ground. It is easy to legislate, but words are ill defined, the debate is confused, and subjective opinions and emotions almost always overwhelm such objective facts as may be available. Just whose taste and decency are we talking about? Who should we appoint to make these judgements? What powers should we give them? How can we believe that anyone is uniquely skilled to make these close calls, to remain themselves uncorrupted as they protect us from corruption?

Clearly, there are specific needs. There is, above all, the need to protect children. [...] History is littered with examples of great works which were thought offensive to conventional good taste on their first outings – Rodin's *The Kiss* – Stravinsky's *Rite of Spring* or Monty Python. Of course not all television – or indeed very much of it – is art in that sense. But it has become the main creative engine of popular culture, and will frequently want to test conventions and break boundaries. Is that really so dangerous? Isn't there an opposite – and who knows, greater – danger in artificially constraining that creativity by not trusting the broadcasters' knowledge of both their producers and their audiences?

A balance must clearly be struck between creative liberty and unbridled licence. It is one of the central conundrums of a mass medium. Should the rules and conventions which govern content be framed to satisfy a simple majority of the population? Or should they prevent broadcasters from risking offence to the most sensitive 10 per cent of viewers? If so, you might as well argue that all swimming pools should be no more than three feet deep, because a tenth of the population can't swim. And in the end, if the broadcasters can't be trusted to get the balance right, what chance have small groups of arbitrarily and generally appointed regulators?

[...]

All the main factors which have shaped our present system will be called into question by the technological developments which lie ahead. The impact of an ever-growing number of channels will make itself felt. It will be much more difficult for regulators to be proactive when there is simply too much output for them and their officials to watch. The Radio Authority has reached that point already, now relying increasingly on audience complaints before they can act. It may be much longer before television reaches the same point [...]

The second change will also be gradual, and also inexorable. [...]

[...]

It is just too easy to say that technology will provide enough channels of distribution to free television from the shackles of neutrality, and let a thousand flowers bloom. It would certainly mark an end to the supposed 'censorship' of the current impartiality requirement, but would it benefit the public, would it benefit the democratic system. We are all free to start a newspaper now, but very few of us have deep enough pockets to do so. Access to the printer on the corner is no substitute for the power of distributing a national newspaper. It's the old market freedom of the sharks to eat the minnows.

[...]

Perhaps in the end such problems are insoluble. Perhaps there is no practicable and credible means of drawing boundaries other than those set in statute law, and even then proof is a contentious matter. Perhaps in a democracy freedom to publish must take precedence over any cultural sensibilities.

Reading source

Grade, 1996, pp.42–7 ■ ■ ■

6.1 Utilitarianism and deontology

Teasing out the assumptions and principles behind Grade's and Short's propositions is not straightforward, but we can identify some important issues at stake. For example: what is the relative importance of claims for the preferences of the majority versus the preferences of a minority? Is utilitarianism, the 'principle of utility' as its main philosophical proponent Jeremy Bentham called it (Bentham, 2002/1789), or, as we now usually know it, the principle of the greatest happiness of the greatest number of people, to govern us? Or is utilitarianism to be replaced, or supplemented, by some deontological (duty or rights-based) principle? This would mean that the wishes of the majority, and the principle of the maximum benefit to all, should not necessarily prevail. Deontologists (those who argue from a principle of duty or what is right) propose that some things should just not be done – even if they serve the interests of the majority and maximise general utility. If some deontological arguments are correct, that people in general enjoy the right not to have some things done, what are these things which should not, must not, be done? Which rights cannot be transgressed and who is to identify these absolute prohibitions? Are measures, which benefit the majority, justified if a minority, or minorities, does not/do not benefit? Are measures, which benefit the majority, justified if a minority actually suffers in consequence of them? Alternatively, how far can the claims of a minority, or minorities, be justified if the majority suffers as a consequence of them (for example, through higher levels of taxation than they would otherwise experience)?

It is important to recognise here that we are thinking about these questions rather differently from the way they are often addressed – that is, through the framework of relevant evidence. For example, Sonia Livingstone considered how far we can identify evidence for believing that the media affects people's behaviour and values (**Livingstone, 2005**). Even if we were to establish that, for example, a screening of a pornographic film, such as the celebrated *Deep Throat* (USA, dir. Damiano, 1972) (see Figure 4.5), damaged everyone who witnessed it, this evidence of effect would not settle the argument (though one might think it highly relevant information) as to whether we should prohibit others from seeing the film. One could argue either that a greater harm might arise from suppression of the film (for example, damage to the doctrine of individual responsibility), or that we enjoy the right to know the content of the film and the makers of the film also enjoy a right to freedom of expression, and that suppression of the film would infringe these rights. Even if it could be shown that no harm was done by screening the film, one could nonetheless argue that a screening should be prohibited if some found the film offensive. In short, not all regulatory questions are capable of being resolved by an appeal to empirical evidence.

Activity 4.4

Consider whether a person's 'right' not to be offended justifies the suppression of information to the majority.

After thinking about this yourself (and remember, thinking is an activity!) you might jot down in columns your ideas for and against suppression. Would people unlike you (for example, of a different age or gender, with a different cultural or ethnic formation) be likely to make different decisions (try asking some of them!)? ▪ ▪ ▪

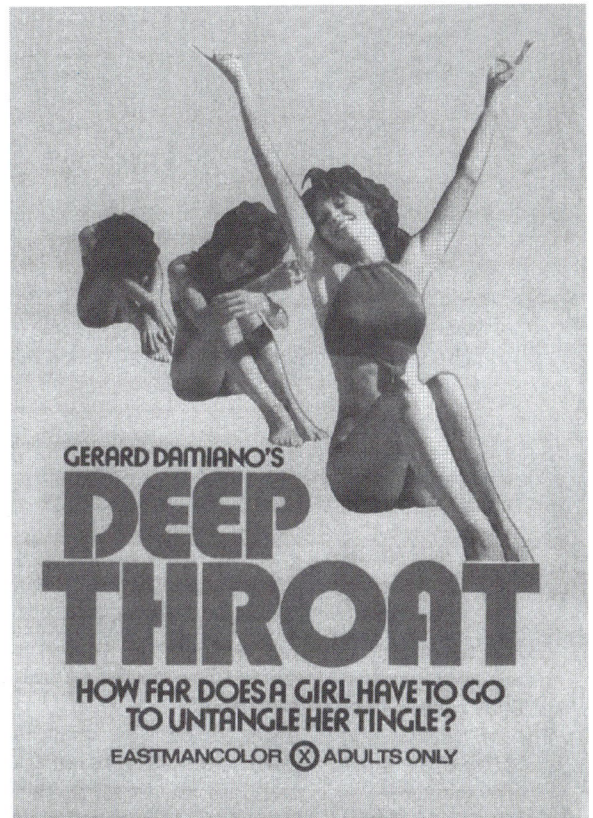

Figure 4.5 A poster advertising Deep Throat, *with its star, Linda Lovelace*

Consider, for example, whether Sky News and the BBC were right to show images of dead British soldiers, whom the government claimed had been 'executed' in the 2003 invasion of Iraq? Was the government right to deprecate the broadcasters' actions on the grounds that the soldiers' families and friends would be shocked, hurt and offended by the images of their dead loved ones?

Anyone's sense of where the balance lies may well be influenced by their emotional closeness to what's depicted. (Would we be more worried if one of the dead were known to us? Or would we be less concerned if they were from a different country?)

Arguably, there are strong claims on both sides of the debate and it is understandable that anyone's sense of where the balance lies is likely to be influenced by their general values and beliefs. Someone who placed a very high value on freedom of expression might well be more tolerant of shocking images than one who regarded protection of the vulnerable to be of overriding importance.

7 Managing conflict: freedom of expression versus the right to privacy

Let us consider another case study of value conflicts in media regulation. We will begin by considering an enormously influential argument for freedom of expression. It was made by the British philosopher, Member of Parliament, and proponent of women's rights, John Stuart Mill. Mill was born in London in 1806 (and died in France in 1873), and had what was possibly one of the most miserable childhoods imaginable for a child of wealthy and well-educated parents. His father, James Mill, and his father's friend, Jeremy Bentham (see Figure 4.6) – best known as the father of utilitarian philosophy – took on the systematic education of the young John. By the age of three, John Stuart Mill read Greek. At eight he was set to teach his siblings. By the age of thirteen he was set to summarise and analyse his father's own philosophical writings. At twenty he experienced a breakdown while editing a major work of Bentham's. As Mill said of himself at this time, 'my heart sank within me: the whole foundation on which my life was constructed fell down [...] I seemed to have nothing left to live for' (Mill, 1924/1873, p.94). It was a brutal irony for one schooled systematically in utilitarianism, the doctrine of organising society so that 'the greatest happiness of the greatest number' prevailed, to find that working for a major utilitarian philosopher brought such personal misery.

Mill's tragic experience neatly poses a central philosophical question, one that resonates as powerfully in media policy as in other domains: what weight should be placed on individuals' rights and what on the interests of the majority? Perhaps the force-fed education experienced by John Stuart Mill, though engendering despair and misery in him, was good in the long run. Perhaps without it James Mill's and Bentham's works would not have been as lucid and accessible as they are. Perhaps John Stuart Mill himself would not have written his book *On Liberty*, his critique *The Subjection of Women*, and his other works. But is, what seems to us, an exceptionally harsh upbringing of a little boy justified by the benefits Mill's subsequent works have brought to humankind? What weighs heaviest – the rights of an individual (for example, to experience a happy childhood) or the benefits experienced by the world at large?

Figure 4.6 *Jeremy Bentham in his box at University College London*

Figure 4.7 John Stuart Mill (1806–1873)

Mill's best-known work, *On Liberty*, was first published in 1859 and dedicated to his deceased wife, Harriet. Mill credited Harriet as 'the inspirer, and in part the author of all that is best in my writings' – Harriet had, almost certainly, a major hand in drafting *On Liberty*.

7.1 Mill and freedom of expression

In *On Liberty*, Mill makes a celebrated argument for the freedom of the press, offering four reasons for its liberty and against suppression of the expression of opinion. He argues:

> We have now recognised the necessity to the mental well-being of mankind (on which all their other well-being depends) of freedom of opinion, and freedom of the expression of opinion, on four distinct grounds, which we will now briefly recapitulate. Firstly, if any opinion is compelled to silence, that opinion may, for ought we can certainly know, be true. To deny this is to assume our own infallibility. Secondly, though the silenced opinion be an error, it may, and very commonly does, contain a portion of truth; and since the general or prevailing opinion on any subject is rarely or never the whole truth, it is only by the collision of adverse opinions that the remainder of the truth has any chance of being supplied. Thirdly, even if the received opinion be not only true, but the whole truth; unless it is suffered to be, and actually is, vigorously and earnestly contested, it will, by most of those who receive it, be held in the manner of a prejudice, with little comprehension or feeling of its rational grounds. And not only this, but, fourthly, the meaning of the doctrine itself will be in danger of being lost or enfeebled, and deprived of its vital effect on the character and conduct: the dogma becoming a mere formal profession, inefficacious for good, but cumbering the ground and preventing the growth of any real and heartfelt conviction from reason or personal experience.
>
> Mill, 1986/1859, pp.115–16

Mill's doctrine is extremely radical – as his statement 'there ought to exist the fullest liberty of professing and discussing, as a matter of

ethical conviction, any doctrine, however immoral it may be considered'
(Mill, 1986, p.75) makes clear. If everything can be discussed and
advocated then it follows that, in principle, anything and everything can
and, if we are to be well informed, should be investigated, recorded and
represented. Mill's principle of freedom of expression opens wide the
door to the representation of falsehood, to making public what might
be thought to be more appropriately private, and to publication of
mischievous and harmful information. Perhaps Mill's 'rights absolutism'
is rooted in his own uncomfortable encounters with utilitarianism. He
does not temper his arguments for liberty by acknowledging possible
circumstances in which the interests of the majority ('the greatest
happiness of the greatest number') might take precedence. Mill's doctrines
touch on the central issues in the cases we will now consider. That is,
what balance should be struck between freedom of expression and
conflicting principles such as the right to privacy and the protection
of the vulnerable?

8   The right to privacy

The extent to which individuals should enjoy a right to privacy, and
whether all individuals (whether or not they choose to put themselves in
the public eye) should enjoy the same right to privacy, was fiercely
debated in the UK throughout the last decade of the twentieth century,
and it remains a live question in the twenty-first century. The Preamble
to the United Nations Universal Declaration of Human Rights
(UNUDHR) of 1948 looks forward, in a very Millian way, to 'the advent
of a world in which human beings shall enjoy freedom of speech and
belief and freedom from fear and want has been proclaimed as the
highest aspiration of the common people'. The foundational value
ascribed to 'freedom of speech' is echoed in Article 19 of the UNUDHR
which states that 'Everyone has the right to freedom of opinion and
expression; this right includes freedom to hold opinions without
interference and to seek, receive and impart information and ideas
through any media and regardless of frontiers'. However, Article 12
of the same UNUDHR prescribes that 'No one shall be subjected to
arbitrary interference with his privacy'. Article 8 of the European
Convention on Human Rights echoes this theme and provides that
'Everyone has the right to respect for his private and family life, his
home and his correspondence'.

How are these two conflicting rights, to freedom of expression and
to privacy, to be reconciled? The weasel word 'arbitrary' provides a
possible solution – it seems to suggest that there are some grounds for
interference with personal privacy, but it is not clear from the Declaration

what these might be. Whatever they are, they are hard to reconcile either with Mill's absolutist claim for the 'fullest liberty' or for the right, specified in Article 19, 'to seek, receive and impart information and ideas through any media and regardless of frontiers'. The conflict between two contradictory principles of right remains. How are 'rights' to privacy and to expression to be balanced? Different societies draw the line between freedom of, and limits on, expression and define the distinction between the public and the private differently at various times.

8.1 Celebrities, privacy and the public interest (or what interests the public)

Consider the case of Michael Douglas and Catherine Zeta-Jones, both prominent media celebrities, whose New York wedding celebrations in 2000 were widely reported, including in the UK gossip magazines *Hello!* and *OK!* Zeta-Jones and Douglas had an exclusive deal with *OK!* for publication of the photographs of their wedding celebrations. *OK!*'s rival, *Hello!* published unauthorised photographs of the wedding. The Douglases sued *Hello!* in the English courts for breach of confidence, invasion of privacy and breach of contractual relations. They were, in part, successful (see Schilling in *The Guardian*, 14 April 2003, and *The Times*, 15 April 2003, p.3). They lost their privacy claims but won their breach of confidence claim (they were awarded damages of £14,600 and £3 million in costs – reputedly less than their expenditure in bringing the case, see Figure 4.8. *OK!* also won £1,033,156. However, at the time of writing, *Hello!* was to appeal against the award to *OK!*). The judge found that 'the wedding was not a celebrity event' and that it was 'as private as was possible, consistent with it being a socially pleasant event'. Taking into account the Press Complaints Commission Code (which prohibits intrusive photography without the subjects' consent), the judge reasoned that there had been a breach of confidence (but not of privacy).

What is the Press Complaints Commission (PCC) and why did the judge refer to its code? The PCC is a self-regulatory agency for the UK newspaper industry. The judge's reference to its code illustrates how intertwined various types and levels of regulation may become. But to return to the wedding!

The Zeta-Jones/Douglas wedding imbroglio raises important questions about celebrities' entitlements to privacy – but answers few of them. It seems significant that the case was brought in London. Under US law – and the wedding took place in the USA – it seems the Douglases would have been less likely to enjoy even the qualified success they secured in London. In the USA, as expert commentators have it, 'the media are protected in publishing truthful matters of public interest. By and large the courts have deferred to the media in determining what

Figure 4.8 *Catherine Zeta-Jones and Michael Douglas leaving court*

is of public interest' (Zuckman and Gaynes, 1977, p.97). But in the UK the Zeta-Jones/Douglas case was treated differently. Celebrities' claims to an entitlement to privacy commands more credence in the UK than in the USA. But we cannot be confident that celebrities enjoy the same entitlements as do ordinary people – not least because the judge in the Zeta-Jones/Douglas trial did not find that the wedded couple's right to privacy had been breached, and nor did he find that 'celebrity events' should be protected.

Activity 4.5

Write down arguments for and against regarding weddings, details of which must be made available publicly (for example, reading of the banns in church and/or publication of intent to marry in a registry office), as private events? Identify what grounds there are, if any, for considering the weddings of public figures differently from the weddings of ordinary people? ■ ■ ■

Consider whether it made a difference that Ms Zeta-Jones and Mr Douglas sold exclusive rights to publish photographs of their wedding to *OK!* for a reported £1 million? Is the 'right' to sue for invasion of privacy and/or breach of confidence worth very much? Celebrities, such as Zeta-Jones and Douglas, may be able to afford to sue, but few ordinary people can pursue successfully a civil court case against a publication that, almost always, is likely to be financially stronger. Perhaps celebrities cannot afford not to sue. For not only may the resultant publicity contribute positively to their careers, but without defending the exclusivity of their contracts, such as that of Zeta-Jones and Douglas with *OK!*, the value of rights to images of other events in their lives (images of their first child, for example) would diminish. But for ordinary people, without the resources to sue, perhaps effective regulation, whether statutory or self-regulation, is valuable. Indeed, one of the strongest arguments offered in defence of the PCC is that it provides complainants unable to afford the courts with a route to redress which they would otherwise be denied.

If one instance of the potential exercise of regulatory power through the law provides at best a qualified protection for ordinary people, what of others? What can regulation, whether statutory regulation or self-regulation, offer? As well as raising sharply the difficulties of establishing boundaries between the public and the private, the Douglas/Zeta-Jones wedding case also shows the unevenness of UK privacy regulation. Because the Douglases were concerned about a printed report, they had no possible recourse to a statutory regulator – for there is no such body for newspapers and magazines in the UK, though the option of a complaint to the relevant self-regulatory body, the Press Complaints Commission, was open to them. Had the report been broadcast, the Douglases would have been able to pursue their complaint (though without the possibility of receiving financial compensation) through a statutory regulator, either the Broadcasting Standards Commission (BSC) or the Independent Television Commission (ITC) which were the statutory agencies at the time of the Douglases' wedding (both have been replaced by Ofcom).

Ofcom now has the duty of protecting the public against 'unwarranted infringements of privacy' (Communications Act 2003, Clause 3), though it has no power (and neither did its predecessors the ITC or BSC) to secure compensation for those whose privacy may be infringed. For compensation, recourse to the courts is required. The issue of compensation is material; for can a statutory regulator, with the duty to protect the public, be effective without power to award damages to the victim(s)? In an important case (*Peck* v. *United Kingdom* 2003, which concerned broadcasting of CCTV footage of a private act) the court found that 'the lack of legal power [...] to award damages [...] means those bodies could not provide an effective remedy [...] The ITC's power to impose a fine on the relevant television company does not amount to an award of damages' (*Peck* v. *United Kingdom*, 2003, para 109. 36 EHRR 41).

Perhaps in this respect at least there is not much difference between statutory and self-regulation, for neither the statutory regulator, the ITC, nor the self-regulator, the PCC, provides a means to secure compensation for those whose privacy has been invaded. We will return to this question of the role and power of regulatory institutions later, but let us return now to the central issue of principle – what balance should be struck between conflicting rights claims: that of a right to privacy and that of the right to freedom of expression?

8.2 Privacy, celebrities and ordinary people

In recent times there has been a growing level of concern in the UK about media intrusion into people's private lives and experiences. Whether celebrities – people in the public eye – should be treated differently from ordinary people is one aspect of this concern (and you may feel that the distinction between a celebrity and an ordinary person is far from solid – for there are many accidental courses of events that could put any one of us in the public eye). Another, and perhaps more fundamental, issue is the balance to be struck between, on one hand, the powers of investigation and publication which the mass media should, and must, enjoy if it is to fully inform the public and, on the other hand, the rights to privacy which we all, perhaps in varying degrees, should and must have if we are to live our lives in peace and tranquillity.

Concern has been fuelled by what a judge called a 'monstrous invasion of privacy' (Calcutt, 1990, p.103) which took place in 1990 when Gordon Kaye, a TV star, was photographed without his informed consent, by the *Sunday Sport*, while recovering from brain surgery in hospital. A similar controversy arose around the subsequent death of another television personality, Russell Harty, at whose deathbed (it was alleged in Parliament) window cleaners were being bribed by newspapers to provide information and photographs. Widespread, deeply rooted, concern about the extent to which the British press invades the privacy of those on whom it reports has led to: two major reports on the press and privacy chaired by the late Sir David Calcutt (Calcutt, 1990, to the 1993); the establishment of the Press Complaints Commission (PCC); successive strengthenings of the PCC's voluntary Code of Practice; and to further official inquiries (such as that launched by the House of Commons Select Committee on Culture, Media and Sport in 2003).

9 Privacy

What is privacy? The first Calcutt inquiry acknowledged that privacy was difficult to define, and argued that the well-known definition 'the right to be let alone' (formulated by the US jurists Samuel D. Warren and Louis D. Brandeis, 1890, in a celebrated article, 'The right to privacy') was too broad. Instead, Calcutt offered a new definition:

> Privacy could be regarded as the antithesis of what is public: hence everything concerning an individual's home, family, religion, health, sexuality, personal legal and personal financial affairs [...] On the other hand, an individual is a member of society and, as such, cannot expect to enjoy total privacy.
>
> Calcutt, 1990, para 3.5

Calcutt also distinguished between the public interest as that 'which is merely interesting to the public' and that 'which should be brought to the attention of the public in order, for example, to expose crime, impropriety or hypocrisy' (Calcutt, 1990, para 3.20). Clearly, the Calcutt doctrine was less friendly to the 'fullest liberty' of expression than Mill might have wished. Nonetheless, so offensive did the public and Parliament find the media's intrusions into the deaths of Kaye and Harty that Calcutt was supported widely. Calcutt found both that British newspapers were insufficiently sensitive to privacy concerns and that press self-regulation was insufficiently stringent. The newspaper industry responded to Calcutt's analysis (and the considerable parliamentary and public concern that accompanied it) by strengthening its self-regulation, not least by drawing on Calcutt's draft code when formulating its own PCC Code of Practice.

9.1 The Press Complaints Commission: self-regulation

In its first landmark adjudication in 1991, the PCC ruled that public figures were entitled to the same protection for their private lives as other individuals, *unless there was some justification of public interest* for intrusion. However, establishment of the PCC has not been sufficient to still all public and parliamentary concern. Nor has successive strengthening of the PCC code fully satisfied either Parliament or the public. The second Calcutt report on the press and privacy, published in 1993, stated:

> The Press Complaints Commission is not, in my view, an effective regulator of the press. It has not been set up in a way, and is not operating a code of practice, which enables it to command not only press but also public confidence. It does not, in my view, hold the balance fairly between the press and the individual. It is not the truly

independent body that it should be. As constituted, it is, in essence, a body set up by the industry, financed by the industry, dominated by the industry, and operating a code of practice devised by the industry and which is over-favourable to the industry.

Calcutt, 1993, p.xi

The second Calcutt Report recommended replacing self-regulation by stronger laws and a statutory regulator. It recommended establishment of a Statutory Tribunal, introduction of a tort of infringement of privacy, and criminalisation of various acts of infringement of privacy. To date none of these measures has been implemented. The situation in Scotland is somewhat different from that in England and Wales and is, depending on how one wants to put it, less media friendly or, alternatively, more effective in protection of privacy. Scottish law defines a breach of the peace more widely than does English law, and thus provides potential remedies against media harassment which are absent in England and Wales.

The PCC code (available on the PCC's website at: http://www.pcc. org.uk/cop/cop.asp) was, and at the time of writing is, considerably more strongly inclined towards newspapers' 'right' to enquire and report than the 'right' to privacy that Calcutt championed. Calcutt had recommended that 'entering private property, without the consent of the lawful occupant, with intent to obtain personal information with a view to its publication' (Calcutt, 1990, p.xi) should become a criminal offence. Calcutt also recommended that 'taking a photograph or recording the voice of an individual who is on private property, without his consent, with a view to its publication and with intent that the individual shall be identifiable' should also become a criminal offence, subject to public interest reservations (Calcutt, 1990, p.xi). Neither practice has yet been either criminalised or prohibited under the PCC code – newspaper reporters and photographers continue to do both.

9.2 Politicians and privacy

Whether or not we conclude, as did the judge, that there was no breach of privacy (but a breach of confidence) in *Hello!*'s report of the Douglases' wedding, and whether or not we believe that a sick bed should be as sacrosanct when occupied by a celebrity as it should be when occupied by an ordinary person, what of politicians' right to privacy? How far does the public's right to know outweigh the putative rights to privacy of someone standing for public office? The UK politician, Chris Smith, UK Secretary of State for Culture, Media and Sport from 1997 to 2001, argued:

I think most sensible people would probably say that if you are an ordinary individual, not seeking the public limelight in any way, then you should be entitled to a certain amount of privacy. If, on the other

hand, you are a public figure and it is in the public interest for
something you are up to, [to] become known widely and generally,
then there is the right for intrusion of privacy to take place.

Smith, 1996, p.50

Smith's argument chimes with practice in the USA where the judgement
in *New York Times* v. *Sullivan* (376 U.S. 254, 84 S.Ct 710, 11 L.Ed.2d
686.1964, in Zuckman and Gaynes, 1977) established that public figures
generally enjoy less legal protection for their privacy than do ordinary
people. This celebrated case provided that 'a public official may not
recover damages for a defamatory falsehood relating to his official
conduct unless he proves with "convincing clarity" that the statement is
made with actual malice' (Zuckman and Gaynes, 1977, p.63). Emerging
UK practice also tends in this direction, and Nikki Tait claims that 'the
courts are less inclined to protect people who, for much of their lives,
actively seek to exploit publicity' (Tait, 2003, p.17).

But not all agree with Smith's line of argument. Mr Justice Eady, a
member of the 1990 Calcutt Committee, argued that:

> [...] a so-called 'public figure' defence [...] would mean, in effect, that
> newspapers could publish more or less what they liked, provided they
> were honest, if their subject happened to be within the definition
> of a 'public figure'. We think this would lead to great injustice.
> Furthermore, it would be quite contrary to the tradition of our
> common law that citizens are not divided into different classes. What
> matters is the subject-matter of the publication and how it is treated,
> rather than who happens to be the subject of the allegations.

Eady, 2002, pp.9–10

Nonetheless, the practice of UK privacy regulation seems to follow more
often Smith's rather than Eady's principle. For example, in 2002 the PCC
rejected a complaint from the celebrity Steve Bing, who had complained
about intrusion into his privacy by a national newspaper. In ruling against
him the Commission noted that:

> [...] he had been involved in a high-profile relationship with a famous
> actress and had subsequently publicly argued with her about the
> paternity of her child. In the Commission's view, scrutiny by the press
> in these circumstances was inevitable.

Press Complaints Commission, 2002

What grounds might there be for dissenting from the PCC's ruling?
Perhaps we might say that the high-profile character of his former
relationship was not of Bing's choosing and that he is not a public figure
in the sense of either Chris Smith or Mr Justice Eady. What action might
we think has a greater legitimate expectation of remaining private than

making love? Moreover, the public argument was, it seems, also not of Bing's choosing. Disputes over paternity are not uncommon and all parties to them may well be sincere. Indeed, it seems somewhat paradoxical that Bing's appeal to the PCC on grounds of breach of privacy should occasion further publicity for the acts which he was concerned should remain private. Paradoxical, too, that the PCC named Bing but delicately refrained from naming the 'famous actress' concerned (Elizabeth Hurley) – someone who had chosen a career which, in the most literal sense, put her in the public eye whereas Bing's celebrity seemingly derived from their relationship. Prima facie, this does seem a case in the class described by Eady – one that divides citizens into different classes and perhaps, in consequence, causes injustice. Does the Bing case suggest, as Calcutt argued, that what interests the public is not necessarily the same as the public interest?

Activity 4.6

Consider the merits of the creation of a legal entitlement to privacy and enforcement of privacy rights via statutory or self-regulation.

As in Activity 4.4, try jotting down in columns your ideas for and against an entitlement to privacy, and for and against the two types of regulation identified. For example, should celebrities' entitlement to privacy be inferior to those of ordinary people? Should the Douglases have sought redress through a complaint to the PCC? What would they stand to gain and to lose by doing so? Does a utilitarian calculus (most people want it and it does not cause most people harm) have superior validity to the 'right' of the weak to be protected? Would people different from you (for example, in age or gender, with a different cultural formation) be likely to make different decisions (try asking some of them!)? ■ ■ ■

10 Conclusion

We have seen, through a series of case studies largely drawn from the UK, the difficulty of reconciling with consistency the conflicting rights claims of privacy, of free expression of opinion and of access to information. There are, moreover, inconsistencies in the procedures, criteria and possibility of redress offered by the law and by self- and statutory regulatory agencies, and differing views on the extent to which acquisition of the status of a celebrity means foregoing some of the entitlements to privacy of ordinary people. The UK is not alone in this uncertainty. In the USA there are striking differences in the legal practices of different states. The majority, but not all US states, acknowledges a right of privacy, but some have explicitly rejected it and only a few have specific privacy laws (though these include two of the most populous states, California and New York).

For Mill, these conflicts might have seemed easy to resolve, for his *On Liberty* sets out very clear principles – which point unequivocally towards publication and publicity rather than towards the preservation of privacy. But not all of us would readily concur with Mill. Publication and publicity might well satisfy *both* Mill's libertarian, deontological, principles *and* also Benthamite utilitarian principles (for the greatest happiness of the greatest number may well be served by publicising what an individual might wish to remain private), yet publication and publicity in any of a number of cases might, we feel, infringe another deontological principle or right – that of an individual's entitlement to privacy.

To summarise, in this chapter we have considered where the boundaries of regulation have been drawn and where they should be drawn, and the different institutions used for regulation (law, statutory and self-regulatory bodies). We have also seen that not only are different values at stake in regulatory decisions (for example, whether deontological 'rights' or the principle of utility should be decisive) but that there are difficult conflicts between rival claims of right and utility. What conclusions can we draw? Three perhaps.

Firstly, there is a class of activity that should be regulated: these are activities that require expert judgement by a specialised agency with well-developed competencies in the matter in question. Secondly, there are classes of activity that are properly dealt with by intermediate institutions – institutions that are neither an arm of government nor wholly private. And thirdly, many regulatory judgements involve striking a balance between conflicting rights claims. They are likely therefore to be messy, inconsistent and subject to rejection, revision and review as social consensus on values changes.

Further reading

Bentham, J. (2000) *Selected Writings on Utilitarianism*, Ware, Wordsworth Editions. A convenient source of Bentham's work including *An Introduction to the Principles of Morals and Legislation*.

Collins, R. and Murroni, C. (1996) *New Media, New Policies: Media and Communications Strategies for the Future*, Cambridge, Polity. This is a systematic attempt to think through the relation of the public and private sector in media and communications and their regulation.

Lord Chancellor's Department and the Scottish Office (1993) *Infringement of Privacy*, CHAN J06091 5 NJ 7/93, London, Central Office of Information. This provides a comprehensive and authoritative account of privacy issues and review of UK legislation.

Smith, A. (ed.) (1974) *British Broadcasting*, Newton Abbot, David and Charles. This inventive account of British broadcasting history contains a collection of excerpts from primary source documents.

Snoddy, R. (1992) *The Good, the Bad and the Unacceptable*, London, Faber. This provides further related material.

References

Bentham, J. (2002/1789) 'An introduction to the principles of morals and legislation', *The Library of Economics and Liberty*, http://www.econlib.org/library/Bentham/bnthPML.htm (accessed 4 December 2005).

Berlin, I. (1969) *Four Essays on Liberty*, Oxford, Oxford University Press.

Calcutt, D. (Chair) (1990) *Report of the Committee on Privacy and Related Matters*, Cm 1102, London, HMSO.

Calcutt, D. (Chair) (1993) *Review of Press Self-Regulation*, Cm 2135, London, HMSO.

Eady, J. (2002) *Privacy and the Media*, http://www.media-ent-law.co.uk/articles/121202-privacy.html (accessed 20 February 2003).

Grade, M. (1996) 'Fair and free communication and the regulation of media content' in Collins, R. and Purnell, J. (eds) (1996) *Reservoirs of Dogma*, London, Institute for Public Policy Research.

Held, D. (ed.) (1983) *States and Societies*, Oxford, Martin Robertson.

Livingstone, S. (2005) 'Media audiences, interpreters and users' in Gillespie, M. (ed.) *Media Audiences*, Maidenhead, Open University Press/The Open University (Book 2 in this series).

Mill, J. (1924/1873) *Autobiography*, (ed. J.J. Coss) New York, Columbia University Press. Also at http://www.utilitarianism.com/millauto/ (accessed 9 September 2003).

Mill, J. (1986/1859) *On Liberty*, Harmondsworth, Penguin.

National Assembly of France (1789) 'Declaration of the rights of man and of the citizen' *Human and Constitutional Rights Documents*, http://www.hrcr.org/docs/frenchdec.html (accessed 9 September 2003).

Ofcom (Office of Communications) (2005) 'Ofcom Annual Report 2004–2005, Operating and financial review', *Ofcom*, http://www.ofcom.org.uk/about/accoun/reports_plans/annrep0405/opfin/ (accessed 2 December 2005).

Peck v. United Kingdom (2003) *European Human Rights Report*, 36 EHRR 41, para.109.

Press Complaints Commission (PCC) (2002) *Annual Report 2002*, PCC, http://www.pcc.org.uk/2002/statistics_review.html#table5 (accessed 9 September 2003).

Ruggiero, G. de (1933) 'Liberalism' in *Encyclopaedia of the Social Sciences, Volume IX*, New York, Macmillan.

Schilling, K. (2003) 'Private lessons', *The Guardian*, 14 April, http://media.guardian.co.uk/ (accessed 7 May 2003).

Senate and House of Representatives of the United States of America (1787) 'The Bill of Rights', *International Information Programs*, http://usinfo.state.gov/usa/infousa/facts/funddocs/billeng.htm (accessed 9 September 2003).

Short, C. (1996) 'Page three, indecent display and the roots of concern' in Collins, R. and Purnell, J. (eds) (1996) *Reservoirs of Dogma*, London, Institute for Public Policy Research.

Smith, C. (1996) 'Freedom and limits in expression' in Collins and Purnell (eds) (1996) *Reservoirs of Dogma*, London, Institute for Public Policy Research.

Tait, N. (2003) 'The glare of publicity proves hard to escape', *Financial Times*, 3 March, p.17.

The Times (2003) '*OK!* Perhaps it was *Hello!* that won the battle but lost the war', *Times Law Supplement*, 15 April, p.3.

Warren, S. and Brandeis, L. (1890) 'The right to privacy', originally *4 Harvard Law Review 193* published in also at http://www.louisville.edu/library/law/brandeis/privacy.html (accessed 9 September 2003).

Zuckman, H.L. and Gaynes, M.J. (1977) *Mass Communications Law in a Nutshell*, St Paul, MN, West Publishing.

Technology, regulation, society and the media

Richard Collins and Jessica Evans

Let us recap on the issues covered in the four preceding chapters. Chapter 1 focused on the influence of technology (a key issue also explored in Chapters 2 and 3), on society, and on media and communications in particular. It distinguished between two influential approaches to understanding the importance of technology: technological determinism and the social construction of technology (SCOT). The first approach attributes priority to technology – it is what technology does that counts. The second reverses the argument and attributes primacy to society. Both approaches testify to the intimate relationship between technology and society and to the importance of technology. Taking printing as a particular case in point, the chapter demonstrated how printing shaped, and was shaped by, society – both technological determinism *and* the social construction of technology were important. And specifically, as argued in Chapter 1, the communications technology of printing standardised (think of the example of the 'wicked Bible') and restructured time–space relationships (technology made it possible for us to 'time shift' our media consumption and removed the need for us to be in the same place as the source of the information we consumed). Communications technology also shifted power to the consumer (for example, in making it possible for consumers to become producers – think of the examples of blogs and podcasting).

Chapter 2 took forward these ideas in more detail and considered the standardisation effect of printing by comparing the language of two contemporary medieval English texts and relating them to contemporary English. The language of the text printed first, Chaucer's *Canterbury Tales*, seems much closer to contemporary English than the language of *Sir Gawain and the Green Knight* – not least because of the standardising effect of printing. But, technological change does more than standardise. New communication technologies restructure social relationships – they exert power. Think of Habermas's arguments about the growth (and decline) of a public sphere, and Meyrowitz's contention that television has eroded the boundaries between the worlds of adults and children. Of course, we could consider these changes as standardisation effects but it probably makes more sense to see them as instances of a more general reshaping of society through the power exerted by media and communications.

This shaping of society by the media is not, of course, a one-way process. As proposed in Chapter 1, society can also shape technologies and the media. An important way in which it does so is through regulation. Here we drew on Habermas's and Sola Pool's analyses of the effects of the media. Both argue that media technologies have profoundly changed society. But, each author draws from his analysis rather different ideas about what society's responses, including regulation, should be. This is an important matter in itself; reasonable people do disagree (but not always reasonably!) about the effects of the media and of society's response. And, as we show in the final chapter of this book, such disagreements are often rooted in different values. The substantive differences in the conclusions that Habermas and Sola Pool come to point to the difficulties of making regulatory decisions. Therefore social choices may turn on the difficult question of which set of values, among conflicting sets of values, should take priority.

In Chapter 3 we shifted perspective and considered the fundamental economic characteristics of media and communication, showing how these provide one of the major rationales for government regulation of media and communications. For example, economies of scale and scope may mean that media firms tend to be large and their ownership concentrated. You will remember the example we gave of the 'five sisters' who account for much of world media production. So, arguably, the fundamental economics of the media and communications sector mean that society has to regulate it if pluralism (which we generally value because it is important for democracy and because competition between a plurality of firms tends to promote efficiency) is to be safeguarded.

In Chapter 4 we took up this seeming paradox (of the state intervening in the media market in order to promote political diversity and independence) and considered both the different ways in which regulation is practised and the delicate choices that regulators often have to make. How are we to reconcile contradictory principles? What is the appropriate balance between state and market in providing media and communication services? In Chapter 3 we suggested that it might be natural to assume the market is likely to be the best instrument through which to realise social goals – it is independent of government and potentially provides choice between many sources and viewpoints. But we also indicated that, on the other hand, there are fundamental economic tendencies towards concentration in the media sector. An optimal regulatory regime seems therefore to demand a balance between state and market.

The way in which the balance between state and market in media and communications changed throughout the twentieth century and into the twenty-first seems to reflect the impact of technological change (opening up or closing down possibilities of pluralism and competition). But perhaps such shifts also reflect changes in social values. The last part of the twentieth century saw a widespread withdrawal of the British state from direct provision of services both in media and communications and also in other essential areas of modern life, such as water and electricity. Instead of state provision British society chose provision of services by private companies, coupled with regulation of service provision using statutory or self-regulatory agencies. These agencies were (and are) used to encourage provision of under-supplied goods and services (positive regulation) and/or to reduce provision of putatively harmful goods and services (negative regulation). In Chapter 4, we also considered how difficult it is to decide on such questions because of the incommensurability of the fundamental values at stake, taking as a notable example the conflict between a right to freedom of expression and a right to privacy.

The terrain we have covered in this book shows how closely knitted together are our three key themes of *power; change and continuity; and knowledge, values and beliefs*. Let us first consider *power*. Technology, we have argued, exerts power in a host of ways. For example, think of the Elizabeth Eisenstein citation on print in Chapter 1 and the related arguments about the analogous effect of the internet: by re-scaling society and in shifting power to the consumer, blogs and media technologies endow us with the ability to choose what and when we consume (consider the effect of the video/DVD recorder, the internet, MP3s, etc.). In subsequent chapters we took up this idea and explored it in the context first of printing's impact on language, then of television making public what had hitherto been private. Habermas's argument that printing made politics more evidence- and reason-based provides another case in point, as does his argument that electronic media have refeudalised society and politics.

All this also clearly affects *continuity and change*. The standardisation effect of technology certainly changes, but it also stabilises, and thus acts as a force for continuity. Printing seems to have changed language and languages. Some languages have fallen out of use because, at least in part, they were displaced by others made more salient by media technologies. But, although Cornish fell away under the onslaught of English (the same argument has latterly been made in a different technological context – the internet – where some speakers of French and other languages have felt their language and linguistic community is being displaced by the predominance of English), the preservation of written texts in Cornish has made a revival of Cornish possible. Printing produced both change *and* continuity.

We might make a similar argument concerning Habermas's ideas of the public sphere and of refeudalisation. Media technology, print and electronic communications (and broadcasting in particular), first create a public sphere and then, through refeudalisation, establishes a media order hostile to that public sphere. The power of media and communications technologies democratises access to information, changing the social balance of power, but also standardises information, thus acting as a force for continuity.

The forces of change and continuity may be balanced by the regulatory power exerted differently by societies at different moments in their history. Societies' choices about what and how to regulate are linked to their *knowledge*, their *values* and their *beliefs* about such matters. If, for example, we concur in the belief that there are fundamental economic characteristics of the media that mean that media ownership tends to become concentrated (founded, we the authors of this book believe, in our knowledge of the media), we can collectively decide either to ignore such a tendency or to seek to do something about it. Whatever our decision may be, it is linked to our beliefs about the importance of pluralism, diversity and independence in the presentation and circulation of information.

Regulation is thus informed by the *knowledge, values and beliefs* of those who regulate. These often differ, not only because people are different but also because the values and beliefs are profoundly different. Such value differences may be reduced (or sometimes amplified) by knowledge. For example, if we knew what the effect on behaviour of the media's representation of violence actually was, then we might hold similar beliefs about what, if anything, should be regulated. Although shared knowledge is likely to lead to shared conclusions, it does not always do so. Knowledge and understanding will not resolve all conflicts. Some values, as we hope to have shown in our discussion of the privacy/freedom of information issue in Chapter 4, are simply incommensurable.

Understanding the intimate interrelationship between *power; change and continuity; and knowledge, values and beliefs* helps us understand some important elements of media history. How, for example, could we understand the differences between the number of printed works published at the same time in different societies without understanding that the power of technological change is shaped by social values and social power? One print historian contrasted the relatively high number of printed works in England to the lower number produced in contemporary seventeenth-and eighteenth-century France. In contrast to England, he claimed, 'The publishing industry of Paris [...] limped along, in the rear, shackled by government regulation' (Blanning, 2002, p.137). The technology of printing was the same in both countries but regulation, informed by different values and beliefs, and relationships of social power, made the power and impact of printing very different in England than in France. Of course, we should beware of assuming that differences in regulation and values accounted for everything;

literacy rates and levels of prosperity in the two societies almost certainly also made a difference. And, nearer to our own times, different ideas about the merits of deregulation and liberalisation of the media (or, put another way, the respective merits of the state and market) have made big differences to the shape and size of the media. For example, in 1982 there were only two telecommunications companies operating in the whole of the UK. One, British Telecom, operated everywhere except in and around the city of Hull where the other, Hull Telephones (later Kingston Communications), supplied service. Nowhere was there competition between suppliers, whereas, at the time of writing in 2005, there are now more than 300 telecommunications companies and most people in the UK have a choice of service supplier (whether these are fixed or mobile telephony, or internet service provision, etc.). In 1982, there were only three television channels (BBC1, BBC2 and ITV) available in the UK; now hundreds are available through cable, satellite, analogue and digital terrestrial transmission (and this does not include streamed video over the internet).

Technological change had a lot to do with these transformations, but so too did a major shift in regulatory thinking. Essentially, the UK government (and many other governments have done the same) decided that the public interest was, on balance, better served by promoting the entry of new services to electronic communication markets than by trying to restrict entry. Technological, social and regulatory power operated in combination to rebalance the relationships of change and continuity. The way in which this happened (and this is by no means the same everywhere) was shaped by the most powerful system of knowledge, values and beliefs prevalent in UK society at that time. Not all agreed on whether the outcomes were good or bad (and nor do all agree now!). We have explored (notably in Chapters 2 and 4) some of the differences in values that have led to different conclusions about the nature and extent of media regulation that is appropriate to secure the public interest.

We hope that we have whetted your appetite to continue with your own studies of the media, its economic circumstances, markets, technology and regulation and the part that all of these forces have played in social change. At the end of each chapter we have suggested how you might follow up some of the issues we have explored. We hope you will read more widely in the field to advance and deepen your own understanding of one of the indispensable constituents of our shared modern world.

Reference

Blanning, T. (2002) *The Culture of Power and the Power of Culture*, Oxford, Oxford University Press.

Acknowledgements

Grateful acknowledgement is made to the following sources for permission to reproduce material within this book.

Chapter 1

Figures

Figure 1.1: The Wicked Bible, Shelf Mark C.24.a.41. By permission of The British Library.

Readings

Reading 1.1: Williams, R. (1974) *Television, Technology and Cultural Form*, Routledge; Reading 1.2b: 'Inside story', *Which?*, October 1977 and 'Video cassette recorders: the rival systems', *Which?*, July 1979. By permission of *Which?*; Reading 1.3: Winston, B. (1998) *Media, Technology and Society: A History – From the Printing Press to the Superhighway*, Routledge.

Chapter 2

Readings

Reading 2.1: From *Jurgen Habermas on Society and Politics: A Reader*, Edited by Steve Seidman Copyright © 1989 by Beacon Press. Reprinted by permission of Beacon Press, Boston; Reading 2.2: Reprinted by permission of the publisher from *Technologies of Freedom* by Ithiel de Sola Pool, pp.5–7, 20–22, 109–116, 149, Cambridge, MA, Harvard University Press, Copyright © 1982 by the President and Fellows of Harvard College.

Figures

Figure 2.1: Copyright © AP/Empics; Figure 2.2: Copyright © Tim Rooke/Rex Features; Figure 2.3: Copyright © Denis Poroy/AP/Empics; Figure 2.4 (photo): Copyright © Stephan Savoia/AP/Empics; Figure 2.4: Ellis, M. (2003) 'Hasta La Victor', *Daily Mirror*, 9 October 2003. Copyright © Mirrorpix; Figure 2.5: *Financial Times*, 27 January 2004. Copyright © *Financial Times*; Figure 2.6: Ann Ronan Picture Library/HIP/TopFoto; Figure 2.7: Copyright © The Dean and Chapter of Hereford and the Hereford Mappa Mundi Trust; Figures 2.8 and 2.9: courtesy of John Frost Newspapers; Figure 2.10: Copyright © Ricky Leaver/Londonstills.com; Figure 2.11: *Sunday Sport*, 17 July 1988, Sport Newspapers.

Chapter 3

Reading

Reading 3.2: Graham, A. and Davies, G. (1992) 'The public funding of broadcasting', from Congdon, T. et al. (eds) *Paying for Broadcasting: The Handbook*, Routledge. Copyright © BBC 1992.

Figures

Figure 3.2: Mary Evans Picture Library; Figure 3.4: Copyright © Rex Features; Figure 3.6: Copyright © Solo Syndication; Figure 3.8: Copyright © Helene Rogers/Art Directors and Trip.

Chapter 4

Readings

Reading 4.1: Short, C., 'Page Three, indecent display and the roots of concern', in Collins, R. and Purnell, J. (eds) (1996) *Reservoirs of Dogma*, Institute for Public Policy Research; Reading 4.2: Grade, M., 'Free and fair communications and the regulation of media content', in Collins, R. and Purnell, J. (eds) (1996) *Reservoirs of Dogma*, Institute for Public Policy Research.

Figures

Figures 4.2 and 4.3: Courtesy of BT plc; Figure 4.4: Copyright © BBC; Figure 4.5: Ronald Grant Archive; Figure 4.6: Courtesy of the College Art Collections, University College London; Figure 4.7: Getty Images; Figure 4.8: Copyright © Photonews Service Ltd Old Bailey/TopFoto.co.uk

Index